DIAMOND

By

Ronald A Hummons

Foreward

Bishop Dr. Raymond H. Rufen-Blanchette, ThD

Afterward

Nicole Y. Riggins

Editor

Ebony Williams

Dedication

I dedicate my book to my son. My beloved, son TrePierre Hummons. Daddy loves you! I miss you!

DIAMOND

FOREWARD

Blacks have developed through their faith and experience an almost superhuman indifference to pain. It is as if the long night of suffering has steeled blacks against the tragic odds that are operating against tomorrow. An Army chaplain, himself a black man of rank and distinction, having been decorated for his courage, indicated that he had more difficulty preparing his white soldiers for possible death than he did his black soldiers. He did not know how to account for this. We are suggesting that our incessant experience of suffering has enabled us to transmute this suffering into a purpose-filled life. We are a people who survived the Middle Passage, slavery, and constant discrimination and who still shout in church and possess "the gift of laughter." By somehow maintaining sanity in an inhuman, racist situation, we have overcome - apparently not in spite of, but because of, what has happened to us. As black psychiatrist W. H. Grier and P. M. Cobbs put it, blacks have taken what was intended to be a noose and made out of it a receptacle of moral power. (Roberts, 1974 Pg. 58)

These words are spoken with such eloquence, so full of power and filled with hope and determination, but the ideation behind the words themselves are part of the pathology responsible for destroying the African in America. They are part of the problem, a false narrative that black folk in America have internalized living a maladjusted reality. This has been the rejoinder for hundreds of years, certainly since the days of chattel slavery in America. These Africans, these black people, are so resilient and strong, almost superhuman and virtually indifferent to pain. Do they even really feel pain? This, as African families were ripped apart on slaves ships, on the auction block and on plantations throughout the South. This, as African women and their young daughters were raped by their white masters giving birth to the children of immoral bondage and the crimes committed against them suffering perpetual subjugation at the hands of their oppressor. This, as they were compelled to deny love and succor to their own children while forced to love and nurture the children of the white master. These are the roots of generational self-hate and dysfunction in the black family in America. Those who have embraced this false narrative, have wittingly or unwittingly, perpetuated the pathology of brokenness and dysfunction among black peoples in America and are completely ignorant to the truth. Black people are people, and like all human beings they feel and experience pain, and experience it deeply. It can be said that the very idea that black people are impervious and indifferent to pain is racist, all by itself.

13.2 percent of the American population, approximately 46 million people, identify as Black or African-American according to 2014 U.S. Census Bureau statistics. Another 2.5 percent in the United States identify as multiracial.[1] This representing an increase from 12.6 percent of the U.S. population as reported in the 2010 Census Bureau data. As of the 2010 Census Data, 55 percent of the African-American population live in the Southern portion of the United States; 18 percent live in the Midwest; 17 percent of this population live in the Northeast; and 10 percent live in the Western portion of the Country.[2] Slavery and 'Jim Crow' have had their day and are gone in America, for the most part, but the ravages of race-based exclusion from healthcare services, educational opportunity particularly in early childhood education in the poorest minority communities, and the deprivation of manifold sociopolitical and economic resources, continue to translate into socioeconomic disparities experienced by African-Americans in the America of today.

---

[1] United States Census Bureau (2014)
https://www.census.gov/quickfacts/table/PST120215/00
[2]
http://www.census.gov/newsroom/releases/archives/2010_census/cb11-cn185.html

Socioeconomic status, position and realities are linked to mental health. The working poor and underemployed struggling to make ends meet, people who are impoverished, the homeless and those struggling with housing affordability, families struggling with food security, families dealing with a parent or other family member who are incarcerated, and families struggling with alcohol and substance abuse issues as a coping mechanism to deal with the depth of such significant issues in their lives are at a higher risk to experience serious mental health challenges.

Compounding this painful reality, despite the successes of the Civil Rights Movement and much of the significant social progress made over the last 50 years, racism and the subtleties of white privilege and advantage continue to be a pariah on the psyche of the black community and other communities of color in the Country having a profound impact on the mental, emotional and behavioral health of blacks in America. This reality, as police departments all over the Country surge in low and moderate income communities of color preying on the victims of the very dysfunction created by institutional inequality, establishing a feeder system the sustains and enriches the unjust and inequitable criminal justice pipeline. Institutional racism, and social inequality and inequity in America feed familial and social dysfunction in vulnerable black communities creating a crisis of black life that the Nation has never stood up to address.

Consider, African-American adults are 20 percent more likely to report issues of serious psychological distress than their adult white counterparts. African-American adults living below the poverty line are 3 times (300 percent) more likely to report serious issues of psychological distress than persons of all racial backgrounds living above the poverty line. African-American adults are more likely to experience and report intense feelings of melancholy, hopelessness, and depravity in self-worth than their adult white counterparts. And although African-Americans are less likely to suffer death from suicide than their white counterparts in their teenage life experience, African-American teenagers are more likely to attempt suicide than their white teenage counterparts (8.3 percent versus 6.2 percent).[3] The abhorrent fact that their white teenage counterparts are more successful at committing suicide is no consolation. African-Americans of all ages are more likely to be victims of serious violent crime than are non-Hispanic whites, making them more likely than their white counterparts to meet the Diagnostic and Statistical Manual of Mental Disorders (DSM-V) criteria for post-traumatic stress disorder (PTSD). African-Americans are, as well, 2 times (200 percent) more likely than their white counterparts to be diagnosed with schizophrenia[4].

The irony of this tragic reality is that the American system of Mental Healthcare practice is culturally impudent and clinically inadequate to address this pervasive phenomenon in the African-American community. Presently the DSM-V recognizes racism as trauma only when an individual meets the DSM criteria for PTSD correlated to a discrete racist event, such as an assault. This is problematic to a significant cultural degree given that Africans in America engage cumulative experiences of racism as trauma; live under socioeconomic and sociopolitical regimes in dysfunctional communities that promote daily experiences of trauma; and manifold numbers suffer from generational trauma as a function and result of the impact of historical racism on their families and the macro community in which they live. A particular discrete social event may simply serve as the 'coup de grace, or

---

[3] U.S. Dept. of Health and Human Services Office of Minority Mental Health (2016). Mental Health and African Americans. Retrieved from http://minorityhealth.hhs.gov/ohm/browse.aspx?lvl=4&lvlid=24

[4] American Psychological Association (APA) (2016) African-Americans have limited access to mental and behavioral health care. Retrieved from http://www.apa.org/about/gr/issues/minority/access.aspx

the 'straw that breaks the camels back' serving effectively as the trigger mechanism effecting traumatic reactionary emotions and behavior.[5] [6]

This construct of trauma in the DSM-V as a discrete event has a profound negative impact on the African-American community culturally, and all communities of color in America seeking understanding, and mental and behavioral health support from the professional community of mental and behavioral health practice. Moreover, existing PTSD measures aimed at identifying an index trauma event typically fail to include 'racism' among the listed choice response options, leaving such events to be reported as "other" or squeezed into an existing category that may not fully articulate the nature of the trauma experience. This leaves the diagnosis of PTSD to be highly subjective based upon the perspective, biases and experiences of the practitioner, making racism, the pandemic of trauma as a result of racism, and the mental and behavioral health service delivery to an entire oppressed cultural people in America to be clinically impudent and inadequate. Less than 2 percent of American Psychological Association (APA) membership is African-American. This reality in mental health care delivery is compounded by the fact that African-American patients have reported experiencing racism and microaggression from the very therapist responsible for their treatment.[7] [8]

---

[5] Williams, M. T. (2013). Can Racism Cause PTSD? Implications for DSM-5. Racism itself may be a traumatic experience. Psychology Today. Retrieved from https://www.psychologytoday.com/blog/culturallyspeaking/201305/can-racism-cause-ptsd

[6] Williams, M. T. (2015). The Link Between Racism and PTSD. A psychologist explains race-based stress and trauma in Black Americans. Psychology Today. Retrieved from https://www.psychologytoday.com/blog/culturally speaking/201509/the-link-between-racism-and-ptsd

[7] American Psychological Association. (2014). Demographic characteristics of APA members by membership characteristics. Retrieved from http://www.apa.org/workforce/publications/14-member/table-1.pdf

[8] Williams, M. T. (2013). How Therapists Drive Away Minority Clients.

If the white system of mental health and mental healthcare services delivery in America will not recognize the 'epidemiology of racism' and the cause and effect of race pathology in America, then this system will not and cannot serve blacks in America. Ask any child who's been bullied how they feel after having been bullied. If the epidemic of 'bullying' is a social disease that must be radically addressed and eradicated in Civil Society, than the pandemic of 'racism', as a clinical matter, must be radically addressed and eradicated even more so. This problem is a function and manifestation of white privilege in the system of mental health run by white males in America working to the detriment of an entire cultural race of people.

According to a study conducted by Ward, Wiltshire, Detry, and Brown (2013), African-Americans hold beliefs related to stigma, psychological openness, and obtaining help when symptoms of mental illness arise, which in turn affects their coping mechanisms and behaviors. Participants in the study, in the aggregate, were not particularly forthcoming in acknowledging psychological issues, but were more open to seeking mental health services in general. 30 percent of the participants reported having a mental illness or receiving treatment for a mental illness at some point in their life experience. The study found that African-American males were particularly concerned about stigma. Participants in the study appeared apprehensive about seeking professional help for mental health issues, which is consistent with previous research. However, participants were willing to seek out some form of help to address an issue.[9]

Psychology Today. Retrieved from https://www.psychologytoday.com/blog/culturally-speaking/201306/how-therapists-drive-away-minority-clients
[9] Ward, E. C., Wiltshire, J. C., Detry, M. A., & Brown, R. L. (2013). African-American men and women's attitude toward mental illness, perceptions of stigma, and preferred coping behaviors. Nursing Research, 62(3), 185-194. doi:10.1097/NNR.0b013e31827bf533

African-Americans in this present day are over-represented in the criminal justice system, and in American jails and prisons as a factor and function of the earlier discussion of police surges and the over-policing of African-American communities saddled with sociopolitical and socioeconomic disparities as a result of historical and institutional racism (Alexander, 2010). People of color account for 60 percent of the prison population nationwide at the same time that they represent just under 16 percent of the total American population. African-Americans, as well, account for 37 percent of all drug arrests, while representing only 14 percent of all illicit drug use. Illicit drug use is frequently associated with self-medication among individuals in crisis and those suffering from some form of mental illness.[10] Stigma, judgement and fear of how they will be experienced and treated by their provider prevents African-Americans from seeking treatment options for mental health issues (Ward, 2005; Ward et al, 2009). Research studies reveal that African-Americans believe that mild depression and/or anxiety would be considered as either 'soft', 'weak', or even 'crazy' in their social circles. This understanding of mental health stigma in the African-American community bears out anecdotally, as well. Moreover, many expressed that discussions about mental illness would be unwelcome and not be an appropriate topic even among family members.[11] In 2011, 54.3 percent of African-American adults with major depressive disorder received treatment as compared to 73.1 percent of their white counterparts. In comparison to 45.3 percent of their white American counterparts, 40.6 percent of African-Americans age

---

10

http://www.americanprogress.org/issues/race/news/2012/03/13/11351/the-top-10-most-startling-facts-about-people-of-color and-criminal-justice-in-the-united-states/, 2012

[11] Williams, M. T. (2011). Why African Americans Avoid Psychotherapy. Psychology Today. Retrieved from https://www.psychologytoday.com/blog/culturally-speaking/201111/why-african-Americans-avoid-psychotherapy

12 and over were treated for substance abuse and completed their treatment course, in 2010.[12]

This is the reality for millions of blacks in America, and just a portion of the statistical data behind this reality.[13] But in my Ministry to the people of this macro-community, we have a saying. He who feels it knows it. Studying and absorbing academic research documentation, statistical data and government reports is one understanding, listening to the stories of those who've lived this experience and who suffer with the daily realities of this trauma is entirely another. Empirical data means nothing without an understanding of the people who've lived it. Ronald Hummons a/k/a "Diamond", has lived and has overcome this experience in America. Although he's overcome, he's as well daily overcoming fighting everyday to give purpose and meaning to his existence by virtue of the things that he has suffered. This book is his story. Brother Hummons can tell you about pain, and whether or not he feels it and has felt it. [14]Growing up in the tough and precarious urban landscape of Cincinnati, Ohio, the son of a 15 year old girl raped by his biological father, Ronald Banner, himself an illegal narcotics dealer and illicit drug user. Ronald was frequently abused by his young mother and was practically raised on the streets of Cincinnati experiencing maternal abandonment, both emotionally and physically.

---

[12] Agency for Healthcare Research and Quality. (2013). National Healthcare Disparities Report. Retrieved from http://www.ahrq.gov/research/findings/nhqrdr/nhdr13/chap2-txt.html#fig231

[13] Mental Health America (MHA) (2018). Black & African American Communities and Mental Health. Retrieved from https://www.mentalhealthamerica.net/african-american-mental-health

[14] Psychology Benefits Society (PBS) (2016). Racial Trauma is Real: The Impact of Police Shootings on African Americans. Retrieved from https://psychologybenefits.org/2016/07/14/racial-trauma-police-shootings-on-african-americans/

Ronald Hummons spent his childhood and adolescence confronting traumas daily, living in an extremely dark space which he discusses in this incredible memoir. To keep from drowning in the dysfunction that literally engulfed him everyday, he developed his own coping mechanisms to escape a person whom he admits he did not know, himself, and developed the alter ego, Diamond, losing site of his born identity Ronald, along the way living as Diamond in order to daily survive. Ronald Hummons is candid in his expression of his life reality, that he did not know who he was. He did not understand relationships, and the only thing that he knew well was how to survive. It was only after being approached by an 'inmate prophet' in the prison system, and coming to his own profound 'Born-again' salvation experience within the prison walls that he was able to achieve some understanding of his own self-worth and obtained a revelation of who he was born to be, discovering purpose in this life. In our conversations he tells me that the birth of Ronald came when he emerged from prison in 2000 and embarked upon a new life. Since his emergence, Ronald Hummons has embraced extraordinary achievement, achieving what most who have not experienced such life adversity have not. He still struggles daily to hold on to that purpose, relevance in self-worth, and newness of life. His is not only a story of redemption, but of personal revelation embracing his own continual journey of self discovery. This memoir is the expression of the dynamic value of the African male in America, in spite of the psychological, emotional and social traps that were set for him, taking ownership, accountability and responsibility to overcome, and tell his own story. Perhaps we are super human after all. This book is not an obituary, it is his coming out, and I affirm him.

"History, despite its wrenching pain cannot be unlived, but if faced with courage, need not be lived again."

Dr. Maya Angelou, 'On The Pulse Of Morning'

Bishop Dr. Raymond H. Rufen-Blanchette, ThD
The Clergy Campaign for Social & Economic Justice (2018)
The National Coalition of Mothers & Families of the Movement & Foundation

DIAMOND

Chapter 1

Diamond—The Long Ride to Prison
July 1994

The guard yelled our names along with a set of numbers that would label my identity for many years to follow - Ronald Hummons, inmate 217714 would be my new name. It would forever be a symbol of my inner demons, reflecting my values outwardly. As we stood in line waiting for our riding clothes, I remember thinking, *what have I gotten myself into?* I prayed every step of the way, while following other inmates to receive what was known as "ghost suits." White painter coveralls were the standard uniforms that inmates were required to wear to take that long ride upstate. The guards shackled both our arms and legs to one another. During the two-hour drive on I-71 North to Columbus, Ohio, my arms ached, the cuffs bit into my wrists and the chains dug into my back. I wanted to cross my legs or stretch my hamstrings, but even without the chains, there was not enough room. Everyone was silent. It felt as if we were all going to our final resting place.

The broken stripes on the highway blurred into a nauseating white line as the tires beat out a dull rhythm. Even though it was only 6 o'clock in the morning, it was already 80 degrees outside. I remember the headlights of cars quivering in the pavement heat. I tried to hold my breath so as to not breathe in the smell of twelve sweaty men in a hot van with no air conditioning. My stomach growled, my eyes were heavy. I didn't get much sleep the night before. All I could think about were movies I'd seen about the penitentiary, in hopes that what I recalled was not going to be my experience. I laid there replaying in my mind the actions that landed me there and asking myself *was it even worth it?* It's funny how you don't think about the value of your choices until you're faced with the consequences. I never thought at twenty-three years old, I'd be chained to two other guys, in a prison van, with Cincinnati in the rearview mirror.

We rode until we reached the outskirts of Columbus. The van stopped in front of a guard house. A sign with the words "Correctional Reception Center" stood just left of the entrance. The C.R.C., where we'd stay while we waited for our permanent placement, received us with heavy link fences topped by triple layers of razor wire. The van pulled inside a set of gates and then into another, each one with taller fences and even thicker wire.

When we walked through the prison door, a 6-foot, 400-pound Samoan with a long beard and shoulder-length hair stopped us. After shouting obscenities at us he led us down a long, dungeon-like corridor until we came to a holding cell. He ordered us to get in and threatened to cut our balls off and feed them to the other inmates if we said a word. I thought this guy was the devil himself.

The fat Samoan called us out two at a time to check for weapons and drugs. He and another guard, a smaller white guy, who seemed even more mean, ordered us to take off our socks and turn them inside out; remove our jumpsuits and turn out the pockets; shed our t-shirts and drawers; open our mouths and lift our tongues; raise our feet and spread our toes; and lift up our nuts so they could check under those too. The two guards shouted insults at us the entire time, which seemed to be part of the procedure.

After the inspection, they led us naked into another room where we were given two t-shirts, two pairs of drawers, two pairs of socks, a brown painter's suit and brown cowhide boots that were paper thin with hard rubber soles. Next, the Samoan led us to the clinic where the nurse conducted mental and physical examinations. We also had to be evaluated by a psychiatrist to make sure we weren't crazy or suicidal.

Having been declared as sane, as the murderers and rapists no doubt in my company, I got back in line with the others. Another guard led us across the yard to Cell Block B, where we would be locked down 23 hours a day for 12 weeks.

Cell Block B was a giant, concrete morgue with two layers of cells circling around it. I was taken to a cell on the first floor, and when the guard closed the heavy steel door between us, it sounded like the shattering of bullet-wounded windows—hundreds of them. And just like broken glass, my nerves seemed to split into pieces when he shut that door. It didn't take long to look around the five by eleven cell. There was a small window just low enough for me see out of it, the rest of the room contained two steel cots, a steel toilet and sink. I thought to myself, *is this it? I'm in the state pen.* I lay down on one of the cots and cried until my cheeks burned. Then I soaked a wash rag in cold water and held it over my face. I held that rag over my face for a long time. After a while, I lay back down and stared at the ceiling. Finally, my senses started coming back to me. The first thing I noticed was how hot it was inside the cell. The sun coming through the window beat down on me like a magnifying glass. I noticed the stench still attached to my body. The stagnant air hung on me like a shroud. I tried opening the window, but that was no good. There was no breeze and no screen for the window. The flies had an easy access into my cell now. They landed on my face like it was a landing strip. I felt like those kids in Haiti that you see in commercials and pictures. I couldn't take it anymore. I decided I would rather endure the 100 degree temperature, so I got back up and closed the window. Then I tried to wash myself with the soap they gave us, but it was blue lye soap, it was so harsh that it burned my skin. When I scrubbed my privates, it felt like the skin would rub right off my balls. We had no deodorant so I would put toothpaste under my underarms to cover the funk.

The food was horrible. For breakfast we only got fifteen minutes to eat a scorching hot bowl of oatmeal and a boiled egg. It was so hot that it was nearly impossible to eat it in the short time allotted. The first time I put a spoon full in my mouth it felt like I shoved hot coals down my throat. Maaaaan, hot oatmeal with no sugar was like eating a peanut butter and jelly sandwich on burnt pop tarts with no peanut butter and jelly. Since the food was so horrible, I stopped going to "chow" and ordered from the commissary menu. Doing this, I lost a lot of weight. I ordered barbecue chips, brownies, soups, and kool-aid. It wasn't much but it kept me full and if you know anything about folks from Ohio, you know how we love our Grippos.

Week two and three, and hell, the first two months passed about the same, broken each day by an hour of recreation on the yard, me slashing a line, to represent another day down on the wall. After a couple of months, the guards brought me a cellmate. He was a young guy, maybe 19-20 years old. I don't know what his problem was, but he spit and hacked and burped all day and night. Plus, he farted nonstop. I thought I would go out of my mind from the noise and the smell. Finally, I couldn't take it any longer. I sat up in my bed, and told him. "If you fart, burp, or hawk and spit one more time I'm going to beat the shit outta you. "I didn't care about going to the hole at that point. I figured maybe there was A.C down there and it couldn't be worse than this. After that, I don't know if he held it in or what, but he didn't make a sound for two days. While lying there in silence, he let a fart slip out and man, I jumped up and leaped off my bed and commenced to whooping his ass. That little fart cost him an ass whipping and me a trip to the hole.

The guards came running in to break us up and took us both to the hole. It looked just like my cell, except it had no windows. I stepped inside thinking to myself, *why am I making this even harder than it has to be?* Being isolated will bring out your inner physiatrist. I lay on my bunk and tried to find solace in my situation, but there was none. Only endless thoughts about a broken child, living in this grown man's body, equipped with only a little boy's manual on life. *How did I get here?* I felt like I was in a nightmare that I couldn't wake up from. They say the gateway into the soul is through your eyes. I got up and looked into the plastic distorted mirror on the wall to see a fragment of my reflection. My eyes were bloodshot red from my tears. My eyes were so empty. I stared into them for the first time and I saw so much pain. I hated the reflection staring back at me. It was like looking in an empty glass jar. I got closer to the mirror and put my face right up against it, hoping to get a glimpse of any light. My soul was so dark. There was no life inside of my eyes. With the every blink, my eyes glazed even more until my vision was blurred from the tears. I soaked my wash rag under cold water and put it over my eyes and laid back on my bunk. I would find some solace in closing my eyes. I hated the darkness, as a kid and in my adult life, but it was through the darkness that I found memories that I could escape to. I needed answers and I knew those answers would only be found from starting from the beginning. I knew it would be a difficult journey but if I was going to get some clarification, it had to come through understanding the whole picture. I decided to write my mom a letter and ask how it all started.

Chapter 2

The Blood Conception
1973-1979

Violence has been part of my life for as long as I can remember. I was even conceived in violence according to my mother. I was born on July 12, 1973, at the University of Cincinnati Hospital. My mother was 17 years old. My father, Ronald Barron, known as "Paul" raped my mother. She went with my uncle to visit his friend at his apartment in Over the Rhine in Downtown Cincinnati. It was then, my mom told me she saw Paul for the first time. He was leaning against the kitchen doorway, his arms folded and his face serious. He had a long jerry curl and a mouth full of gold teeth. He was light-skinned with a full nose, and she would have thought him handsome but for the look in his eyes. Chills crawled down her back as he spoke

"Power to the People," he said to her, his voice barely audible. She repeated the phrase; it was the early seventies after all and the Civil Rights Movement was well underway. Her brother asked her about school, and she showed him the report she was doing for her history class on The Great Depression.

My uncle laughed. "Jenni's the scholar in the family."

"Why do you care about American history?" Paul asked, his eyes locking on hers. "Our history dates back to Africa where we were kings and queens." Paul was very militant and was a Black Panther in the late 60's.

"Well, I happen to like..." my mother started.

"Hey, Paul, relax, man," my uncle said, cutting his little sister off. "I got to go out for a minute. Will you two be alright?"

Paul continued to stare at her and replied "Yeah, we'll be fine." My mother got up to leave with my uncle but he told her, "Wait here baby girl, I will be right back." Reluctantly, my mom sat back down on the sofa and anxiously waited for her big brother to return as promised; except he didn't come "right back."

After my uncle left, Paul moved close to her while his eyes slid up and down her body and spoke real low. "You lookin real good, baby." He put his hands on her shoulders and began kissing her. She tried to pull away, but he only kissed her harder. His hands went under her shirt and reached up her back for her bra. "Stop it," she said. "I don't even know you!" "Shut the hell up." He pushed her onto the couch and held her around the neck with one hand as he pulled her clothes off with the other. She fought as hard as she could before letting go. She let her body go slack like a corpse and looked away, refusing to witness the violence happening to her; she went numb. Paul had no consideration of the pain he was causing her, only the satisfaction of having his way with the little girl he once admired. The feeling of control enticed him almost more than the penetration.

After being violated in one of the worst ways a woman could experience Jenni hid the scars of rape, thinking that if she stayed quiet no one would notice, not knowing that scars weren't the only thing Paul left her with. It wasn't enough for him to leave the scent of the man who violently raped her, he also left his seed.

When Paul was done, he zipped up his pants and left. He didn't wait around for her brother to come back. Neither did she. Later that evening her brother called to tell her that she had left her history paper over at Paul's apartment. She told him to throw it away. She didn't find out until she was five months along that she was pregnant with me. She was anemic, so it wasn't unusual for her to skip periods. The only change she noticed was weight gain around her midsection, but my mother was so small that she didn't associate the extra pounds with pregnancy. She had trouble fitting into her clothes, so she borrowed my grandmother's girdle, the kind with the side snaps. She finally went to the clinic, not because of pregnancy, but because of some other illness, a cold or ear infection.

Needless to say, she was shocked when the doctor told her she was pregnant. "Pregnant?" Mom and grandma asked at the same time. This wasn't great news. This couldn't be possible, she thought to herself. The only man she'd been with was Paul and it was only that one horrible time. Her legs turned to jelly walking to the car as they left the doctor's office. The fear and anxiety of having a child given to her through rape was unimaginable. There was no way she was going to give birth to a life conceived by the monster that attacked her. She was devastated! All my mother ever dreamed of was to finish high school and go to college. She would be the first of five siblings to finish high school, but college was replaced with a young girl having to learn how to care for her baby.

She hadn't seen Paul since that fateful day at his apartment, and my uncle never talked much about him. Because my grandmother would not consent to her having an abortion, my mother said she drank quinine water and a bottle of castor oil because she heard that would cause a miscarriage. After the second abortion attempt she became violently ill and had the runs for days. I am sure she hoped that I would come out in the toilet. No such luck for her, and no such luck for me! I suppose my grandmother saved my life, and approximately 4 months later, I was born. My mother said she had a very difficult labor, and was in excruciating pain for twenty-four hours. Finally, my grandmother had a fit and demanded the doctor perform a C-section, which he did. My mother loved me as soon as she saw me. It must have been hard for my mama, loving a child who was unexpected, unwanted, a child with the same brutal genes as the man who raped her. My grandmother kept asking about my father—who he was, why he wasn't around, asked if he was married. Out of frustration, my mother told her about Ronald Paul Barron, my dad. My grandmother, Barbara convinced my uncle to tell Paul about me. My father came to visit me, but he left the hospital without saying a word.

Six months after my birth, my mom moved out of my grandmother's house into an apartment with her best friend Veronica. My grandmother begged her to stay, but you have to know my mama—she has a mind of her own. She didn't want another woman, even her own mother, telling her how to raise her child. My mother lived on public assistance while she attended school and looked for a job. My grandmother and aunt Paulette were the ones who watched me while my mother finished her senior year of high school.

Paul never showed up again until I was eight months old. He knocked on the front door saying he wanted to see his child. Grandma Barbara, God bless her soul, was ready for him. She was never a woman to hold back her thoughts.

"What're you doing here? Get out! You've hurt this family enough!" My grandmother yelled at the man that raped her daughter.

Paul, with his cold stare, didn't flinch. "I came to see my child," he said. "Where is he?"

"You ain't gonna touch my grandbaby," she said. "Stay away from here!"

He pulled a wad of cash out of his pocket. "I thought Jenni might need some help."

My grandmother glanced towards the bedroom door. I must have been sleeping. Not flinching my grandmother replied, "I think you've helped enough. If you don't go, I'm calling the police."

Paul laughed and put the money back in his pocket. "I'll be back," he said.

A month later, my mother had just put me down for a nap and was cleaning up in the kitchen, when Paul walked through the front door she had left unlocked in case my grandmother stopped by. She didn't want her knocking and waking up her baby. "What do you want?" she asked.

"I want to see my son." The light from the front window kept her from seeing the expression on his face. "He's sleeping. I just put him down and I don't want to wake him up."

A backhanded blow across her face sent her reeling to the floor. "Don't you ever tell me I can't see my child!" he yelled.

He walked into her bedroom where I was in my crib. My mother said I woke up crying and screaming, but she couldn't move to get me. Curled up in a ball on the kitchen floor, she could hear Paul's laughter above my cries.

Since that day, Paul came over almost daily, at all hours. Veronica stayed with her boyfriend more than she did at their apartment, but, when she was home, she complained about Paul's visits. She would complain to my mother, "That guy gives me the creeps. Can't you tell him to leave you alone?"

"No! I can't!" she said. "It's not that simple with Paul. He won't go away, and you know what he'd do to me if I called the police."

One night when he came over, a guy my mom had met from school picked her up for a date. Paul saw her getting into the guy's car and became crazily angry and chased after the car with a two by four. No doubt, he would've busted out the windows and God only knows what else had he caught up with them. Fortunately the guy drove off fast enough leaving Paul standing in the street shouting obscenities. He didn't even bother walking her to the door. Mom said that was the last time she saw that guy.

Paul came back that evening and forced his way into the house threatening to kill her and take me away. My mama ran into the bedroom after him, begging him to leave me alone. "Please, Paul! Don't," she cried. Paul, ignoring her, lifted me out of my crib. "Put him down!" my mother screamed. Then, for some unknown reason, he changed his mind and put me back in the crib.

"You can keep the damn kid," he said. "I don't want him."

Before walking out the door he slapped my mama in the face knocking her to the floor, then he left.

After that incident, my mother fell into a debilitating depression, she was paralyzed to the point that she could not take care of me. She lay curled up in her bed for two days. Mom said I cried and cried for her, my sobs growing into screams, but she was too despondent to respond. Essentially, she had died inside, and like a dead woman, my cries fell upon deaf ears. That's why she decided to move back to my grandmother's house, at least until she was fit to care for me and for herself.

While living at my grandmother's, Paul began to stalk my mother. Sometimes he would follow her home from school, other times he would force his way into her home, mostly while my grandmother was not home. He was arrested several times but always managed to get out of jail. One day on her way home from school, he spotted my mom walking home. He ran up to her and began asking her if she had been with that guy again. She was frozen in fear and was not able to speak. Next came the punches to her face and mouth. Paul had knocked my mama's front tooth out from the root! Disoriented and dazed from his blows, she could not fight him off as he drug her down Armory Ave. to his apartment where he locked her in the closet. He said he would keep her there until she agreed to marry him or else he would kill her. His sister heard about what had happened and called Paul insisting that he release my mother. Eventually he did, hours later. This terrorizing would continue for years to come. Even though his presence disrupted her life, and guys were afraid to date her because of his threats, she did manage to finish high school and push him out of her life.

My uncle had been right. Jeanie was the only one of her mother's five children to graduate, but when her graduation day arrived, her older sister Paulette was the only family member who came. Her mother didn't even come to her graduation, which hurt my mother deeply since Grandmother Barbara was the only real parent she had. Her step-father died when she was fifteen and she didn't know her real father, a white man her mother had an affair with, and who was out of her life almost as soon as she was born. But my mother was happy because Paulette, since passed away, brought me to her graduation. It was important to my mother that I be there. I was just a baby, but this marked a new day for us. At least that was what my mother hoped.

My mother did go on to college at the University of Cincinnati. She got public assistance to pay for daycare and I went with her to her classes. I was only a toddler, but I do remember drawing pictures with the few crayons my mother gave me. She kept some of the pictures I drew that year. One shows a little boy with curly hair sticking up like a halo and a tall woman holding his hand, smiling. "Ron" is printed several times on the top of the drawing, and all the "R's" are backwards. It's hard for me to imagine that I was ever that little, ever that innocent. We all start out so naive and trusting. Then life, the cruelest of teachers, snaps away our primal joy.

Mama didn't do very well in college. She didn't fit in, a young black woman with a two-year-old sitting among middle and upper class students, most of them white, many who had never lived away from home before, many who did not have to worry about grocery or fuel bills, let alone a baby! She made her best grades in her social work classes – other people's troubles she could understand. That's where she met Walter Cummings. He had a brilliant mind and graduated from U.C.'s Health Administration program Magna Cum Laude. But there was something about him that didn't click and she kept her guard up. She didn't date him long, yet he kept hanging around long after she tried to break it off with him. He finally gave up and left her alone.

With the help of public assistance, my mother was able to put me in daycare. I only remember two things about daycare: the brown brick building with a fenced in concrete playground, and the time one of the caregivers had to take me to the hospital. It was the first of the many grand mal seizures that marred the first twelve years of my life and left me with 3 concussions before the age of 11.

Caring for a child and going to school became too much for my mother, so she dropped out. At the time, she wasn't on the best terms with her mother, so we moved out of my grandmother's house to a little apartment on Chapel Street in Walnut Hills. I was almost four by then and I remember the apartment well. There was a kitchen, a bedroom, a living room and a bathroom, and a family of roaches! I still have nightmares about those roaches. Eventually my mom was able to rid our apartment of the little brown creatures by setting off roach bombs. We had to leave the apartment for hours because it was harmful to inhale the fumes. When we returned, there were dead roaches everywhere! Mama got the broom and swept them up. They filled the entire dust pan! My young mom turned that roach-infested, drab apartment into a comfortable little home for us. The outside of the building was average, it was a red brick building with a backyard to play in, and a balcony off the front bedroom. I have good memories of my cousin Kim and I tossing a football and riding our tricycles in the backyard.

I love to look at the pictures of my days on Chapel Street. It was the happiest time of my childhood. One photograph shows me sitting with a friend eating cereal at the kitchen table. I'm in my pajamas with my mouth wide open, shoving a spool full of corn pops into my mouth. I was always grinning and laughing. Sometimes my mother would walk with me down Victory Parkway to McDonald's and as a treat, she'd let me order any one thing I wanted off the menu. I always ordered a vanilla milkshake. Summertime I'd go outside and play with my friends. Once I punched a little guy in the nose and my mother scolded me, but I was a good little kid. I didn't misbehave very often. When I was good, mom would heat up a frozen pizza for me and my friends. Later, my aunt Paulette moved into our building with her daughter, my cousin Kim for a spell, and I rode the bus to school with her every day. We were first cousins but we acted more like brother and sister. We were a small family then, but we were a close family.

Then Walter showed up again. I don't recall too much in the beginning, like when he was dating my mom. He hardly ever talked to me then, but I didn't mind so much because he represented the missing component of what a real family should be. I would have a real dad, just like on TV. They dated for a year before Walter proposed. My mother tells me now she didn't want to get married then—she still had hopes of going back to school and getting a college degree. She told Walter she wanted to wait until after she has an established career, but he was persistent and even enlisted my grandmother's help, who repeatedly told her how great it would be for me to have a father around. She said to my mom "Besides, you need to give that boy a name so that he isn't illegitimate." So, out of guilt, I suppose, my mother succumbed, and she accepted an engagement ring from Walter.

My mother washed our clothes in the bathtub, on a washboard she bought at the Goodwill store. She would bring me in the bathroom with her and let me scrub some of the smaller items, like socks and t-shirts. One evening while I was watching my mother scrubbing clothes, not long after her engagement, she asked me what I thought of Walter.

"He's okay," I remember saying.
"Do you really think so, Ronald? Really?" she probed me further. I was just a little kid, almost five, so I didn't understand why she was asking me those questions, or why she seemed so sad. I remember another woman came to our house, I think her name was Dottie, she talked to my mother for a long time.
"Honey, the bible says a man who finds a wife, finds a good thing and obtains favor with the Lord. You wanna find favor don't you baby?" I remember her asking. "Do right by God and do right by Ronald."

My grandmother agreed with Dottie. "Girl, you got a college man who wants you?" My grandmother finished scrubbing a dirty cake pan. She placed it in the rinse water before she faced my mother. "You ain't gonna get any better offer than that. You got it made, girl. You're going to be taken care of for the rest of your life," she said. My mom told my grandmother that she didn't love Walter, but my grandmother said "You will grow to love him." My mother sat in an old chair that she had draped with a blanket. She covered her face with her hands.

"I don't love him. I don't want to get married," she said

quietly.

"You're just scared of marriage honey, but you got a good man. It'll be fine." My grandmother answered.

"But, Mama…" My mother started.

"Don't 'but Mama' me." My grandmother blurted. "You want to live like me? Working your fingers to the bone just to keep your head above water? You want a man like your daddy? Or maybe you should call Paul. He'd make a good daddy, now wouldn't he? You owe it to the boy to give him a father."

"Please, mama," I said, encouraged by my grandmother. "I want a daddy."

"You want some more cake, Sugar?" "Yes, Grandma," I said. "And I want a daddy, too."

In the end, my grandmother and I convinced my mother to marry Walter. They set the date for September 29, 1979. Right before the wedding, Walter, my mother and I took a walk down Victory Parkway. I was on my bike a few feet ahead of them and feeling so proud that I had a daddy. But then, Walter turned to my mother, and right in front of me, asked if she had ever thought about giving me up for adoption. I stopped my bike and looked at my mama. She angrily said to him, "how can you say that in front of my son? He's old enough to know what's going on. He's my son. Why would I want to do that?"

"Well," he said, glaring at me as if I were an intruder. "Just the way he was conceived. You didn't want the child, you wanted to go to college and build a life for yourself. He kept you from doing all the things you dreamed of."

My mother pulled away from him. "Yes, but I have him now and I love him. Besides, he didn't ask to be born!" My mother spat back at him.

I started to pedal away from them, but mom grabbed my arm. "How can you say these things? It's like you don't want him around." She asked.

"He's not my kid," he said quietly.

"If you don't want Ronald, then you don't want me. C'mon, Ronald." My mother yelled.

After that, mom gave Walter back her engagement ring, and even though Walter didn't want me around, I was still disappointed that she didn't want to marry him anymore. I thought that once he married my mother and we all lived together, he would change his attitude towards me. A few days later, Walter dropped by our apartment, carrying a box of flowers. He told mom he was sorry and gave me a candy bar. He lifted me up in his arms and asked me if I still wanted him to be my daddy. I didn't know what to say. I just looked at him without giving a response. My mom put her arms around both of us and kissed me on the cheek. "I guess you're going to have a daddy, after all." "You won't be sorry, Baby," Walter said.

But my mother didn't take her eyes off of me.

Chapter 3
The Middle Years

1979-1987

I was five when Walter married my mother. Some relatives came up from Alabama to attend the wedding, with the exception of my great-grandmother, Madea. She was in her seventies and not getting around too well. Mom was her favorite grandchild and Madea was very upset she couldn't make the wedding. It was an exciting time for me, mom even bought me a fancy suit because I was the ring bearer. My aunt Paulette caught me admiring myself in the mirror and laughed so hard she couldn't catch her breath. All the relatives gushed over me as if I was the one getting married. The singing, the dancing, the food, it couldn't have been a better day. At midnight, Grandma Barbara took me home, and even though I could barely keep my eyes open, I didn't want to leave. I don't remember one thing about Walter that day, but I do remember how beautiful my mother looked in her wedding dress.

After a week, Walter and mom came home from their honeymoon, they vacationed some place in South Carolina. My mother said it was no big deal, just a little trailer at Walter's foster mom's home. While they were gone, my mother's sisters had moved all our belongings from Chapel Street into our new home, including all the wedding gifts. The house was flooded with presents, and my mother asked me to help her open them. Walter wanted nothing to do with the presents, he was too busy watching the football game.

"I don't want to open any stupid wedding gifts from a bunch of old aunts," he said. "I'm trying to watch the ball game. Let the kid help you."

My mother seemed angry with him, but I was thrilled. I hadn't seen so many glittering packages in my life. That first night together, after I said my prayers, my mother tucked me in bed, and Walter told me good night. The world felt like a safe and happy place.

      Things were fine for a while, and I thought we were going to be a real family, but right after their honeymoon, the nightmare began. The first time he ever whipped me, Walter beat me so hard he drew blood. When he took me into the bedroom and told me to lie face down on the bed, I didn't know what was happening. Then, the belt smacked into my bare skin. I put my hands out to cover my arms and legs but he pushed them away. I couldn't catch my breath. Each time, I could see his arm rise, hesitate and then drop. The shock of pain riddled my little body. My mother heard my cries and ran into my bedroom and stopped Walter from beating me. "Walter! You hit him so hard you made him bleed!? Why would you hit him like that?" Walter quoted a scripture from the Bible. "The blueness of the wound cleanses the belly of evil" he said. But what was my evil? I still didn't know what I had done wrong. I had just won the first grade spelling bee and was excited to show Walter my certificate. I may have spilled some milk or juice as I set my books on the table, but I really had no idea what made him so angry that day.

      That was the first of many beatings Walter would give me. They became so regular, I planned my days around them. "I'll be good, Dad. I'll be good, I promise" I would tell him. It didn't matter. And I tried to stay out of his way but the beatings continued. I remember looking out the corner of my eye during his biblically justified beatings, hoping my mom would bust through and save me but she was never there. Though my mom loved me, it seemed as if she could only see in my face the resemblance of my father, her rapist, and she emotionally detached from me. That was my first experience of abandonment. Looking at my face and seeing the resemblance of her rapist, she once again, went inside of herself and became numb, blocking out the memory of Paul and shutting off her emotional bond with me. Physically, my mom was always there for me and provided for me, but emotionally, she severed her bond with me. My mom had cut the emotional umbilical cord that tied her to me, and me to her. With me looking like her rapist, she didn't know any other way to cope, except to emotionally distance herself from me.

Not long into the marriage Walter quit his job and we had to move out of our nice, two bedroom home in Hyde Park, and into the basement of the church we attended. It didn't seem like a bad setup - after my mom turned that one room basement into a cozy efficiency. It was also convenient that the Christian school I attended was right next door. I could walk home for lunch and didn't have to worry about missing the bus. Walter had been promised a job as the assistant principal at my school, and my mother started night school at the University of Cincinnati. That meant I was alone with Walter most evenings during the week.

"Who left that light on?" Walter asked, knowing I would have been the only culprit. "I was doing my homework, I forgot." Then I'd hear the slither of leather. "Get in here, Ronald!" "But, Dad. I'm sorry." I could feel the lashes in my mind. "I did my homework," I said quietly. "Ronald! Get over here! Lay on that bed!" Then the strap came down. I realized there was nothing I could do to please him. I remember him breathing heavily each time he hit me, the belt continued to come down. The whole time Walter would tell me it was for my own good. It would keep me out of trouble, he said. Walter was a college man, my adoptive father. He must've been right, and my mother wouldn't let this happen if it wasn't right. I must deserve it, I thought. But deep inside, I knew better. In the place where I went each time he beat me, I knew better. The more he beat me, the easier it was to go there and the harder it was to come back. "You'll thank me for this one day." He told me. I began to doubt my own reality. There was no safety in my home. Walter said with his eyes, "You're not mine." So, I never completely believed anything he said. That was how I kept my sanity. I was pretty sure that, all in all, I was a good kid, but every time the strap stung my back or arms or legs, it became a little harder to believe. I wasn't sure what love was, or who I was.

One day, when I was about ten years old, Mom came home from work after I received one of Walter's love beatings. I was in my bedroom. My back was bruised and my hand was swollen as big as a baseball glove. Mom stood in the doorway to my room and her eyes filled with tears.

"Walter!" she screamed.

"What?"

My mother walked furiously out of my room and slammed the door behind her, but I could still hear them.

"Did you see his hand?"

"He ignored me when I came home."

"That doesn't mean he deserved that. He's hurt." My mother started yelling! "How could you do this Walter!?

"Your son needs discipline. He'll appreciate it someday." Was his cold response.

Silence. No response. *C'mon, Mom, say something. Tell him it's not right. That he's full of crap. Say something. Make it stop. Silence. Please, Mother. Please.*

The door opened and my mother walked in. Walter followed. He looked so hard at me I felt it. Ronald, we need to take you to the doctor, honey."

"Yeah. We'll see about that hand," Walter said as he pulled the car keys out of his pocket. Mom told Walter, "When Children's Hospital sees his hand they are going to call Children Services and you're going to be arrested." So instead of taking me to Children's Hospital, Walter drove us to Jewish Hospital. My mother was tending to my hand so she didn't notice until we pulled into the parking lot that Walter drove past Children's Hospital. Apparently he believed what mom told him, that he would be arrested. On the way to the hospital, Walter told my mom several times that it was an accident. We finally pulled into a parking lot on the other side of town. I didn't know this place, but it seemed very busy.

When we arrived at the emergency room the doctor asked

what happened. My Mom explained that it was an accident and my hand was hit. So the doctor said "Oh so it was accident Ronald?" I didn't say anything. Accident? Say something, Mom. Tell him it wasn't an accident. But she stood there in silence. I realize today that she was counting on the doctor to tell Walter what he had done constituted child abuse. That's why she wanted Walter to take me to Children's Hospital. That was her attempt to protect me. However, her attempts failed and she failed me when she didn't speak up.

When I would use my hands and arms to cushion the blow, Walter told me to move them, but I couldn't. I knew that I couldn't take any more pain on my back. I felt like I was on fire. I couldn't take my hand away. He swung so hard that when the buckle crunched into my fingers, it sent shivers of electricity over me. I screamed. "Next time, move your damn hand like I tell you, boy." When I moved my hand away, he still kept striking at it, as if he wanted tear my hand right off of me. My hand was still swollen when Mom filled out the paperwork. Another doctor saw me about ten minutes later. I sat on a gurney and there was a curtain between me and the groaning man beside us. People were scurrying all over.

"Hurt your hand, did you, Ronald?" the doctor asked.

"Yesir."

"Your mom says you were getting a whipping and you put your hand in the way and it was an accident. She said he only hit your hand once." The doctor stepped between Mom and me. "Is that right?"

I glanced at my mother at the end of the bed. She just stood there but didn't say anything.

"Yesir. It really hurts" My mother put her arm around me; her shoulders collapsed in relief.

The doctor looked at my Mom, then back at me. "I know it does, son. I know it does."

I got some bandages and a sling for my hand, but I didn't get anything to replace the mother that I had just lost. In the back seat on the way home, I vowed that I would take care of me if nobody else would.

There was nowhere I could escape from Walter. After being unemployed for some time, he landed a job as director at my school. Walter found time during the school day to knock me around. He would call me out of class and take me to his office and swat me like he was training a dog. More often than not, he made me take my pants down. After he beat me, he would handle my genitals in a way that made me want to throw up. The more he did that, the harder it was for me to concentrate at school. I would sit at my desk and just stare at the pages. I was distracted by fears of the sound of Walter's voice. He knew what he was doing. It was intentional. What was once my greatest love became my biggest struggle. I loved getting my education but the more my grades dropped, the more reason it gave him to beat me. I couldn't hear what the teachers were saying anymore. All I did was watch the door, waiting for him to appear. "I need to see Ronald," he would say. Teachers weren't ever going to say "no" to the principals.

But there was one teacher, Mrs. Laura, my third grade teacher, who did what she could. I don't know how much she knew or suspected, but she did ask me more than once why I was so frightened of my dad. "Oh, I'm not, Mrs. Laura," I would say. She would look at me with sad eyes and ask me again. When I couldn't answer and became all tongue-tied, she'd take me in her arms and say, if I ever needed her help, she would be there for me. Unlike the other teachers, she never complained to Walter about my declining grades. She knew better. Mrs. Laura would give me extra time in class to study and to complete my homework assignments. Sometimes, she would let me sit in her office during lunch and recess to catch up on my studies. My mom didn't know about Walter beating me at school. That wouldn't come out until later, but she did notice my grades had dropped. She knew that I was a bright kid and that I wanted to go to college to be a doctor, so she bought me a chemistry set with the microscope. I was so proud of my microscope, but how was I going to become a doctor if I couldn't focus at school?

Between my adopted dad being the principal and living in the church basement, I wasn't the most popular kid. I played on sports teams, but that didn't land me many friends either. In the sixth grade, I played football for a Sycamore league team called the Sparks. I was really too little to be any good, but I was strong and full of energy. I played linebacker and the coach told my mom that I floated like a bee, and when the runner got past the linemen, I would sting them and make them pay. My coach made me feel proud and almost forget that Walter couldn't afford to buy me the shoes or equipment the other guys had. Walter drove our family into poverty when he quit his job at Veterans Hospital. That's how we ended up having to move into the church house basement.

When football season was over, I played basketball. Again, being short, I wasn't one of the best players but I never lacked for effort and I could jump pretty high. When I posted up in the lane, I could hit the shot enough that the other players kept throwing the ball to me. I was still getting beat by Walter at home, so before I went to a game or practice, I'd wrap Ace bandages around my legs to hide the bruises. In football, my uniform covered everything up. During one game I got a rebound and dribbled up the middle of the court. When I made it to the foul line at the other end, I was open so I took the shot. Right at the moment I released the ball, I could feel my bandage started to unravel. I continued to shoot with one hand and grab at my covering with the other. The ball missed the rim completely, the bandage fell off and my bruises were exposed for all to see. Some of the players near me started laughing and pretty soon others joined in. That was the last season I played basketball.

The toughest part of the school day for me was when the last class bell rang. I'd stand outside watching the other kids go home; they'd get on the bus or get in their mother's cars, waving at their friends as they left. After a few frantic minutes, I would be standing alone on the playground. The whole while, I would peer into the distance like I was looking for my ride. For a long time I thought I was fooling my classmates, but, one day, a bunch of kids shouted, "What are you standing around for, Ronald? We know you live in the church basement!" Everybody knew. I was so embarrassed. One of the kids that bullied me on a daily basis started to make fun of me because we were so poor. "Church mouse," he teased. The other kids laughed and made me feel even worse.

From that day on, I went directly home after school. My mom wondered why I didn't have many friends. I didn't tell her I was too embarrassed to invite any of my classmates to our basement home. I also didn't tell her how bad my feet hurt from wearing Walter's too-big leftover shoes. I wore a size 5 ½ and he wore a size 9. One day during lunch break, I was running around the playground when my sock came out of a big hole in the sole. I didn't even notice but as I was running I tripped over the sock and went head first into an 8ft concrete staircase. My head hit the ground so hard that I blacked out. As I slowly gained consciousness, I could hear kids yelling "Call an ambulance!" Dawn, one of my peers had asked if she should go get the fireman at the fire station right across the street. "No he'll be ok. He just bumped his head but he's coming around." Mr. Crane said. Mr. Crane was one of the teachers there and was trying to downplay my injury so that the school wouldn't be held liable. "Mr. Crane he doesn't look too good." Nita said. "Help me get him downstairs and to his desk and he he'll be just fine." he replied. They carried me down the stairs and sat me at my desk and placed my hands on the desk.

After sitting there for a few minutes, the students said they heard a loud boom. I had fallen over and fell to the floor. This time I didn't regain consciousness. After waiting for almost over an hour, the staff decided to call the fire department. By the time they got me to the hospital my brain had swollen and the damage was critical. "Why didn't you call as soon as he was injured?" One of the fireman asked Mr. Crane. "We thought he'd be ok." He replied. The fireman looked at them in disbelief. I was rushed into ICU with a traumatic brain injury. The doctor said my brain had swollen and they had to try and relieve some of the pressure. While I was being treated, a priest came into the room where my mom was, she bursted out in tears. "Oh my God, please don't tell me!" She screamed. "No Mrs. Hummons, I was coming to see if I could pray with you. His injuries are pretty serious and they're doing everything they can to save his life."

I came out of ICU but I would never be the same. I had amnesia for almost a week before I started to recognize anyone. The kids from school came to visit me once I regained my memory. Some I could remember, others I couldn't. After leaving the hospital, the headaches started. I would get such bad migraines as a result of my concussions, it felt like my brain was bleeding.

I later learned that the New Life Temple School wouldn't help with any hospital bills. They told my mom that she signed a waiver of liability if anything happened to me while in their care. The school wasn't even formed correctly and turns out, their license was illegally obtained. There was a hole in the play area, where I once fell. There were no guards or rails around it at all. If an average lawyer would have been alerted to this case, they would have had to shut the school down. The following year the school did close down for good. I'm not sure why, but the school's academic standards didn't line up with other schools, so everyone got held back one grade.

Most of the kids were fortunate enough to attend a private school, but my mom decided to enroll me in one of the worst public schools in the city. My first day was the worst, and to top it off, I showed up in a pair of blue buddies with big, red fat laces. The other students picked on me so badly. I had never been so humiliated. "How the hell you got on buddies with fat laces?" One of the kids asked. I just sat there ashamed. They all had on

Nike, Adidas or Puma. Everything they wore was named brand, but we were too poor to afford the new styles or trends.

I felt so out place. Isolation became my friend. I wasn't tough, wasn't a thug, and definitely wasn't a cool kid. I was just little Ronald. The kid that wanted to get a good education, scholarships, and go to college to become a doctor so that I could help people. Instead, I became the kid who was bullied, abused, abandoned and left on his own to figure this out this thing called life.

I thought I'd just make the best out of the new school but all I did was trade one school bully in for an even bigger one. Damon Miles was his name. It seemed he may have been held back a few times, because he looked like he was twenty two years old. I was a french fry compared to this guy. We were in the same grade but I think he must have breastfed off giants. For no reason, Damon started picking on me one day. "Why yo hair so damn nappy?" He asked me. "And look at yo shoes. You ain't got no mamma or daddy? My mom would never send me out the house looking like you." I was so afraid, I couldn't move or say anything. For some reason, every time he opened his mouth I saw Walter's face. The fear I felt when he picked on me would make me feel frozen in time. It seemed I was 50 pounds lighter and many inches shorter than he was, so why he chose me to pick on didn't make sense.

One day, in front of the whole class, he spit his gum out on my sweater. "Now say something and I'll beat yo ass." I didn't even look at him. I just stared at the ground almost in tears. I was the sweetest kid ever and gave no reason for this treatment. As I got up to leave the room I accidently bumped his arm trying to go around him. He turned around and shoved me halfway across the room. As I stood up, the teacher came in the room. "Everybody take a seat." Mr. Migossi said. Damon looked at me and told me after school he was going to finish what he started. I knew I couldn't stay at school so I left early. Damon was in a gang so trying to escape this guy seemed almost impossible. I decided I would tell my mom about him. I never felt any security with my mom after her allowing Walter to hurt me the way he did, but I was praying she would hear me this time and save me. "Mom, there's this kid at my school who's bullying me. I've left school early the last couple of days to keep from being killed. He won't leave me alone." I told her. "Let's go talk to your dad about it." Was her only response.

After she told Walter, he called me into his bedroom. "So your mom tells me you got a bully harassing you. You want me to show you how to make him leave you alone?" "Yes." He turned around and took weights off the end of a barbell and handed one to me. "Take this. This is all you need to make sure he never messes with you again. When he's sitting in his seat walk up behind him and bust his head open!" *What the??, This dude just told me to go and catch a first degree felony.* He wrapped it in a sock and placed it in my bookbag. I took it to school the next day. It was so heavy in my bag, that when I sat it on the floor, it made a clinking noise. Damon heard the noise and asked what I had in the bag. I was scared to tell him. There was no way I could carry this out. I wasn't a violent kid and even though I wasn't a punk, I also didn't like to hurt people. I lied to him and said it was a gun. He looked me dead in my eyes and told me I'd better use it or he would use it on me. I left school early again and ran home. All I wanted was for my mom to protect me. I was hoping she would pull me out of this school and put me around kids that were more like me. Somewhere I could just focus on getting my education without having to deal with all the drama, but once again I was left alone to take care of myself.

After getting beat by Walter for leaving school early, I'd had enough. I ran away. I was placed in a home for kids but I wouldn't stay there long. I got into a fight my first day with a guy named Mike, but things were different this time. When he walked up on me, I instantly went into fight mode. After I slammed him on the ground I started to kick him in his head and body. I was in rage. It felt good and at the same time, scary. Who was this shy kid that loved God and all things good? I got kicked out of the home and went looking for my biological dad. I figured he was my last hope for a normal life. I didn't know about the rape at that time. I was only eleven years old, and all I knew was that was a man out there that I thought loved me and would call me his own. I didn't even know his last name, I just knew we had the same first name, Ronald. Maybe he could restore my true identity.

When I was six years old, Walter legally adopted me but I didn't know that I was adopted. My birth certificate changed, and I was given Walter's middle name "Arvell." I never got his love or acceptance, just the bruises and wounds that were justified by the Holy Bible. I suppose there was something in it for my mother to have Walter adopt me; she could block out her painful memory and shame of how I was conceived. But she could not block out the truth about who my biological father was.

Because my mom hated everything about him, she tried to hide his whereabouts from me. "He's worthless, Ronald." Was her reply when ever I asked about him.

I would respond with, "I can't take being beat anymore. People at school laugh at me. They point at my bruises."

She finally gave in and agreed to call him. She said as she dialed the phone, "But, Ronald, he can't help you." I could hear the phone ringing. Then someone answered. "Paul? This is Jeanie." My mother looked at me and mouthed the words, "Are you sure?" I nodded. "Your son wants to meet you."
I heard a sharp voice on the other end of the phone. "I told him," she said to my father. "He thinks living with you would be good for him. He's your son too and he deserves to know his dad." After several minutes, mom hung up. She turned to me. "He says it's okay."
I must've had a great big smile. "You have to wait until school's out for the summer, and then you can go. Just for a few weeks though"
"I'm not ever coming back," I said to myself.

Chapter 4

Birth of Diamond/ Death of Ronald

We met on the front steps of the Hamilton County Justice Center.
A place that he frequented from being locked up so much. I raced
there as soon as school let out for the summer. I didn't take time
to sign yearbooks or say goodbye to my friends. I didn't want to
be late for the big reunion. We got there a little after four and I
didn't recognize him right away. This wasn't the man I'd seen in
my dreams. I used to imagine he would look like Dr. Huxtable
from The Cosby Show.
    "Hey, Dad," I said.
    He just looked at me with a cold stare. "Let's go. I got
things to do."
        My dad had a jerry curl and a lot of gold teeth; he
looked like a mix of Goldie from the Mack and Flavor Flav. But
he was my dad and none of that mattered. I just hoped that my
life would be better, now that I found him. Man, was I wrong.
We walked a few blocks to his apartment and every dope boy,
dope fiend and hooker knew who my dad was. Once we were
inside, I sat down in a chair near the window in his bedroom. A
knock at the door, "Who is it?", my dad yelled, "Pat! Hurry up
and open the door, it's cops everywhere downstairs!" She
responded. Pat was one of my dad's smoking partners. She came
back to the bedroom and sat down on a mattress on the floor.
"Who is this cutie?" She asked. That's my son, he told her. "he
looks just like you Paul." "Yeah that's what everybody been
saying since I got him down here. Bitch fire that shit up." He
replied. He pulled out a plate with a broken car antenna and a
piece of brillo pad on it. Then Pat opened up a small baggie and
gave it to him. It looked like little pieces of popcorn. They put a
small piece of a yellowish looking rock on the end of the antenna
and lit It. I had never seen crack before but I figured out rather

quickly they were smoking dope. They smoked right in front of me. I leaned in as close to the window as possible so that the smoke wouldn't get in my nose. I couldn't believe this, my dreams of a different kind of life burned up like that little rock in his homemade pipe. That night, as I laid on an old, dirty couch in the living room, I cried myself to sleep. Maybe mom was right about my dad, but I still wasn't ready to accept reality. What other options did I have? Stay there with her and live in fear? All were questions and answers no kid should have to ponder.

The next morning my dad wanted to introduce me to some of my cousins. While we were walking to their apartment, he handed me a brown paper bag and told me to put it in my pocket. I had no clue what was in it but when we made it to Lincoln Courts, where my cousins lived, I learned quickly what it was. When I handed him the bag back he opened it and pinched a small piece off and gave it to some guy for $20. That became the norm. He would hide dope on me so that if the cops pulled up, he wouldn't go to jail for it. My dad was trying to slowly make me a copy of him. I could tell my quiet, gentle, sweet spirit wasn't what he hoped for in any child of his. He wanted a tough kid. Someone he would be proud to call his own. One day when we were headed to the free store to get some food and hygiene products, I started to ask him a question, "Dad". He turned and looked at me with this dark cold look and said, "don't ever call me Dad again boy! Call me Paul." I held back my tears. I knew at that point my dad, I mean Paul, hated everything about Ronald and I needed to be more like the kids in the neighborhood.

Ronald was dying a slow death. That good kid was on life support and I knew the only way to save him was to find a safe hiding place and create identities that could protect him. I needed an identity that people would love and accept. Survival for me meant creating a mask to help me fit in. I needed something that would represent everything I wanted to be. Diamond! Diamonds were beautiful, valuable and the toughest of them all. That was everything I wanted to be.

It was like playing a movie role, in real life. My new character had to be confident and somewhat arrogant. Growing up I was made to feel so ugly. I didn't have the clothes and shoes the other kids were wearing and they made sure to let me know how bad I looked by teasing me every chance they could. I was so insecure because it seemed as if everything that made me who I am, was hated by the ones that were supposed to love me the most. My hair was so thick and nappy. The kids used to call my hair sheep wool because it was so thick. I was short and skinny and felt as if there was nothing appealing about me. I was the ugly duckling. My mom had totally detached from me due to my dad raping her, and I ended up looking just like him. My own dad hated Ronald because I didn't represent what he was about.

There was nothing "street" about me. I was just a gentle spirited kid who liked insects, reading books about science and going to school and church. How could nobody love me? I couldn't understand it. How could I love this worthless piece me that my mom and dad seemed to despise? I wanted to be someone that everyone would love. I thirst for it. I needed it. I didn't know what it was or how it felt but I associated it with acceptance and I wanted it however I could get it. Diamond was the vehicle to get that hunger in my soul fed. He would be the beautiful, flawless, hard, valuable sub-self that I would live through. He would be my reinvention to take care of the little boy inside me that was afraid. Diamond was his name and with this new identity I needed a new look.

First, I had to get rid of what everyone called "bad" hair and change it to "good" hair. I bought a duke texturizer kit and made my hair look like the mixed-raced kids'. After I washed it out I looked in the mirror and couldn't believe my eyes. My transformation was underway. Now, I'd have to get rid of the nice guy act and take on a hard, street type of personality. That was the hardest part because I wasn't tough. I wasn't a punk either but I didn't really like to fight so trying to be tough came with a price. I created a fake temper to mask the fear I really felt. I would make myself so mad and develop such a temper that it made it easier for me to engage in fights and eventually hurt people. I did get my ass whooped a lot before I learned how to really fight.

This guy Diamond appeared flawless but there was nothing real about him. He was just a character I created to keep the monsters away. It was hard at first to keep it up, but I thought it was worth it to gain my dad's and everyone else's approval. I wasn't good at developing relationships. I didn't have any models that showed me what real friendships looked like. Relationship building for me was being accepted and admired, so I used Diamond to gain that acceptance and admiration. I had the hair and the look that people liked, especially the girls. It was time to create relationships. The relationships I created were always seasonal because they never had any real foundation. But this was the only tool I had for making friends, so I was going to use it.

The streets were new territory for me. I had never carried a gun or sold drugs, but I learned fast. One night, a week or so after my twelfth birthday, my dad was pressed for some dope and wanted me to help him get it.

"Here," he said. I held out my hand and he placed a handgun in it. Then he grabbed some things out of the closet. "Put this on." He gave me a ski mask and a green trench coat, several sizes too big. "Slip that gun in your pocket. It's time for you to put some work in around here."

My skin burst out with sweat. "But…"

Dad looked at me. "What? You scared?"

"No." But I was. Boy, was I scared. What was I supposed to do with a gun? Shoot somebody?

Paul tied a bandana around his mouth and put on a coat. He grabbed a yard-long pipe and opened the door to the apartment. "C'mon."

My feet wouldn't move.

"C'mon now!"

I thought we were going out into the streets looking for a victim, but we weren't going far at all. We went downstairs, in the same building. They lived right under us. For my first robbery we simply walked down a flight of stairs, busted into these guys' crib, and found them sitting in the back room, smoking weed and watching TV.

My dad kicked in the door. Boom!

"Get on the floor, muthafucka!" he yelled at our neighbors. "Hold your gun on them," he said to me. Dad waved the pipe around. "Get on your knees! Put your hands behind your head!" The guys obeyed. "Where's the dope and the money?"

"Man, we ain't got shit." One guy responded

"You think I'm playing? Hit him in the head with the gun!" My dad yelled at me. I was frozen. I couldn't believe what was happening right in front of me. I didn't want to hurt these guys or anyone else.

As I watched all this, it felt like a TV show. I wasn't a robbery boy. I was just a kid. The gun trembled in my hand as I was obedient to what my father told me to do. We were probably in there for only three or four minutes, but it seemed to go down in slow motion. Tears ran down my face under the ski mask. I remember shivering. Dad took the money and crammed it in his pocket and rummaged through their pockets looking for the drugs.

Then Paul said slowly, "Any of you bitches move and we'll blow your head off." Then, it was over.

We ran out the door and up the stairs. Paul dumped the money and dope on the sofa. Through the vents, we could hear the guys we had robbed yelling at each other. They had to know who we were, but I sensed they wouldn't call the cops. I saw how they looked at my father, like he was not somebody to mess with. Besides, what would they say, "Yes, sir, Mr. Officer, those guys upstairs stole our dope and money." Uh, yeah, I don't think so.

My dad counted the money. It looked like a lot to me.

"This ain't shit. I know they got more down there. Those assholes holding out on me. C'mon, we're going back down there."

What?! I yelled in my head. I felt like passing out. "Won't they figure out who we are and call the police if we go back down there?" I asked.

He grabbed me and said, "boy the only way you gonna get what you want in this world is to take it. We're going down there and I don't wanna hear shit else about it."

He walked with urgency toward the door and then stopped. My dad turned to me and raised his eyebrows. I followed him. We ran down the stairs pushed the broken down door in. My dad went in like Rambo. I never saw more surprised faces. The one guy my dad hit with a pole was half conscious and bleeding all over the place. This time he made them take all their clothes off and turn their socks inside out. That's when I learned dope boys hide dope in their drawers and socks. I had to check their socks and underwear while my dad checked under the mattress. Sure enough, I found money where I searched and my dad found dope and money where he searched. Suddenly, one of the guys jumped up and tried to tackle my dad. The pipe my dad was carrying smashed into the guy's skull and blood spattered everywhere. There was blood on me, all over the walls and floor, and dripping from the pole my dad hit him with. So much blood poured down his head that it came pouring out of his eyes and mouth. I had never seen so much blood before. I stared in disbelief. It felt as if I was having an asthma attack. My chest tightened and my breaths were shorter. I was shaking uncontrollably. My vision went blurry and it felt like I was looking through the bottom end of a coke bottle. His body seemed to hit the floor in slow motion as he fell backwards with his legs bent underneath him. Was this man dead? Did I just help my dad commit murder?

We ran back upstairs, locked the door and counted the loot. I didn't want to touch the dope. "You did good," Paul told me. He counted the money and said that he would take me to the store tomorrow to buy me something nice.

I sat by the window and watched through the curtains as the ambulance came to help the men we had just robbed. I still don't know if that guy died, I just remember seeing someone carried out on a stretcher.

The next day I was excited about going to the store. New shoes, a shirt, a walkman, I had no idea what I might get. "Let's go," he said and waved me toward the door. All right, let's go. We stopped at the corner store not even half a block from our apartment building. Dad walked in and grabbed a brownie and a bag of Grippos potato chips off the shelf. He turned to me, "Get a drink." I got a red Faygo and put it on the counter. Dad plopped two dollars in the man's hand and waited for his change.

I was speechless. *You've got to be kidding*, I thought. *I helped you rob somebody, put my life in danger, and all I get is a bag of chips, a quarter brownie, and a soda?* I ate that brownie with a heavy heart.

When we walked out of the store, Dad turned to me. "Every one of these stores is owned by either Asians or Arabs. They overcharge us and wonder why they get robbed all the time.

Later, I worked up the nerve to talk to my father about the robbery. I went into his room where he was laying on the mattress on the floor.

"Paul, can I ask you something?"

He didn't respond. Then a barely perceptible groan left his lips and his head tilted toward me. His eyes were glazed. If I was almost invisible when he was coherent, I was now as transparent as the plastic baggie he kept his crack in. I remember feeling my throat tighten the way it does before I cry. But I didn't. I just turned and walked out.

Usually it didn't matter if Paul was high or not. He ignored me either way. He'd sleep until almost noon, snort a little coke, and then head to Washington Park and drink beer with his friends. If I were sitting on the couch, he'd walk past me without saying a word. The only time he spoke to me was when he needed something from me. And what he needed, I, for the most part, never had and never would have. More often than not, our conversations consisted of "I'm going out," and "Don't forget to lock the door if you leave." If I'd lock the door I wouldn't be able to get back in until my dad came home and let me in. Sometimes when I couldn't get in I'd sleep in the hallway or in Peasley Park, while talking to my friend Sam about how big and successful I was going to be when I grew up. We would talk all night about what life would be like when we grew up and got up out the hood. Daydreaming about a better life was a way I kept some sanity. It's funny that even in the midst of complete poverty I always had visions of greatness.

One night, I was roaming the streets trying to find somewhere warm and dry to take cover. The rug I used to prop the door open was removed and I accidently locked myself out. I walked down the street trying to find my dad when a car pulled up. I heard a small voice inside me say "Don't get in that car," but I was scared, cold, and hungry. I didn't know what to do or where to go - the driver knew my dad so I figured it would be ok. It was raining and cold outside, so the man took me back to his house, fed me and gave me a room to sleep. The events that took place in that apartment would change my life forever. Later that night, after I dozed off, I was awakened by the sound of a door slamming. "Lil Paul, get yo ass up and go in the living room." I didn't know what was going on. I thought maybe he was going to take me back to my dad's or something. I got up and went and sat on the couch. He came back out but he wasn't dressed to take me anywhere. He came out in a house robe and a hammer in his hand and walked towards me.

I was so scared. I trembled in fear. I remember praying to God that if He was real, please protect me. What the hell did I do to deserve this? This guy knew my dad and I thought they were cool but I guess all he saw was this little 90 pound, 12 year old kid. This guy had to be at least 6 ft. tall and a good 250 pounds. He sat next to me and stared at me for a second before saying anything. "Look at me". He said. He had opened his robe. I didn't want look at him so he said it again, but louder this time, "Look at me!" I slowly looked at his dark-skinned ugly face. "You know what it feels like to have the claw of a hammer sunk in your head?" He asked. "No sir". I replied. "Well I need you to do everything I say or you'll find out." "Please don't do this". I pleaded fearfully. He raised the hammer up and said, "shut the fuck up! This will be over before you know it. Get that dick up and fuck me from the back" "Oh God, NO. I'm BEGGING you, please don't do this, PLEASE!" I pleaded as tears rolled down my cheeks. "God please help me, please". I said quietly. The man told me I just needed something to drink to help take my mind off it. As soon as he got up and went into the back room, I jetted to the door. He ran behind me all the way to the street but by the time he made it downstairs, I was gone. I ran for my life. I ran so fast that I could hardly catch my breath. I went to my dad's apartment building and slept in the hallway until morning when he finally showed up. He had removed the rug that I used to prop the door open and told me not to ever do that again. I didn't tell him what had happened the night before because I honestly didn't think he would care. This guy didn't give a damn about me or my wellbeing. I felt disgusting. I wanted to go jump off the bridge into the Ohio River but I thought, even the river would reject me. I had to accept that this was my life now. The image of living like the Huxtables on the Cosby show had faded away. Instead, the images of the show "The Wire" had become my reality.

The first time I ran into my father and his women on the streets, it didn't take me too long to figure out what was going on. He had a stable of women that used to prostitute for him. Apparently, pimping was an income stream to support his drug addiction. Paul saw me but he turned away. "What's that kid hanging around here all the time for?" one of his girls asked.

"Bitch don't worry about that, you just worry about getting this money" my father said.

"He looks an awful lot like you," she said, her voice stretching into laughter.

"He's my son," He said.

My father pushed the woman out of the way. His face was twisted when he got to me.

"I hope you're taking lessons? " He said. "Do they work

for you?" I asked. "They do whatever the fuck I tell them to do. I own these bitches and they know if they don't get my money, I'm gonna beat that ass." Then he put his finger in my face, emphatically pointing at me with each word. "When you get that college shit out yo head and grow the fuck up, then you'll realize being a man means to get it at all costs." This was my life lesson from my dad, Pimpology 101.

Finally, it was the end of August—time for school. That meant going back to mom and Walter's house. I had developed a love/ hate relationship with school. I loved getting an education, with plans to go to college someday, but with so many distractions of everyday life, I found it impossible to stay focused long enough to get the lessons. I didn't feel like I had fit in at school. I was very isolated. I've always felt alone, even with people around. I never felt like I belonged anywhere. I wasn't popular or accepted by any of the groups. Loneliness became the norm. I decided I didn't want to go to school anymore so I would get off the bus and cut school. A bakery down the street from my school, had daily free samples of doughnuts, so I would go there in the morning and swiped as many samples as I could get. I ended up getting picked up by the police for truancy and they drove me to my mother's house. She and Walter had moved out of the church basement into an two-family duplex. Walter had taken a job working for an automotive firm.

At first, it was a relief to be with my mother. I thought things would be better this time around. But my stay at my mom's didn't last long.

"Get out here, boy!" Walter screamed through the bathroom door.

"Yesir?" I was in no hurry for him.

Then he started banging on the door. "Now! Now!"

"I didn't do anything."

He hesitated for a second. "Is this your mess in the kitchen?"

"I'll clean it up." I heard him walk into the living room so I opened the door and went to my bedroom.

Walter was soon standing in my room yelling at me. I feared this man, he knew it and thrived off it. He was a bully and it fueled him but I had enough. I wasn't going to take his fear tactics anymore so I put up a fight as best as my small 110 pound frame could. I had committed an armed robbery and hung in the streets with prostitutes and dope dealers. Walter didn't look so scary anymore. When he came at me, it wasn't Ronald he approached, it was Diamond.

Walter tried to push me onto the bed but I was ready for him. I grabbed his belt and held on to it for dear life. He grabbed my wrist with one hand and tried to pull the belt from me with the other. "If you don't lay down and take this whipping, I'm gonna have you locked up in a home for juveniles!"

"What's going on in here?" My mom asked.

"I've had enough!" I shouted. "You ain't gonna beat me anymore!" I yelled at Walter. "Marrying you was worst thing my mom could've done!" He lashed out at me with all his might, but I fought back.

"No more!" I cried between blows. "You ain't gonna beat me no more!" Then I swung at Walter's belt with both hands and tried to run out of the room. He caught me in the doorway and pinned me down. I squirmed and fought until I was able to break free and run out the door. I ran as fast as I could down the street. My heart pounding and out of breath, I finally took shelter at a bus stop. All I could think of was how Walter and my mom looked at me. So much disgrace in their eyes. To me, I was just a kid who loved science and math, a straight-A student who used to spend afternoons in the school library. When I wasn't in the library, I was out digging in the ground looking for old bottles, arrowheads, fossil rocks, anything old I could find. I wasn't a bad kid. I was Ronald, the kid who was the ring bearer in my mama's wedding, the little boy who used to watch his grandmother make delicious coconut cakes and pies. I felt like I didn't have anyone.

I was so depressed, I could have slept in that shelter, but it started raining so I caught a bus back to the Light House shelter for kids. After a week there, I ran away and went back to my father's to find out he'd gotten evicted. It was Fall, so the evenings would get cold, so I walked miles to find shelter. After walking up Eastern Ave for over an hour, my legs began to ache, I needed rest. I was exhausted. Exhausted from life. All I wanted in my life was to be safe, loved and cared for. I didn't want to be alone anymore. I ended up slipping into a tunnel I found off the road. It wreaked of liquor and eurine. The further I walked down the blackened walkway, I was startled by a deep groggy voice, "you lost kid?" an older, white-bearded gentleman asked. "No sir, I was just trying to find a place I could rest for a minute." ''You got any cigarettes?'' he asked. "No, I don't smoke, sorry." He murmerred something, then went back to sleep. As I leaned up against the wall and slowly slid down into a squatting position, tears began to stream down my face. I kept quiet so the man in the tunnel wouldn't hear me, but the tears didn't stop. I put my head between my knees and fell asleep. I was so cold, and the stench made it hard to breathe. Once I woke up, I started devising a plan.

I returned to my mother's house. Hiding outside, I watched for her and Walter to leave for work. When the coast was clear, I snuck in, using my door key. I noticed money on the kitchen table, along with my mom's jewelry on her nightstand. I went into my room, got some clothes and supplies, put them in a plastic trash bag and left. I had every opportunity to steal that $20 and take the jewelry as well, I left it all behind, as I shut the front door.

For most of my early teenage years, I bounced back and forth between my mother's house and Paul's little apartment until he got evicted. Paul and I kicked in doors of abandoned houses to find shelter and would sleep on the floor, until we were found out by the landlord. I remember one house in Kentucky, where we climbed through the window. I was so short that as I pulled myself up, I accidently cut myself - a piece of the glass was lodged in my arm. My dad didn't even care. There was no toilet paper to stop the bleeding so my dad handed me a dried up paint rag that was used to wipe the paintbrushes the workers had used to clean with. It was so cold in that house. We would roll the carpet up from the corner of the room to cover up with to stay warm.

  The next day, my dad left. I walked the streets looking for food but I wasn't that familiar with Kentucky. It started getting dark, so I went back to the house to see if my dad came back, but he wasn't there. I stayed there all night and he never showed up. I didn't know what to do. I was officially all alone. I had a cousin in Kentucky named Khalid that lived with his mom. I would go there to get something to eat sometimes. He didn't know how bad I really had it because I was too embarrassed to say anything. No one knew I was staying in this abandoned house, sleeping under the carpet and washing up at Burger King because there was no running water. My cousin and I got really close. He knew everybody in Kentucky and took me around to introduce me to other cousins we had there. Later, I told Khalid about a guy that was giving me problems. He pulled out a big 357 millimeter. I had never seen a gun so big - it looked like a cannon. He gave it to me and told me if I ever saw that guy again, pull it out on him. I felt empowered, like no one could ever hurt me again.

  One night, my stomach pains were so bad from hunger that I figured I had to do something drastic. With my new armory, I knew a sure fire way to get some food in my belly. I walked down the street until I found an apartment building with a dark entrance way. The building sat right on the corner and was in a perfect location to rob someone who stopped at a red light. I wore a black hoodie and dark jeans, clothes that made it easy to hide in the darkness. I tucked the 357 in the pocket of the hoodie and I patiently waited for either a jeep with the top down or a convertible. After waiting for over an hour, finally a jeep pulled up and stopped at the light. In it was a young guy, listening to heavy rock, sitting there unsuspecting. I crept around the back of his jeep before the light changed, jumped in and put the gun to his head. "Sir, I don't wanna hurt you, so please just give me whatever money you have." I said nervously. "I only have a couple of dollars in my glove compartment, you can have that." He responded. "I'm so sorry. I'm starving and I'm just trying to get some food" I told him. "Please don't do anything stupid to make me hurt you. Reach in the glove compartment real slow and pull the money out." He pulled out $3.00 and handed it to me. I hopped out the back of his vehicle and fled into the night. I ran down the street to Burger King. I hid the gun in the bushes before I went in. I ordered a cheeseburger, a small fry and a cup of water. I ran back to the abandoned house and ate that food like it was gourmet. I so badly regret robbing that guy. I was probably more afraid than my victim. That was the first time I'd ever done a robbery by myself, but I didn't have a choice. I later learned my dad got locked up for a probation violation. Being abandoned and left alone seemed to be a pattern I became expectant of. You don't realize how abandonment and rejection affects you when you're young. It becomes a subconscious fear and an automatic self-sabotage mechanism we develop as a way protect ourselves from the pain, especially when it's dealt by someone we love. I feared people leaving me. It confirmed my feelings of being unworthy and deepened the wounds left from being abandoned. I started to depend more and more on Diamond to manage my fears of never being enough and unworthy of love.

Chapter 5
The High School Years
1988-1990

In high school, I felt I was one step closer to achieving my dream of graduating, going to college and becoming a doctor. Even with all the dysfunction in my life, I still held on to the dream of being a doctor. I always had the desire to help people and change lives by healing them and making their lives better. I loved everything to do with science, math, and art. There was a science fair competition at my school that I participated in. I developed a volcano that actually erupted. I spent days studying everything about volcanoes. I built a huge dirt mountain, and then filed it with baking soda. On the day of the competition, I poured vinegar in it which caused it to erupt. I was so proud of my experiment. The art of science was amazing to me. It was like being a god. To be able to create something from dirt and make it into a beautiful creation, probably had a deeper effect on me than the other kids, because in my world, I was ugly and the ability to create something beautiful gave me such a sense of empowerment and purpose. Art was another tool I used to create beauty. The ability to take a blank canvas and apply different color paints and create a picture that I had in mind gave me a subconscious belief that my life would one day be beautiful, and that I would be someone that was special and do great things. I had a power that I didn't know existed in me. I was like a child mutant that was born with powers I didn't understand. I could think of something and from that thought I could create it. I had a God-given gift that made me so powerful that I could change my life and the life of others.

I had trouble staying focused in school. I went to Woodward High, a Cincinnati Public School. Unfortunately inner-city schools weren't like they are today. When I was young, it seemed teachers worked for paycheck, not for the purpose of having a life changing impact on kids' lives. I was blessed with two teachers that did actually care. Mr. Moore, my science teacher and Mr. Kraft, my English teacher. It wasn't about a paycheck for them. You could tell they were genuine and really wanted to see kids progress in life. One day I walked in Mr. Kraft's classroom and there was a kid that looked like he should have been in college. He had to be every bit of 5'10, 200 pounds, and me being 5'0, 130 pounds, that was a huge difference. His name was Brandon. He was a tough kid who had a reputation on the streets for putting guys to sleep with one punch. I don't know what the hell made me walk over and tell him to "get the fuck outta my seat." There were no assigned seats, but there a desk that I usually sat in by the window. As far as I was concerned, that was my assigned seat. When he didn't move, I felt like I had to make a statement so I pushed the table back on him and gave him a look like I was six feet tall and three-hundred pounds. That had to be the biggest mistake of my life. I was so embedded with the identity switch of Diamond that I forgot it was all made up. I really wasn't the tough guy Diamond pretended to be. If Ronald were in control, he would have just sat at a different desk, but Diamond was short so he had to be louder, tougher, and act bigger to cover up his insecurities and self-hatred. Diamond had to prove a point and he paid for that point. Two days later, Brandon saw me walking down Race Street and came up behind me and said, "what's up now nigga? You were talking all that shit and acting like you was a gangsta in school. Ain't nobody here to protect yo bitch ass now." I was scared as shit. He had about eight other guys with him and I knew there was nothing I could do, I froze in fear. I had nowhere to run and no one to run to. My uncle was with me, but there were so many guys that I couldn't be mad at him for not helping. He swung and knocked me down. I got up and started throwing punches but they weren't that effective against this giant of a kid. Next thing I knew, everybody else joined in. One dude got me on the ground while another dropped down on my head, leading with his knee. They stomped my head into the concrete with timberland boots, and after so many blows I started to blackout.

Then the police came screeching up. Everyone ran away. Out of my good eye, I saw an officer looking out his window at me, lying in the street.

"Is he dead?" he asked.

"I don't think so," and off they drove.

Next thing I remember was waking up in an ambulance, beaten and bruised. The cops were asking me questions about who did this to me, but I was dead set on getting revenge. I was changing more and more into this new identity I'd created for myself. Diamond was going to be this gangster that I envisioned for him. He was going to take care of me and the more that people hurt me, the more I built a self-mechanism that became immune to emotions. I was dying on the inside. I was becoming cold and emotionless. I wanted to kill that dude so badly. I told the cops I didn't know who it was that had beaten me almost to death. They didn't believe me, but they had to close the case.

After leaving the hospital, I rode the bus to my mom's house. I showed up with black eyes and bruised from head to toe. She seemed so cold when she saw me. I just wanted her to welcome me with open arms and take care of me. I needed my mom at that moment. I needed her to show me love, but because of her own personal issues, she couldn't. Once again I was abandoned, rejected, and left alone to deal with wounds that would have an impact for many years to come. I left there and went back Downtown. I kicked in a door of an abandoned apartment and slept on a pissed stained mattress on the floor. I was so lost. I couldn't believe this was my life. I was in so much pain that I could barely move. I could barely see out of my left eye. It was black and swollen shut. My nose was partially fractured and it bled at the slightest touch. I knew at that point I needed to form a crew. I needed some guys that I knew would have my back if anything was to go down.

After taking some time to heal, I went back to school. I was determined to make something of myself. I didn't want be anything like my dad. I still had dreams of being a doctor and I knew getting my education was my only ticket there. During all of first quarter, a sophomore girl named Tina, stalked me all day. She would show up to all my classes, pop her head in, then disappear. I thought she was cutie, but I had my eye on another girl named Stacie. One day at lunch Tina cut in line to get behind me.

"Why are you trying to avoid me?" She asked.

"I'm not avoiding you, I didn't even know you liked me." I replied.

"Soooo, the notes I sent you and me blowing kisses at you in class didn't give you a hint?"

Okay, she had me.

"What are you doing after school?" She asked.

"I don't have any plans, just going home I guess."

"Meet me after school in the back parking lot. I'm going to show you how much I like you."

I agreed to meet her after school. As I walked away, I thought, *Oh, my God, what have I done*? I hadn't ever French-kissed a girl before. *What if she laughs at me when I try to kiss her? I could never show my face again,* I thought. I couldn't breathe. You'd think a kid whose dad was a pimp, would know more about sex. Right after school, I ran into the bathroom and found an empty stall. Inside, I made a fist, bent my thumb forward, spread my fingers a little, and kissed my hand. My first French-kiss ever was with my own hand. Then I split an orange in half and practiced on that. It didn't even matter; when our lips met you'd thought I was a master at kissing. With Tina, I just closed my eyes, put my arm around her waist and pulled her to me and kissed her, soft and slowly - she love it. After that, I couldn't keep her away from me. Man, oh man.

When I was in school, dancing was the thing to do. If you were part of a dance crew, you were the man. I had a younger cousin named Rashad that could dance his ass off. I saw him dancing in a talent show once, after seeing him I knew I had a love for dancing. He would show me some moves and we would work on routines with my older cousin Kim. There was nothing you could tell me. I had mastered a new skill to make Diamond more popular. I started my own dance crew called Rated R. We named it that because all our names started with an R and we were hot. On Friday and Saturday nights, we'd go to Golden Skates, a local skating rink where we would skate part of the time, dance and spend the rest of the night fighting. We all had dreams of making it big.

Having a crew only guaranteed that I would be in more fights and we were, every week it seemed. Then I began to drink. We would skip school and go to the gas station across the street from my school. The workers there didn't care about us being underage, they would sell alcohol to anyone. We would buy a 40 ounce bottle and split it. I really wasn't a drinker but to fit in I would take a few gulps. I really didn't like the taste but my crew was none the wiser. Diamond had to maintain his act. Since I was the leader of my crew, I couldn't look like a lame. Skipping school became the norm. Kim and I would go Downtown to get a double up bag of crack. A double-up was basically a way of doubling your money. We were young and new to the dope game, but we were doing it before our classmates even knew how to sell dope. My dad had taught me a lot about the streets and the dope game. The rest, I just winged it.

One day, my homeboys and I skipped school and went driving around in a dope fiend's car we rented in exchange for free dope. We were drinking a 40 ounce of Old English, clowning and talking about girls. Just as we approached the bridge over the interstate, my friend Tyrone lost control. We swerved and crashed into a truck, towing a boat. The boat fell off the trailer and flew over the railing onto the highway below. We flipped over twice. It looked like we were on the inside of a kaleidoscope. When the world stopped spinning, we realized where we had come to rest. Our car leaned up against the railing. One more turn or even half a turn and someone would have been picking us up off the pavement below. We could've died. Every time the car would flip, those who were sitting in the front, their faces smashed against the windshield. Glass had broken from the window and cut up their faces. They had blood leaking from their ears and eyes. My only injury was a small scratch around my waist, where the seat belt dug into my skin a little. I had never told anyone this but I don't know if it was an angel or intuition, but something told me to put my seat belt on a few minutes before the wreck.

We abandoned the car and hailed a cab back Downtown. My dad moved in with one his girlfriends and she would let me crash there at times. Paul stayed high most of the time. I don't remember him ever being sober. If it wasn't crack it was heroin, if not heroin, it was alcohol. I really never knew my dad; only the shell of a man that used to be a revolutionist. Every now and then, I would go to my mother's house, even though she was seldom there. Mom was working longer hours, trying to make ends meet since Walter had lost his job. One evening I had several shots of Jack Daniels to help ease the pain of the migraines I suffered, and to help me sleep. I didn't know why but it was as if my brain had a loose connection. I would feel really tired by the time I laid down but when I closed my eyes to go to sleep it felt like I had drank a cup of coffee. I would toss and turn all night. I wasn't a drinker and couldn't stand the thought of using drugs but I was so exhausted, I thought a shot or two would help. The next morning, I woke up on my mother's sofa, my head was killing me.

"Get up!" Mom yelled. "How much did you drink last night? You could barely stand up." She pushed my shoulder. "Get up!"

She rolled up the shades and the bright light made my eyes shrink back into my head.

"Ronald, you don't even drink. What's going on with you? Get your butt up. We need to get you some help"

"I can't, not today." I turned away from the light. "I feel like crap."

Mom pulled my arm until I fell off the couch. "Let's go!"

"No, mama, I gotta go to school".

"I ain't taking you to school," she said.

She drove me to the Jewish Hospital Dependency Unit. I resisted when I saw where we were going.

"Ronald, please go in. It's a good place and they can help you." Then she whispered, "What happened to my baby."

I shook my head and rolled my eyes, but I agreed to let her check me in. I could use the chance to get some rest.

The counselor sat us down to do an evaluation. She began to ask me questions about my drug use but obviously there wasn't much to say. She ran down a checklist of drugs and I answered each one honestly. I had never tried weed or anything else and my drinking had just started that same year to help my insomnia, and I only did that a couple of times. She asked if I thought I had a drinking problem since alcohol was the only thing I had ever tried. I told her no. The counselor was confused as to why I was there. Next she began to ask about my home life. My mom interrupted, "That's not why we're here." Then I said, "I told you what he did to me." The counselor looked at me, then at my mother, then back to me again but she said nothing.

My mom sat quiet for a moment. "Ronald, are you sure it wasn't an accident?"

"Accident? You mean like the one when I 'accidentally' put my hand in the way of Walter's beating me like an animal? I'm your son and you let that man do those things to me!" My mother seemed to be at a loss for words. I had to look away before I could continue.

I turned to the counselor. "And you know what? The man, my adoptive father, who abused me, people look up to him, they think he's an upstanding member of the community, a Christian. It's all a bunch of bullshit!"

"But, Ronald," I heard Mom say as I ran out the door. I found the stairwell and hid under the stairs. Then, I ran out the side of the building and caught the bus back Downtown.

The next time I saw my mother, I was in front of a judge. The charge that time was theft. I got fined five hundred dollars, she paid the fine along with court costs. I had to promise to stay out of trouble and get my diploma. "Sure," I promised. Within a few months, I was arrested again. Mom didn't always have bail money, during those times I would sit in the holding cell for days until they released me

"When you turn eighteen, there won't be anything I can do in court, you'll be an adult." Mom talked and I pretended to listen. She went on, "You better stop before you end up in an adult prison." I lifted my eyes toward her.

I didn't feel guilty about it. I blamed her for my screwed up life. I wouldn't be in this situation if it wasn't for her - that was my perception but what I failed to realize was that even though my childhood was screwed up and a lot of traumatic things happened, at the end of the day, I was now almost grown and the judge wouldn't care about my difficult childhood. I had to be responsible for my choices since I would be the only one to deal with the consequences. But my choices were shaped out of a dysfunctional upbringing that became my norm. All I knew was survival. My actions looked irrational to others, but in my world it was the only way I knew how to stay alive. My brain was wired in a way that kept me in a constant, hyperactive mode. Before I could process a thought, I was already bringing action to the problem and usually it was an action that would come with consequences. Afterwards, when everything stopped moving, I would look at the choices I made and people that were affected by them and feel so much regret.

I finally landed a place of my own, ironically it was around the corner from the building I grew up in Downtown. It was a shit hole but it was my home. I shared it with a friend who dropped out of Job Corp. Our apartment was the party spot. We kept girls, liquor and dope there. He wasn't from Downtown, so he couldn't sell dope in the neighborhood, but since it was my territory, I sold little ten and twenty dollar pieces of crack. One day I lost my pack of dope and I had to make up for it. When one of my customers paged me, requesting a $60 piece of dope, I made up some fleece, put orajel on it and tried to pass it off as the real thing. When I opened the baggy and handed her the product, the customer took a small piece off and tasted it. Next thing I knew, the guy she had with her went to lock the door. When I turned back to face the woman, she pulled out a straight razor. "You ain't going nowhere." She said. "Bitch please!" I pulled out my gun and walked backwards towards the door, she asked for her money back and I said, "What money? This is my money now." I didn't realize the mistake I had made. All this time I had been living across the street, serving one of the biggest dope boys' mom on that side of town. I didn't realize who she was, I just thought that if she needed dope, she'd just get it from her son. I also didn't know that he had a rule, and that rule was he wouldn't sell dope to his own mother.

Later that evening, I saw Icey, the woman's son. "Diamond, what up bruh? Come here real quick, I wanna talk to you about something." He seemed cool so I thought maybe his mom didn't say anything to him. I walked in the hallway, he shoved me up against the mailboxes and put a gun to my throat. I tensed up thinking he was going to blow my brains out. "You know that was my momma you sold that fleece to don't you?" He asked. "I do now. I swear I didn't know it before I did it. I was just trying to get my money up so I could cop an eight-ball." He pulled the gun from my neck and reached into his pocket and gave me a baggie of crack. It had to be at least 6 or 7 grams, just enough for me to get back "up." "Take this little homie and don't ever do no bullshit like that again." After that, I had all the respect in the world for Icey.

I started gaining attention from some of the girls Downtown, but there was one girl all the guys talked about. She didn't seem to have any interest in any of the guys in the hood, though. Her name was Monica, and if I could help it, she was going to be mine. She was taller than I was, had high cheekbones and a great body. I would watch her walk home from school but would never speak. She was younger, but so damn fine, I was determined that she would one day be my girl.

That weekend I was jumped by some guys from the hood. I wore my shades to cover up the bruises. One day while I was sitting in the park Monica walked over, "Hi" She said. "Hey" I replied nervously. "I see you staring at me all the time so I thought I'd stop and speak. "Hold up a minute. What's your name?" I asked her, "Monica." She replied, as if I didn't already know. "My name is Diamond but everybody calls me D." She reached and took my glasses off.

"Oh my God, Diamond. What happened?"

"I got jumped by some guys on the West side but I'm cool." I winced when she raised her hand to my face. She said. "You need someone to take care of you."

"That would be nice," I told her.

I thought she was the most wonderful girl in the world, and we were inseparable after that day. Monica was a straight-A student and was chosen to be in the Young Scholars Program at Ohio State. It would take her away from me for two weeks in the summer. While she was in Columbus, there was a rumor that she was sleeping around. I found out from the letters Monica sent to her homegirl. When she got back, I confronted her.

"I think we should break up," I said to her on the front steps of her apartment building. I couldn't believe I was telling her that.

"I don't think we can, Ronald."

"Why not? After what you did?"

"I'm pregnant and it's yours."

I was stunned. "But how can you know?"

"I just do. I'm carrying your baby."

"I don't believe it. I want a DNA test."

"Fine!" She stormed back inside.

When I called her the next day, her mother answered the phone.

"Diamond, don't you ever come around here again."

"What did I do?" I asked angrily.

"You running around here talking about this baby ain't yours. You know Monica ain't been with nobody but you". And then she hung up.

Monica's family gave me a second chance, and no matter

how hard I tried, I couldn't provide for my daughter. I gave up the dope game and worked as a delivery man for local furniture store, but didn't make much over minimum wage. I tried to stay away from the streets as much as I could, and spent more time with Monica.

After a year, Monica told me I could never see my daughter again, not unless I made my child support payments. I honestly couldn't be mad. I sucked as a dad. I loved my beautiful baby girl. But it was hard enough taking care of myself, let alone another life. I did the best I could but my best wasn't enough. By this time I had dropped out of school. Like Biggie said, "It was all a dream." I hadn't lived up to the promise I made my mom. No high school diploma and no college plans in sight. It was time to go hard with this street shit and get paid.

Being a school dropout didn't sit well with me. Even though the street life had become such a huge part of my life, I knew I was different from other kids. There was something inside me that wouldn't let me give up. I went to our school board to sign up for the G.E.D test. They gave a pretest to school dropouts for free. If you passed the test on the first try they would give you a certificate to go to take your GED test, also for free. Despite dropping out of school in the 10th grade, I still passed the G.E.D test on the first try. I didn't know what I would do with it. I was just proud to have that accomplishment under my belt. I figured no college would ever except me with a G.E.D but whatever, it was mine.

One night, I went to my dad's to lay low for a while. I pulled an all-nighter on the block and needed to close my eyes for a second. Dad was high as usual, a heavy-fisted pounding on the door startled me. It sounded like the police.

"Who is it?" my dad asked.

I heard a garbled answer. Dad got up.

"What you want?"

"I need to ask you something," the voice responded.

I stuck my head around the corner of the kitchen wall and

watched as Dad opened the door. A young dope boy from the hood named Que stood there. He had on a Yankees hat and a white t-shirt.

"I thought you was gonna let me use your car," He held the gun at his waist and my dad glanced down at it. I knew my dad would let the dope boys use his car sometimes so that he could get dope and so they could drive to hit their licks. "Not, today. Last time you brought it back on empty," my dad told him and he tried to close the door but the guy stuck his gun in the crack of the door and pulled the trigger. Blood exploded out of the back of my dad's neck and I heard the bullet shoot into the wall behind the sofa. Que ran away and I yelled for help as Dad staggered back and collapsed on the floor. When the medics got there, Paul was so high on crack that his adrenaline helped him manage the pain. He actually walked to the ambulance with the help from the EMT's. The dope had him so numb I don't think he felt anything. The bullet had gone out the back of his neck.

Que, the guy that shot my dad was still was on the loose. Everybody kept asking if I was going to get him back. I really didn't want to though. We had a saying in the streets, "Charge it to the game." Basically that means if you're in the streets and living that life and you go to jail, get shot, or robbed then you should expect some or all these things to happen, and not to trip when it does. I was under so much pressure to retaliate. Diamond didn't have the courage to say no. Diamond was a people pleaser, he allowed other people's opinion to shape his perception of who he was trying to be.

"Bruh if you don't go see dude and put some heat in him you know they gon think you soft right?" Calvin said.

"I know what I gotta do. I'm gon handle this shit tonight. Meet me at my crib at 9pm and let's handle this nigga." I replied.

I don't know who the hell I was trying to be. This Diamond character was getting real and there was nothing Ronald could do to stop it. Some of my friends were true thugs. They would shoot you in a minute and not blink an eye but me, HA, I was no killer. I didn't even like the sight of blood. I had to carry this out though. I knew my crew was expecting me to take action. I was scared as hell but I didn't show it. My hands shook as I loaded the tech. The bullets kept falling out the clip every time I'd put one in.

"You aight bruh?" Cal asked.

"Yeah I'm cool. It's just cold in here. You ready to go get this nigga?" I replied

"Bruh I'm ready."

I hopped in the back of Calvin's flatbed truck. The plan was to roll up on the dude's block, Cal would whistle once the guy was in sight, then I would raise up and unload the tech on him.

"Stay down D. I see that nigga. Wait, wait, whooot whoot!" Cal whistled.

I rose up. As soon as Que saw me, he dashed off running. I really didn't want to shoot him but I wanted to let him know that he wasn't going to just get away with shooting my dad and there would be no consequences. I was trying to make a statement that would later cost me.

"Hit that nigga D!" Cal yelled.

"BLAAT, BLAAT, BLAAT. He cut through the alley. Go around the block and cut that nigga off." I replied.

We got around the block but Que must have hidden in the bushes. He was nowhere to be found.

"Let's get back to the pad so I can drop this gun off." I told Calvin.

It felt good to shoot at somebody. It was empowering. I don't think I ever felt so invincible before. Guns can make a shy guy come out his shell real quick. I just wanted to give the impression that I wasn't to be fucked with. I wanted people to know that I wasn't scared to let them bullets fly. I didn't realize real gangsters don't get scared, they get even.

"YEAH NIGGA, WHAT'S UP NOW!?" Que yelled.

I turned to see him and about seven other dudes shooting at Calvin and me. I had on sweats so I couldn't carry the tech but Cal had on jeans so he could tuck it easier, but the barrel was so long it got caught on his belt. We were running in between cars

and trying to stay low. Calvin finally got the gun out so we started shooting back. I heard the bullets flying past my head. We made it to the main street where we knew they wouldn't follow.
"Bruh, you alright?" Cal asked.
"Yeah I'm good." I replied, but I was breathing so hard that I didn't even realize I'd been hit.
"Oh shit. I'm hit. I didn't even feel that shit." I said.
I was grazed in my left shoulder but it wasn't anything serious, thank God.

Just when I thought the craziness in my life was over, I met a girl that spelled crazy with the four letters, N-I-N-A. I had just turned nineteen and some friends took me out to celebrate. We ended up at a party in Walnut Hills, my little sister Drea came with a friend. "Hey sis, who is ole girl you came with?" I asked. "That's my homegirl Nina. You wanna meet her? She ain't like these hoodrats you used to though bro." "Don't play me like that. You know I only like classy hoodrats." We laughed as she walked me over to meet her. "Nina this is my brother Diamond, Diamond this is Nina. I'm gonna get a drank while you two love birds get to know each other." "So Nina, what are you doing here? You look out of place." I asked. "She responded in fluent French. I couldn't understand a word that came out of her mouth but I was enjoying watching them come out.

We exchanged numbers and after the party, I tried to get her back to my crib. "Come to your crib for what? She asked. "Just to chill. I just wanna get to know you better." Shit, I was trying to smash but she wasn't the type of girl that would go for the 'I wanna fuck you' line, so I had to be the sweet, gentle butterfly and come at her like a gentleman. We talked late into the night and early morning. Nina was intelligent and sweet, and she had a good job at the YWCA. Appearances can be deceiving though. I learned that Nina had also grown up in an abusive home, and people say if you grow up with abuse, then later you either seek it out or become an abuser yourself. I didn't need to watch Dr. Phil to figure out that she had some serious issues dealing with her past. She was recreating her childhood and I was reinventing mine. One day we were sitting on the sofa when she said she had something to tell me.

"You've got a what?" I asked her.

"You know, a split personality."

"Who clsc arc you?"

"Nyla." She leaned toward me and I leaned away. "Hold the fuck up. We not gon act like you didn't just tell me you got other people living inside yo head."

"Nina, Nyla, whatever your name is. What do you want me to call you, Nyla?"

"Don't call me that." Her face tightened up.

"Okay . . . Nyla." I laughed a little, still thinking she was kidding around.

Before I could say anything else, in an instant, Nina, or whoever she was, picked up a beer bottle and fired it at me. As soon as she picked it up, I was on the move, she was halfway across the room when I saw her arm swing forward like Roger Clemens. She missed, barely, and I felt it brush the hair above my ear. When she saw the bottle shatter against the wall, she ran to the kitchen and started rummaging through the silverware drawer. I heard her say "yes" and the rummaging stopped. With a demented look, she sprinted out of the kitchen toward me, carrying a big knife. She lunged at me and I managed to avoid her and grab the hand clutching the knife. After I took it from her, her face changed and she sat back down on the sofa.

"What happened to you?" she asked.

"Oh, right. Like you don't know."

"Nyla?"

I nodded.

"I'm so sorry. I black out sometimes and I'm not in control anymore."

She gave me an interesting glare and said. "Sooo, you hungry?"

Being the master-of-great-decisions at that time in my life, I didn't even kick her out. Several months later, she stabbed me in the thigh and I had to go to the hospital for stitches. Because of the hospital reports, that story was published in the local newspaper. Life with Nina was tough, but I was just as messed up as she was, so I tried to make her better. I didn't know this at that time but people that are co-dependent have a need to save other people from their dysfunction, while ignoring their own issues. Codependency was reliance on other people for approval and identity, and as Diamond I needed as much approval as I could get. I decided I was going to save Nina. We got an apartment together and things seemed to be cool. We argued like some wild banshees but we would be good by nightfall. One day I got a phone call to that would change my life.

Ring, Ring! "Hello?"

"Hi, can I speak to Diamond." The voice on the phone asked.

"This is Diamond. Who is this?"

"This is Michael Pane from the group Shilowave. Have you ever heard of us?"

I couldn't believe it. I was a big fan of old school music and I used to watch his band play live at a local club. They were produced by Roger Troutman and Bootsie Collins in the '80s.

"Of course I know who you are Mr. Pane. How can I help you?"

"I saw you and your dance crew perform in the Cincinnati Apollo and I wanted to know if you'd like to tour with me and my band and choreograph the tour overseas?"

"Yessss!!" I said to Nina. "We about to get paid. I'll tour for a few months and make the money and send it back for you and the baby. You and Tre can have everything you want."

"Don't go getting all optimistic about things," she said. "You haven't danced in a long time, and you don't know these new dance moves. How long would you be gone anyway? We've got a baby to take care of."

"For a couple of months. I'll be back in plenty of time for Christmas. C'mon, babe, this could be good for us." It was decided. I was going to Thailand.

Chapter 6

One Night In Bangkok
September-November 1990

"You got a passport?" Michael asked me.
        "No."
"You gotta get a passport. Im driving some of the band members
up to Chicago tomorrow to their passport office. They issue
same day passports. Be ready to leave at 6 a.m."
        Two weeks later I was on a plane to Thailand.
The flight to Bangkok was long, some twenty-four hours from
Chicago. First, we flew to California, then Korea and finally to
Thailand. I was exhausted. Some of the guys slept but I got stuck
next to a big guy who snored for most of the trip. Finally, we
arrived. I was so excited. Even though it was November, it was
very hot - the temperature was around 105 degrees. When we
strolled into the terminal, I was stunned at how beautiful the
women were. All I had ever seen were people in Cincinnati:
white, black, and a few others mixed in, but no one as beautiful
as I saw there.
        After we claimed our luggage and crammed into a van, I
had my first views of Bangkok. Congested, run down, poor
people all over, I could have been back in the projects except
there were no blacks around. The streets were thick with people,
like bugs scurrying away from the light. Our hotel, the Pentium
Mansion, from the name seemed like it would be an elegant place
but then we pulled into the front lot, it was a dump. We walked
inside and I swear I saw twenty roaches within the first minute. I
hate roaches. The rugs on the lobby floor were old and had scuff
holes in them, and the furniture wasn't much better. It looked and
felt like nothing had been replaced in fifty years. But, hey, at
least it was cool being in a foreign country, so I checked in and
went upstairs to lie down. I fell asleep instantly and didn't wake

up until the next morning.

When I woke up, I thought it would be cool to tour the neighborhood. It was still early but the heat was already unbearable. Hot, steamy, over 100 degrees, I felt like I needed another shower after ten minutes. Then I noticed something more oppressive than the heat – the smell. The air punched me with all sorts of foul odors, so thick, you could taste them: urine, feces, rotting meat, and spoiled milk. All of that before I left the hotel. Then, I stepped out into the worst slums I would ever hope to see. I thought we had it bad back home but my little apartment with Nina looked like the Hilton compared to this. Small sheets of rusted tin held up with sticks, were home to entire families. Grandparents, parents, kids, all sitting up under there to escape the scorching sun, it seemed, only to collect water from the filthy river that ran behind our hotel, the same one they went to the bathroom in and the same one mange-ridden dogs ran in. As I passed by the makeshift homes, I tried not to look into them but I couldn't help myself. Faces leered at me from the shadows. Thin, haunting faces.

It took me more than just a walk to get my bearings in Bangkok. That first day, I decided to check out the stores, so I walked into the first one I saw. Since I hadn't exchanged my dollars for baht's, I only had my fives, tens and twenties from home. Later, I found out I had paid way too much for a candy bar and a drink. I also bought a box of condoms, and learned a valuable lesson: always read the box. Especially in a country where I'm considered tall.

"Man, look at this thing, you've got to be kidding. It will never fit," I had met the most beautiful girl I'd ever seen and I wanted her in the worst way, but my health was more important, there was no way that condom was ever going to fit. "Ain't no way," I said. "I couldn't put this thing on my finger."

"Try again."

"I'm good babe. I didn't know they made condoms this small" I shook my head. My excitement was quickly fading. "My circulation could be cut off. It might be dangerous." I looked at her. "Sorry, baby."

Another day, several of us were playing cards when someone said they were hungry. Pretty soon, everyone was up and out the door in search of a Bangkok hot dog stand. We had heard food was cheap at the corner stands - that sounded like a good plan, considering our budget. A man, who was outside in front of the hotel, pointed to a cart up the street. The closer we got to it, the more our disbelief grew.

"What in the hell is that?" one of us said.

Something attached to a string was baking over an open flame. Grease and blood ran off of it and splashed onto the small grill. It could have been a rat for all we knew. Turned out it was a squid. The owner of the stand said something in Thai and we all shook our hands in front of us.

"I'm not that hungry. I'm going to McDonald's."

After that, I stuck to McDonald's every day.

I had a hard time falling asleep because our hotel was infested with roaches. And not just regular roaches but roaches the size of baby turtles.

The roaches didn't even try to hide. You would see so many during the day, you didn't want to *think* about how many were tucked away behind the walls. When it was quiet at night, you could hear them crawling. A soft clicking, scraping sound as they ran all over. Then you could hear them fly, that thumbing-the-edge-of-a-book kinda noise. One night, I was having the best dream. A beautiful girl was running her hand lightly over my face. She's swirling her fingers in my ears. She's touching my lips, my eyes, my hair, my nose, down my chest. She's all over me and I'm getting excited. To my surprise it wasn't a girl. It was big fucking roaches. I jumped out of bed and I felt them crunching under my bare feet. "Man, I'll never sleep in Thailand."

Day one of our tour was a week away – hard to believe I was getting paid to dance. In the afternoons, we rehearsed at the Leo Grottos, a nice place even though the stage was small. First, the band decided which songs they were going to do, and then I would create dance routines to go with them. The singers practiced on one part of the stage, while I worked with the dancers on the other. I did all the choreography for the group while we were on tour. It was hard but a freeing experience; I loved it. Once performances started, we didn't get a day off for two weeks. Practice every day and then do at least five sets each night. All any of us did was practice, perform, eat and sleep.

During that time, though, we were making money and becoming celebrities, which made me really popular with the ladies. When we finally gained some down time, some of the band members and I took a motorcycle taxi to the mall. Once we got there, we went crazy spending all our money. The prices were so good; we bought something of everything—silk, jeans, perfume, and leather jackets. A few really good-looking women were also there shopping. My buddy and I tried to pick up a couple of them but they couldn't understood us, or so they acted. They would giggle and then chatter back and forth with each other. I finally gave up.

After one of the shows, I met a woman who was half-Australian and half-Thai but she was an American citizen. She looked like a model, more curves than the Pennsylvania Turnpike. "I saw your picture in the paper," she told me.

"That's cool," I replied.

"Can I sit down?"

"Sure." We talked for a while. She loved being seen with me. "I've got to do another show in a bit. Will you be here when I get done?" I asked

"No, but you can take my number...here." She handed me her phone number.

I called her the next day. I asked her if she wanted to take me shopping. She agreed.

That afternoon, when she pulled up in front of the hotel, her eyes about bugged out of her head when all five band members piled into her SUV. She thought it would just be me, so she didn't understand what was going on and before she could say anything, we were all crammed in like sardines. At the mall, she paid for all of my things. I told the other band members to put their things on the counter for her to pay for as well. Steam was coming out of her ears. I guess I should have told her what we say in the hood, "It ain't no fun if the homies can't have none". After she dropped us back at the motel, she sped away. I never heard from her again.

Another night, after a show, there was a woman, maybe in her thirties, dancing by herself in the middle of the dance floor. She had long blonde hair and wore a black evening dress; she was quite attractive. She was spinning around and around, looking at the ceiling, so I walked out and started dancing with her. I turned toward my buddies, they were all laughing and hooting at me for being out there with this sexy American white woman. Then someone tapped me on my shoulder. I turned around and it was her. She moved closer to me and started grinding and hanging all over me. I looked over her shoulder, even the D.J was pointing at me and smiling. Then she put her arms around me and kissed me. My buddies stopped laughing. Of course, I kissed her back, she was very attractive and she was loaded. Her husband owned mall in California. Next, her eyes rolled back in her head and she jerked her body all over the place. Quickly, she reached out and put her hand on my forehead. She leaned in to me.

"Use the power wisely," she said.

"What?"

"Use the power wisely," she repeated.

"Uh, yeah ok. Whatever you say." I would've agreed to anything to get some of that, but I think she was involved with the devil or demons or something. But the power of booty can overthrow the fear of the devil any day, so I gave her my number. She never did call but I saw her ads for her 1-800 psychic company.

The people who came to our concerts were well off, so it wasn't unusual for some very wealthy folks to be in the audience. This woman's husband was the owner of a big computer company—

I'm talking major bucks. We instantly connected. I really enjoyed talking to her in my broken Thai and her broken English. Later, when I took her back to my hotel room, I asked her why she was in Bangkok. "My husband's in Alaska. He doesn't even know where I am," she told me.

"What do you do, travel the world hanging with dancers?"

"Oh, no," she laughed. "I'm on my way to Burma. My mother and sister are stuck there. There's a war. I need to get them out."

She told me about how she and her husband slept in separate bedrooms. "People think because I have all this money, everything is just peachy. Well, it's not."
I never did have sex with her, I just liked talking to her. The next day she caught a flight to Burma. Our paths never crossed again.

After we had been in Thailand a month or so, the band relaxed a bit and sometimes during the last show of the night, they would let me get on the mic. One night, I was rapping to a song when Michael, the owner, came running up on stage and snatched the mic away from me. "Don't be trying to steal my spotlight," he yelled. I was ready to knock his head off. The band members grabbed me. "It's not worth it," they said. They were right, but I was ready for a flight back to Cincinnati. There was only one problem: the guys who were paying us had our passports and airline tickets. Some band members had left them hanging and the promoters made sure it didn't happen again. But not having your passport with you could get you in serious trouble.

I went on a date one night and was caught in the worst traffic jam. With cars stopped, police walked back and forth, looking for suspicious characters. One cop strolled up to our cab and motioned for my date to roll down her window. She did and he started talking ninety miles a minute in Thai. It was all gibberish to me.

"He wants to see your passport," my date, Dari said.

Sweat started pouring down my face. Stories I heard of

Thai jails came to mind and they weren't good stories. *Damn, damn,* I thought. *How could I be so stupid?* "Tell him it's at my hotel." She leaned out the window and spoke to him.

With no expression, he looked at me and then turned to his partner who was checking cars facing the other way. They chatted for a few seconds and the second cop walked over to my side of the car.

Dari looked concerned. "They don't believe you." She paused and looked straight ahead. "You're not going to get me in trouble. I'll tell them I don't know you."

"Oh, great. Thanks." One cop was on his radio. An image of prison flashed in my mind and it wasn't an American prison. "Tell them I'm on tour and our manager keeps all the passports."

She got his attention and I waited while they spoke. I heard a couple of words I recognized. Then she frowned. *Oh, no,* I thought.

"What?"

"They pretty much said, 'Yeah, right, and we're Milli Vanilli.'"

The cop on the driver's side laid his hand on her door and said something to Dari. She turned to me, "What group?"

"Shilowave."

Both policemen heard me and their faces turned to instant smiles. "Shilowave?" the officer next to me asked, as he stood up straight and yelled across the top of the car. "Shilowave!" More teeth flashed and they stuck their heads almost inside the car.

"Yes, Shilowave," I said. I nodded and waved at them. The one next to Dari jumped back from the car, and then the other cop did also. By now, there was room to move, traffic had thinned a bit. With backs straight and whistles blowing, they motioned for us to move on. As we pulled away, they waved and yelled Sawadee.

There was never an end to bizarre happenings in Bangkok. I had a day off and I went to a different club to see what it was like. People recognized me as being the lead dancer for Shilowave, including one little scrawny guy with black hair scattered all over his head. Before I could even sit down, he came over and slammed his elbow on the table and held out his hand. He wanted to arm wrestle. I thought he had to be nuts. I was pretty strong from all the dancing for this puny squirt to try me. Now, all these folks started gathering around and girls were giggling and talking in Thai. He kept smacking his elbow down on the table and saying unknown phrases, that seemed in a disrespectful tone. I shrugged and leaned in closer to him. His eyes bugged out of his head, and his breathing became heavy. His buddies patted him on the back. When I put my hand out to grasp his, the crowd let out a big "aaaaahhh." He grabbed my hand and I could feel pressure immediately. Someone put a hand on top of ours. Across from me, this nut's veins and tendons were about to come loose from his neck when, suddenly, the hand grasping the top of ours let go. Everybody was going crazy, screaming, and banging on things. I all but broke his arm off at the wrist, as I quickly slammed his forearm into the table. He grimaced and held his arm with his other hand. The other people looked at me like I did something to him. Maybe this wasn't a good idea, I thought. Then I left quickly.

That Friday night a stagehand grabbed me after the show. "There's someone who wants to meet you," he said. We always had at least an hour break and I needed a drink. I walked over to the table where two guys and a woman were sitting. The men were smiling but the lady seemed timid. You never knew what people were thinking in Bangkok. The men introduced themselves in Thai (by then I knew the basics) as brothers and told me that their sister, Sujari, had watched my dancing and really wanted to meet me. I smiled at her, nodded, and pulled out a chair. As I thought about it, I did remember them from the night before, sitting closer to the front. One of the brothers asked if I wanted a drink.

"Sure. Jack Daniels," I said and sat down in the chair between Sujari and her brother. The tables were small, and we were almost sitting on top of each other.

We talked a bit but not much. I spoke to the sister through her brothers.

"She's visiting us here on business," a brother said. "Our sister's very successful in India and in Thailand. A bank manager. Nice, yes?"

"I'm impressed," I replied. I looked at Sujari and pretended to politely applaud. She smiled. Suddenly, she reached across the table and grabbed my hand. She pointed to the dance floor where a DJ was playing her song.

"She wants to dance with you."

"That much I understood."

We danced for several songs, including one slow one. She leaned against me and I lightly put my arms around her. We returned to the table when the song went off. The brothers were grinning like it was the first time they had ever seen their sister dance or the first time she had ever walked for that matter.

"Very nice, very nice. We have more drinks," they said as we sat down.

"Great, thanks."

"Our sister, she dances well, yes?"

"A good dancer. She's real cute."

The two brothers spoke silently to each other and they both turned back to me in unison. "You like our sister?"

Uh-oh, I thought. "Yeah, kinda."

The taller one grabbed my hand and put it on top of Sujari's. He stared at me with a serious face. "You marry."

"What?!" I yanked my hand from under hers so fast her forearm thumped the table.

"Yes. You like. She cute. You marry."

I pointed at him and said, "You're crazy."

He snatched my hand again and tried to pull me back to Sujari. "You like. You like. Marry! Marry!" By the last "marry," he was grimacing in one direction and I was straining in the other. I broke free and we all jumped out of our seats at the same time. I can't believe this, I thought. "I have to go," I said. Then all three of them started pulling on my sleeves.

"Marry. Marry," they pleaded.

"Stop it!" I shouted. "I'm not marrying anyone."

When I said that, they all collapsed back into their chairs like blow-up dolls that had just been popped. Sujari looked like she was going to cry. So did her brothers.

I backed away with my arms in front of me. "I'm sorry."

When I got to the door of the club, I sprinted across the street to our hotel. Catching the elevator up to my room, I checked the lobby before I got inside, just in case. Upstairs, I locked my door and lay on the bed, longing for home. When I went back to do my next show, their table was empty.

Every so often, we'd go down to the Pitau strip, where vendors sold all sorts of black market things: fake Rolexes, Polo knock-offs, Louis Vuitton, Gucci - you name it, they had it stored somewhere. A few famous restaurants were in that area too, but the fake designer shoes and great food wasn't the main reason people went to the strip. It wasn't called the "strip" for no reason. There were prostitutes all over the place and strip clubs with glass windows so you could see right in. Sex was for viewing or for buying. Some of the street corners had boxing rings set up—girls slugging it out or guys having kickboxing battles. It all was almost too much to absorb. Mike, one of the band members, Ruby and I were watching the female boxers pound on each other when someone brushed against me.

"Sorry," I said.

"Don't be," a feminine voice said.

I looked at her. Black hair and eyes, slender, possibly Italian, certainly not a local.

"Are you next?" I asked her.

"Next?" she lifted her eyebrows.

She laughed. "Funny. I'm a lover not a fighter" She stepped close to me and put her hand on my arm.

"I don't pay for no ass" I said.

"I'm not for sale," she replied.

An hour later, we were in my hotel room.

"You really look good," I told her.

"Just good?" "I mean great."

"Okay, then. Great."

"Tell me I look great. And mean it."

"You look f-a-a-a-bulous."

"I need something to drink and eat." She sat down on the bed and reached for the remote. "Go get me wine and a sandwich." She waved at me.

"Huh? You're kidding right?"

"No, now." She waved again.

"Bitch you must be crazy. This ain't Africa and my name ain't Toby, bitch."

"What kind of man are you, you arrogant fool. Don't you know how to be a gentleman?"

"Hey, look. You're the one who wanted to come up here, I was cool just chilling with my friends." I was getting pissed.

"Bring me food or I'll scream." She opened her mouth and kept it frozen in place.

"Scream then. It won't matter here. We hear it all the time." I paused a moment. "Look, you need to go. Now."

"I'll leave when I'm ready," she said. Then she started channel surfing.

I reached over her shoulder and snatched the remote out of her hand. "Guess what? You're ready." I pointed toward the door with the remote.

"No."

"Wanna bet?" I took her by the wrist and pulled her up.

"Don't touch me. You don't know who I am."

"I know what you are and that's gone bitch," I said as I grabbed her other arm. I began pulling her to the door.

"Stop! Stop! You American shit! My father and brothers will make you pay for this."

I continued to shove her out of my room. She broke a hand free and put a finger to her forehead. "My father is head of the Mafia," she told me delightedly. She pulled an imaginary trigger. "Bang, bang. Bang, bang." Over and over, she repeated the words all the way into the hallway. When I shut the door on her, I could still hear her. I leaned against the inside of the door. Turning around, I looked through the peephole. She was still there.

"See how you dance after tomorrow. My father will send his regards," she shouted.

I called our manager.

"I told y'all a hundred times not to mess with these girls over here." But he had a different girl in his room every night.

"What do I do?" I asked.

"Get your stuff. You're switching hotels." Right before he hung up, I heard him say "Dumb ass."

Who knows if she was serious or not, but she sounded convincing. Now I'd had another good reason to go home. Actually, it was the best reason.

The last week of our tour, a man with quite an entourage sat down front during a show. I recognized him from the cover of music magazines; he was the Prince of Bata. He had a lot of influence in the music world. We performed well that night. Afterwards, he invited me to his table.

"Would you like to choreograph with some of my groups?" he asked.

"Groups?"

"I own a record label with several groups signed to the label."

Hell yeah, I thought. One contract ends and another begins. And I could work for a prince.

"Where do they tour?"

"Why, here, of course. In Thailand."

Oh, no! Tell me I heard wrong. "Here?"

He nodded. I hesitated.

"I can't," I told him. "I need to go home."

"Understood," was his calm reply.

That night with the Prince the band members, we partied all night. I felt like royalty myself, like Achilles, hidden away in a harem trying to avoid the inevitable, which for me was the responsibility of my girlfriend and son back home. I didn't think too much about her, though. I just missed my kids. I sent money home and one hastily written postcard, but I never called; it was too expensive. Scoring with as many women as I could, I thought I was a real man. But I wasn't a man. I was a scared kid using women to fill the empty space inside of me, like a drug high. I didn't know what love was then; love was something elusive that I lost the meaning of.

After four months my assignment with the Shilowaves ended. By then, I was more than ready to go home. I'd had enough of Thailand and it of me. But much has happened since then. The recent tsunami disaster brought back a lot of my memories. The stories of courage and kindness I saw on TV told of Thai people I didn't know. I met some of the best people in my life there and I would miss them and always remain friends with some. If it weren't for my kids I swear I would have stayed there forever. Besides my children, I had no life to return to. I loved being there and I vowed to return if I lived long enough. For now, it was back to my reality.

Chapter 7

Pimps, Drugs, and Money
Diamond

September 1992- July 1994

When I was about twelve or thirteen years old, my dad showed me the finer points of selling drugs. He showed me how to cut, cook and weigh it, and most important of all, how to sell it. I couldn't have found a better teacher. And even though I watched him use, I never did. He tried to get me to smoke weed but I was so afraid of becoming him that I didn't have any interest in it. Although I didn't make much money selling it at that time. I made a little bit of money, but nothing serious, it was great training for a later time in my life.

After my tour in Bangkok, I came up on an apartment back in my old hood Downtown. I went out on the block just to check out the landscape and see if I saw any of my old homies. The first thing I noticed was this thick white girl and a dark skinned dude walking into my building. I overheard them talking about a plan on how to get money. My ears burned, they were speaking my language. The next day I saw the same dude, by himself this time.

"What up bruh?"

"What's happening?" He responded, his eyebrow raised.

"They call me D, short for Diamond."

"I'm Hank."

There was something about him that seemed dark. He was the type of guy you wanted on your team but he also was the guy that was cut throat. Whatever it was, we connected. He was a pimp and a coke boy. The white girl was his lady and she was all about the money. He trusted her with his dope and money. I thought to myself, I know what my next come up will be: women.

Hank and I had a conversation one day about Cincinnati

dope boys and Indianapolis coke boys.

"This dope down here is bullshit," Hank said. "Back home, we don't cut or cook like you guys do," he said, referring to adding baking soda to the cocaine. "We got way better quality." He tilted his head north. "Back home in Indy, we use just enough soda but not too much. We need to flood the streets with something that will put all these niggas outta business." "Ok then, Al Capone, what's the plan?" Hank laughed at my gangster reference and then told me his family from Chicago was his connection. We met up with him a week later. You can tell he was an O.G by the way he talked.

He put an eight ball of crack on a scale. I checked the digits to make sure it was right.

"How much?"

"Three hundred, it's worth it. I guarantee you'll be back" he told me.

He was right.

Once I got back to the block, word got around fast that we had the best work. All the fiends loved it and became loyal customers. Hank and I got more popular and the other dope boys hated us. We were taking business from them and we had to watch our backs more than ever. Good money was in my pockets and in just a few months, we went from selling a few grams at a time to ounces in no time. The money started stacking up. It was crazy how much we made in a short amount of time. I felt like I was living the American dream. Sure I knew it came from selling drugs, but like my dad said, you gotta get it how you lived. At one point, I didn't even have to leave my apartment; people would show up day and night, banging on the door.

"Diamond! You home?" one girl yelled at two o'clock in the morning. I sat my beer down, pulled on a t-shirt and walked across the room. I peeked through the eyepiece. Down the hallway hung a light bulb that further distorted the view through the curved glass. A woman was standing back far enough that I could make out who she was. It was Donna, one of my regular customers.

'Bitch, page me before you just come up here. Don't just pop up at my door. What's up?"

"I just need a little to hold me over till tomorrow." She stepped forward and thrust her face into the gap. I jumped back. "I got three-dollars in change. Just give me a crumb pack," she repeated.

I wasn't turning down any money so I gave her the crumbs that were at the bottom of one my baggies of crack.

"Don't come back up here knocking at my damn door like you the police, without paging first."

Most days I sat in my apartment, sold drugs and counted money. I was making so much "doe" on the streets. I'm surprised no one tried to rob me. Word was out that me and Hank were "eating" out on the streets and we were trying to put the game on lockdown. But, after a while, it all got real old. I mean the cash part of it was great, but I needed to get out and have some fun. One day I went over to White Castle for a burger. A girl in a green SUV pulled out just as I was turning in. She kind of gave me that look, she looked nice, so I nodded. She drove around the corner and came back into the parking lot. She rolled her window down, we talked for a few minutes, and then she handed me her number. As I reached out of my car to grab it, I noticed she had written it on the back of her bank statement. Before I could read how much money she had in her account, she snatched it back from me.

"Wait a minute. I can't let you see that yet."

When she said the word "yet," I knew she was sitting on some real cash. If I read her right, she was saying she wanted to share it with me but I had to put in some work. I wasn't going to let this opportunity get away. I had been cooped up in my apartment for way too long. I called her up the next day and we went out for pizza and drove back to her place.

I knew this cutie had money and I thought I could hit a lick that evening. Within an hour, I was working that ass hard, while I thought about how much money she was sitting on, that made me work even harder. Every stroke was a dollar stroke, I didn't mind though. She was cute and a classy little chick. We fell asleep afterwards - well, she did. I didn't sleep much so I just lay there and waited for her to wake up.

"Hey babe. How you feeling this morning?" I asked
"Feeling like I'm real glad I turned back around yesterday," she said as she rolled back on top of me.
"Yeah, me too." I replied. Then I looked her right in eyes and with a straight face I said,
"I'm gonna need some money,"
Without blinking, she responded, "How much?"
"Oh, I don't know. About five-thousand."
I just came up with a number that sounded good.
She hesitated but then said, "All right. I have to go to the bank but I'll bring it to you."
It was a Saturday and she had to drive past the mall to find an open bank. By then, I had already gone home. She pulled into my driveway about noon with five thousand dollars in an envelope, a down payment she called it. I'm thinking to myself, this is too good to be true. Having sex with a cute girl and getting paid for it. I didn't mind doing something strange for a little piece of change. I continued to hang and chill out with her, but things started to get to serious. She wanted a title and I couldn't do it. I was a dope boy and I had no space for relationships. I needed to take a break for a while.
"Baby, I need to take care of some business out of town. I'll be back in a week or two."
"You are seeing someone else?" Shannan fastened the clasp on the front of her bra. She pulled the straps over her shoulders.
"Naw babe, I'm too busy for that. I need to spend time getting my life together. I need a little break, that's all."
"You gonna call me when you get back?"
"You can count on it, babe." I gave her a little hug before I left. It's always good to leave your options open.
Between being a jigahoe and trapping, I was making tens of thousands and blowing most of it. Who knows where it went. I

was taking trips, buying cars, feeding my crew and blowing it by the thousands. I was never taught money management skills so as a young black man from the hood, I never understood the purpose of money. I abused it just like everything else in my life.

I really wanted to get myself together, but the money and the respect I got from the guys in the streets gave me purpose. People respecting and loving Diamond gave me a false sense of acceptance. I loved and I lived for it. But the funny thing was, as much love and attention Diamond got, the more empty I would become. I had no real identity and this made up character was only feeding me lies that created bigger holes in my heart and soul than ever before. I was the lead actor in a movie. Every morning I woke up there was a director saying, "Action!" I would start the role of Diamond. I didn't know how long I could maintain this role but I was fighting against a sub-self that didn't give up control. I wasn't even sure if I didn't want Diamond to have control. I had built such a dark and scary world for myself that my realities became my truths. I decided that if I was going to do this gangsta shit then I had to be all in, do or die. I wanted to give my life some sort of normalcy but I didn't know where to start. I never thought I was good enough for college since I didn't finish high school. I got my G.E.D so I decided to do something with that.

As a teenager, one of my side hustles was cutting hair in the upstairs boy's bathroom at school. I was a great barber from the time I was a little kid. Since we were poor and I couldn't afford to go to the barbershop, I learned how to cut my own hair. I decided to register for barber school but they had a twelve month waiting list so my cousin convinced me to go to cosmetology school. Back then you didn't see street guys going to cosmetology school, it borderline was considered gay - but when I went to visit the school and saw all the fine girls with no dudes in sight, I thought to myself, hold up, how is this gay? I'd rather be here and look at a bunch of beautiful women, than in barber school with a bunch of guys. I registered for cosmetology school and I started a month later. In the back of my mind, I harbored the thought that while I was in school, I'd save enough money from selling dope, retire from the streets and open up a barber shop. My goal was to bring some legitimacy to my life and raise my kids without the worry of going to jail or getting shot.

One day in late May, a year after I had started cosmetology school, there was a lady in the chair next to me getting her hair done. The girl cutting her hair asked me if I had change for a twenty. I pulled out a stack of hundred dollar bills about an inch thick. The lady's eyes almost popped out of her head. "You make all that from tips doing hair?" she asked. I smiled and gave her a wink. After her appointment, she came over to my station.

"Hey, I have a couple of daughters," she whispered. She hesitated while I turned my attention to her. "They strip up in Detroit but they're not making any money." She raised her eyebrows and smiled, "I think you could show my girls how to make some. They're out sleeping with everybody anyway. They might as well get paid for it."

I had seen women approach my dad about being their pimp - now, the same opportunity presented itself to me. "Here's my number, have them call me." I told her.

One of the girls called me that evening. "My mama gave me your number. My name's Kym. She said you really got it going on, that you might be able to help me."

"I think maybe we can help each other," I told her. "You want in?"

"Hell yeah. I'm down, but I don't have a car." She paused and then continued, "Can you pick me up?"

I wanted to check her out and get down to business, and within the hour we were driving back to my apartment. In the car, I told her if she was going to be in the game with me, she had to obey my every command.

"These streets will eat you alive and I don't have time to be getting locked up because you trying to do your own thing out here. You obey and do what I tell you and we'll be ok. We'll get this money together, do what we have to do, and stay out of trouble. But only if you can abide by my rules." She didn't respond. "You understand?"

"I'll do whatever. I need to come up on some ends." Once we arrived at my apartment, she put her hands on her hips. "You wanna see what I'm working with?"

She danced for me. In the streets there were rules, and rule number one, don't get high on your own supply - that included my girls. I never slept with any of them. She frowned a little when I told her I didn't want to have sex. "This ain't about a relationship, it's about money. I don't need any involvement with my girls. I don't need none of y'all catching feelings. Agreed?"

She nodded. "I guess that makes sense."

"But just so you know, you definitely hot," I told her. "We gonna make some serious doe."

Kym giggled and started putting her clothes back on.

"You ever done this before?" I asked.

"No, but I'm ready to try." She looked up at me. "Can't be too hard to figure out."

I thought that was funny and laughed out loud. "Alright, when you get ready, we'll hit the streets. We'll go up to Walnut Avenue first."

About an hour later, we were Downtown, parked on the street. We got out and walked. I took her up and down for a couple of blocks and showed her where to walk, how far to go and how talk to the tricks as much as possible without getting arrested. I taught her how to be a hooker.

"What if someone pulls up? What do I say?"

"Just be casual. Ask them what are they looking for. Let them engage you, you don't be the aggressor. When they start talking about the price you turn it back on them and let them initiate. Don't mention money until they've answered a couple of questions. And ask them if they're a cop."

"Like they'll say so."

"Ask them again if they avoid the question. If you ever get a funny feeling about someone, walk away. I'd rather lose a little money than have you in jail all night."

Then I told her where to go handle her business and to end the deal quickly. "The sooner you're out of their car and back on the street, the more tricks you can turn. Get 'em off, get their cash, get back on the corner. The three G's of hooking."

"What if someone starts to mess with me?"

I'll be right across the street if something happens. My part of the partnership is to protect you." I took her hand in mine, looked into her eyes, and nodded toward the opposite side of the street. "I'll be right over there."

She worked most of the night and turned probably 15 tricks. For a first night out, she did great. I gave her a cut of the money back at my place and then I took her home. I felt like she was going to be a good hoe-fessional. Or as my daddy would've said, "She'll be a fine hoe." He used to smack his stable girls around if he thought they had been disobedient, but I couldn't see myself doing that. I hoped it never came to me having to hit a girl. All I wanted to do was show these young, cute girls how to get some money for doing what they loved anyways. If you were going to be a hoe then you might as well as get paid for it. These young girls running around talking about, can you pay my cell phone bill, but got $50 worth of cell payments in between their legs and I was going to show my team of girls how to get it. Didn't seem to be a lot of harm in that; nobody was getting hurt.

"I guess you have a job," I told her on the way to her house. She was pleased with her new hoe-fession. But she couldn't stop talking about her Johns.

"And so," she told me, "the third guy was all hairy. Man, it was like doing a bear. And that last guy, I almost laughed when he pulled down his drawers." She went on and on. Finally, I had to say something.

"Did you fill out a tax form? You know I have to take out taxes on how much you make?"

"You're kidding right?" She asked.

"The government is taxing pussy now?" I said. "I'm just playing."

I laughed all the way to her house and most of the way back to my apartment.

Kym must've given her family a good report about her night because the next day her sister called me and said that she wanted in. Kym had told her sisters and cousin that I knew how to make money. I mean, one night turning tricks and Kym was recruiting for me. I said, "whatever, let's get it." These girls didn't live in the hood like the hoes my daddy pimped; they lived out in the suburbs in a nice part of town. They graduated from good schools and were attractive on top of that. So, that night, I picked up Kym and one of the other sisters, and drove back to the same corner we worked the night before. Kym showed her sister Shana how to walk, talk, the whole bit. By the next morning, they had turned a lot of tricks and made good money for me. They turned in over six-hundred dollars; I left with three-hundred and they split the rest. I was thrilled, but not nearly as much when the next day, their cousin called.

"Gold. G-o-l-d," she spelled out for me.

"Alright Gold, don't tell me, you wanna be on the team?"

"You know it. I'm trying to get paid."

"Well, you want to start tonight?"

"Oh yeah, I'm down."

So Gold came over and stripped for me. She was fine as hell and the way she moved, I was thinking that she might be my main girl. She did better than great. Gold turned more tricks than the other two put together. She was the Energizer Bunny of hooking; she never stopped. It was like she never wanted to stop getting money.

. Two days later, I found out there was another sister. The phone rang and the girl on the other end of the line identified herself as Daisia. She was another sister, and, as it turns out, the sweetest of them all. Sweet as in gentle, and cute. I didn't think she would be comfortable doing the job but she was fine with turning tricks. One day, another cousin called. We talked for a bit and then she told she was six months pregnant. Even a pimp has morals at some level and I wasn't having it. Still, I had three sisters and a cousin. Every night was like a family reunion on Walnut Street.

We were partners. They worked, we got money and we went home. Not too complicated. From 13th to Walnut Street, I worked my stable. Sometimes we would walk to Main Street, but not very often. The guys from my neighborhood knew what I did and wanted to check my girls out but I wouldn't let them trick with anybody in the hood.

"Hey, Diamond," one of my homies yelled. "Can I get a discount?"

"Hell naw. You can't afford nothing over here."

I would walk down the street with two girls on each side, my shades on, and people couldn't help but watch. My girls would work all hours of the day and night but after a couple of months, we decided to do something different. I told them to give their good clients, like ballplayers and lawyers, my cell phone number. These guys would call and ask for a particular girl, and I would drop them off different locations. If they wanted one for the whole night, the price was a lot more but not so much that we ran off our good customers.

Damica, a black-skinned girl, was the next addition, then a short, Latina girl. Not long after the new girls joined the group, we began to scout for other places to work. At first, we stayed around Cincinnati, but then I started driving to Kentucky and stopping at truck stops. These places turned out to be gold mines; guys who had been on the road for days would pay top dollar for a quick couple of minutes. I would let the girls out as soon as I turned into the parking lot and then pull down by the vending machines and bathrooms. I would buy the same snacks every night, a mountain dew, chocolate cupcakes and a bag of chips. It was hard out there for a pimp and I had to keep my appetite up.

"Now what?" The girls asked the first time.

"Just go from truck to truck. Ask if they want some company, get in and handle your business. Shit ain't that hard."

"Oh, alright," they said. And off they went.

We ended up turning out some serious cash at truck stops. An hour after we'd get there, the entire set of drivers would be happy, then everyone would pile back into my car. Down the highway we'd go to the next truck stop. I told the girls we were making America a better place. After all, happy truckers make better drivers.

When Hank and I would go to Indianapolis to pick up dope we would work our girls all the way there, from truck stop to truck stop and motel to motel. My girls were down for whatever and they loved and respected me enough to get it however I told them to.

Anywhere guys had money, I worked my girls. Hotels, nightclubs, corners—wherever the cash took us was fine with me. Occasionally, we rode further south into Kentucky. One night, we met a girl from Tennessee, or so she said. Brittany, nice-looking and built like a woman instead of an eighteen-year-old girl. Her father had put her out so she wanted to join the team and put in work. All the girls were happy with the addition. When we got back to Cincinnati, I realized she had no place to go. I let her stay with me and I told her she had to follow the rules like everyone else.

"You gotta start on the street. Then you can move up to hotels and clubs."

She was okay with the rules but she wanted to get some action from the boss, I shut her down A.S.A.P.

"Business is what it's about boo and I don't need no misunderstandings," I told her.

"That's fine," she said and paused. "I've never done this." She turned her eyes away from me, she seemed like she was replaying something in her head. Then she looked up, "When do I start?"

"Tonight some time. I'll take you to Walnut Street and show you where to walk and all that." I stood there for the longest and just looked at her. "You sure you want to do this?"

"Yeah. But I'm really tired. Can I crash on the sofa?"

"Sure," I said, and we went to bed. Separately.

At one o'clock in the morning, not a lot of people are riding around. It's mostly folks doing something they probably shouldn't be and the ones trying to catch them doing it. Guys looking for a hooker knew to cruise up Walnut to find what they needed. That night, it rained and the streets were slick and shiny. Steam rose from the pavement and the lights reflected on the roads. Brittainy and I got out the car and I showed her our territory and where to turn fast tricks, the same routine I had given the other girls.

"I'll be right over there." I pointed across the street.

"Okay," she said. "I'll be alright."

A few minutes later, a purple Suzuki Jeep slid up to the curb. Its tinted windows made it hard for me to see who was inside. My windshield constantly fogging from the moisture in the air from the rain. I rubbed my hand against my window and by the time I could see, Brittainy was in the car. A wave of anxiety curled in my stomach; it felt like something was not right but the Jeep hadn't moved. Just when I relaxed, it started to pull away and then turned the corner to Race Street. I cranked up and followed them. The usual spot where the tricks would go down was around the corner in this parking lot. As soon as I turned the corner, following behind him, he sped off. His tires were spinning before I realized what was happening and I followed as best I could. A car pulled in front of me from a side street and I got caught in traffic. I lost the Jeep. *Maybe I overreacted*, I thought. *He'll bring her back in a few minutes.* I went back to the corner where she got in and I waited. The more I looked at my watch, the slower time went. A car horn woke me up and it was now seven in the morning. Brittany was nowhere to be found. I knew she had a cousin in the Cincinnati area, so I rummaged through the stuff she'd left at my place until I found a number with the 513 area code and called it.

"No, I haven't seen Brittany. Why do you ask?"

"She was staying with me and she never came back last night. All her stuff's here. Her pager, everything."

"That doesn't sound like her. To leave her things and not come back for them."

"If she calls or comes by, have her call Diamond."

"Diamond?"

"My real name is Ron, I'm a friend. I think she might be in trouble. I'm kinda worried."

"Oh, my god," she said slowly. "She's too sweet. It would be so easy for someone to take advantage of her. She's from a real small town in Tennessee. The last time I saw her, she had just turned 16."

"So, you haven't seen her in a while then?"

"Summer before last."

I counted to myself and hung up. Brittainy never showed up at my place. Or her cousin's. Or back in Tennessee.

.

After the episode with Brittany, I wanted to jump ship on the pimp game. If I did any pimping, it was going to be me. I knew how to find the girls with money and get whatever I wanted from them. Diamond was a real piece of work back then. I found it easy to use women who had money, women like Shannan. If women wanted to cash in on me, I was more than eager to help them do it, but no woman cashed in as easily as Shannan did. It was time for me to call her again. Besides, I hadn't seen her for almost six months and a nice yellow Cadillac had caught my eye.

"Why haven't I heard from you all this time Diamond?" she asked.

"It ain't been that long. I've been out here in these streets trying to get this money." I smiled at her. "You didn't miss me?"

She put a hand on her hip. "Yeah I did." Then I hit her with my reason for reaching back out to her. "Hey dig...." I started to say.

"Here we go. I knew it. What is it you want, Diamond?"

I pulled her close to me and whispered in her ear. "I saw this canary yellow Cadillac for sale and dude is willing to give it to me for the low." I kissed the side of her neck. "Can't you see us riding through Downtown in a big Caddy?"

"You would look good in the passenger seat," she agreed.

I moved in for the kill. "Let's go see it. It's got a nice system, white top, sweet rims. It was made for Diamond."

"Let's talk about it, at least for a little while" she said, her hand sliding down my sweats.

All I could think was the work I was going to have to put in to get this car. This was the ride of my dreams. When I was a kid, nothing came easy but now, between pimping, selling dope and jigahoeing, I thought I had it all.

When I pulled out of the parking lot in my new canary yellow Cadillac, system blasting, I felt like the poster child for pimping. All the guys on the block watched me cruise by. I was the man. Shannan rode with me that first day.

"Give me a kiss, Diamond," she said while she draped herself all over me.

I pushed her arms down. "Hey, chill. You can't be making no scene out here."

She acted like she owned me just because she bought me a new car. Besides, if I let her kiss me, she might think she was my girl and that wasn't the case. She was someone I kicked it with and would cash in every now and then, nothing more. If the money wasn't there, I wouldn't have been there either. It was time for me to step up my hand in the dope game.

I moved from dealing on my block to selling from my pager. I traveled all over Cincinnati and Kentucky to make a sale and eventually throughout all of Ohio. We had connections from Dayton, all the way to New York. Canton, OH became a big drop spot until some dudes there tried to set me up and rob me. Anytime customers needed a fix, they would page me, day or night. It was nothing to drive halfway across town at two o'clock in the morning to unload some work. I was all about the money, so I sold and sold; the supply of fiends was unending. Women desperate for crack would make runs for me in exchange for a small bag. One girl, Carmen, was so good at delivering that she made the west side of town my biggest moneymaker. But what helped most was that my dope was the best in town. Sometimes, I'd tell myself that, when I reached a certain amount of cash, I would quit for the day or the week. But I couldn't. I always needed a little bit more. You know how addicts will always say they can quit anytime they want? Well, I said the same thing. Now that I look back, I was hooked on selling just like they were hooked on using.

"Hank, let's have some fun," I said as we pulled around the corner. Up ahead, a deal was going down. I turned up my system.
"Man, that song gets no play in my ride," Hank said.
"We in my ride now homeboy, so it's going to be played in here." I turned on Master P's, Ice Cream Man. My speakers were so loud that the fiend that was getting served couldn't help but look in our direction. When he saw my caddy, he pulled his money back and crammed it in his pocket. I could see the two guys arguing; the fiend then walked across the street while looking toward us. I drove down the street, did a U-turn, and pulled to the curb. Hank was a real G, he didn't give a fuck about anybody, he got out and served the fiend. His attitude reminded me that guys we know from down our way wanted us dead. We didn't care, we just kept getting money.

One morning, I woke up with a woman I didn't like and hardly knew, cuddled up beside me, saying she loved me. I stared down at her and all I could think was, who am I? The bits of memory that surfaced from my childhood felt like a story someone had told me, like it wasn't my story, like it wasn't real.

One day, I drove up to my mom's in my Cadillac. I honked the horn a few times and she finally came to the door. At first she hesitated like she didn't know who it was. I had my windows tinted so I figured she didn't see that it was me inside. But even after she recognized me, her face didn't change. She walked down the steps, shaking her head back and forth, her arms folded. She stopped several feet from the car.
"Ronald, Ronald. Is this what you've become? Who do you think

you are?" Her head still rocking as she spoke.

"But, Mom," I tried to say.

She took the wind out of my Cadillac sails and got me thinking. What if, when I was a kid I had gotten caught up with someone like me? By now, I would be one of those crackheads I helped create, roaming the streets in the late night. I decided to go back to cosmetology school and finish up. But I wasn't going to give up the street life just yet. It paid the bills and it gave Diamond the resources he needed to continue to provide a cover for Ronald.

Chapter 8

Cosmetology School
May – September 1992

I had been in school for a few weeks when the flu bug hit the salon. A good many of the juniors and seniors were out sick, but since those of us in the junior classroom barely interacted with real people, most of us were unaffected. The heavy footsteps of the owner thudded down the stairs. "We need somebody!" he said.

I assumed he meant for sweeping hair and cleaning up, so I spoke up. "Right here, sir."

"You? Hell no, Hummons."

No one else said a word. The owner looked around the salon, searching for other options. I guess he didn't see any. He turned back to me. "Alright, Hummons." I reached for the broom. "Get your equipment."

I froze. "Why?"

"Well, unless you've learned something I don't know, you can't cut hair with a broom."

I stammered, "Me?"

"You'll do fine. Let's go, people are waiting." He turned and stomped back upstairs.

I shrugged to the others, took note of the relief in their eyes and followed him.

"Here," he said, "this is your booth for the day. Don't break or lose anything. We'll send someone easy your way." He walked away shaking his head.

I turned and faced my station. Several hand mirrors, a pumping chair, a jar filled with combs and a bunch of other haircutting tools I didn't know how to use. I plopped down in my chair and prayed for a guy customer, only looking to get a haircut.

"So, what do I do?" I asked the girl next to me. Over her

shoulder, I could see customers coming in. They were given numbers and asked to have a seat.

"The customers will tell you what they want." She pointed to the wall. "Besides, you're covered." A big sign hung over each of the mirrors: *Student stylists. Service provided at your risk.*

"Great. Just great. Quite the confidence builder."

Maybe, I thought, I'll get some little kid that needs a fade. I could use the electric clippers and never have to break out a pair of scissors. That would be great; if the workers up front were smart, those were the customers they would send my way. After a half hour, I still didn't hadn't been assigned my first customer. The girl next to me had three customers, while I sat there waiting, playing with the chair pump. Up and down, up and down, my stylist neighbor gave me a funny look. "You okay?" I'd ask her.

"Shut up, Diamond."

"That's no way to talk to a fellow stylist."

I looked up to find a real human customer, marching my way. She wasn't a floating styrofoam head, or mannequin, but was a real person. A thin, black girl with enough hair for three people. I thought, *please turn left, right, walk past me, walk past me.* "Hummons?" she asked. "booth 23?"

I reluctantly glanced at the number above my mirror. "Yes. That's me."

She sank into the seat, anxious to get service. Smacking her chewing gum, she declared, "I want some crimps'."

What!? I thought to myself. *What the hell are crimps?*

"Excuse me?" I asked.

"I want my hair crimped. I ain't had it done in a while, and I know it need my ends clipped too." She grabbed a magazine off the counter, continued smacking her gum, flipped through the pages and waited for me to begin.

I looked at my assortment of devices and implements; nothing had "crimping iron" written on it. It's got to be one of these, I figured. Smack, smack, smack, she continued. I thought,

I need to at least act like I know what I'm doing, so I started combing her hair. Luckily, her chair faced away from the mirror. She didn't realize I was stalling. I kept peeking back over my shoulder, searching for the crimping iron. About that time, one of the assistants strolled up to me.

"Here's the iron." She laid it down on the counter.

Relieved, I picked it up and put it in the stove. "Thanks."

I would see girls practice crimping each other's hair, but I'd never really paid that much attention. I never thought I needed to.

No problem, I can do this, I assured myself.

"How long is this gonna take?" She asked.

"Thirty minutes," I guessed.

"Man, you must be fast," she said.

"Yep, that's me."

She smacked her gum and flipped a page.

I knew the iron needed to be heated up so I plugged the stove and place the crimping iron inside. While I parted her hair into as many sections as possible, the iron grew hotter and hotter. We engaged in small talk for at least ten minutes. I figured it was time to get started. I reached over and grabbed the iron. When I pulled it from the stove, it looked like glowing embers in a campfire. For a second there, I felt like a blacksmith. I though, *this is easy. The hotter the iron, the better the crimps.* I sprayed massive amounts of Pump It Up spritz (holding spray) on her hair, then combed it through. I saw other girls using it so I thought that was the way to do it. I noticed the section of hair I sprayed was getting really stiff. I figured, the hair is ready for the iron.

With the overheated iron, I clamped it down onto the parted section. In amazement, I watched her hair disappear before my eyes; the iron melted right through, like a dying weed in a fire.

"Auuuugh!" I yelled in my head. By the time I realized what was happening, she had a big gap in her hair. *Man, oh man, I'm going to get in trouble for this*, I thought. A puff of smoke

swirled from the iron and the singed hair. Shortly after, the smell of burned hair emerged.

My client, unbeknownst to her, was now sporting a new horrible hairstyle called "Ronald Canyon." She looked up from her magazine. "What's that?"

"What?"

"That smell. Smells like something's burning."

"Oh, that. Someone left hair in the stove. Stinks don't it?"

"Mhmm. Glad it ain't mine."

"Yeah, no kidding."

Soon, the odor of death had wandered down the row of customers and stylists. "Ewwww! What is that? Diamond, are you burning hair?"

"Nope not me."

I quickly grabbed a brush and combed a section of her hair over the gap. "I'll be back in a minute." I walked toward the front hoping to find someone using crimping irons. I spotted a stylist using them, I secretly watched. I noticed she had a towel wrapped around the hottest part of iron to cool it down before applying them to the hair. *A towel, how simple*, I thought.

After destroying a smaller section of the customer's hair, I finally got the hang of the crimping. I kept looking at the disclaimer on the wall, in case I needed to point to it in a panic. I managed to cover up most of the gap and the customer never even noticed. She had a good length of hair, luckily she left satisfied.

For several days after, I kept an eye on the door. In the event of the customer bursting in with an UZI, I already had an escape plan. To my surprise, she never returned. No complaints, not a word. Soon, my anxiety faded and I settled into styling and became more comfortable.

"She needs a conditioning treatment" the little girl's mother told me. To her side, slightly behind her was a young girl, probably about ten years old or so.

"Okay. Well, have a seat right up here young lady." I

swiveled the chair toward her.

"Candace. Her name is Candace."

Candace didn't move from behind her mother.

"Come on, Candace. It's alright, hop on up."

"Go on, girl," her mom said. "Get in the chair. I ain't got all day to wait on you." The lady's thick fingers grabbed her daughter by the wrist and pulled her into the chair. "Yeah, she needs a conditioning treatment."

"So it seems."

The mother looked at me, her eyebrow raised. "You ever did this before?"

"All the time. She'll be fine, you can wait out front."

"What if I want to stand right here and watch?"

"Well, you're not really allowed. Policy." I pointed toward the sign.

I watched the hairs of her mustache stick out as she pushed her lips forward.

"I'll be out front," she said and walked away.

I waited for her to be seated and occupied with a magazine. I turned my attention to Candace. "Now, let's get your hair conditioned."

Candace didn't respond at first. She looked at me with her head tilted. "You ever done this before?"

"Is that a hereditary question?"

"What?"

"Nothing. Now, before I get started, do you have to use the bathroom?"

She stared at me with a confused expression.

"Well, do you?" I asked.

"No." She settled back.

I went to the dispensary for supplies. No one was there to give them to me, so I decided to get the supplies myself. I figured it couldn't be too hard to find the leave in conditioner. I grabbed the first big tub of white cream from the shelf and added a scoop in a clear cup, along with rubber gloves and a tint brush. I looked as if I really knew what I was doing. Looking at Candace's thick hair, I thought I would need to really work it in. Candace watched as I placed all the items on the countertop. You would think I was prepping her for a liver transplant with the way she watched my every move. She asked again, "You ever done this before?"

"Actually, I don't work here. I snuck in when they weren't looking."

"Mom! Mom!"

"I'm kidding. Stop it with the yelling."

With my gloves firmly on, I applied what I thought was conditioner to her hair. It took several minutes with all the hair she had; it was thick as any I had seen. Next, I put a plastic cap on her head like I'd seen other stylists do, after they applied conditioner.

I set the timer on the dryer. For someone her age, I figured fifteen minutes would be plenty of time. "Okay," I smiled to Candace, "so in fifteen . . ."

"I've got to pee."

"What? You said you didn't have to go!"

"I didn't. But you talked about it so much; all I could think of was the bathroom."

"Can't you wait?" I peeked at the clock: fourteen minutes, thirty seconds. "Just a few minutes?"

Candace put her hands in her lap and started bouncing in the chair. "I don't think so. Ooooooo . . ."

"C'mon! Hurry!" I yanked the protective robe from her and pulled her out of the chair. I looked over; 6:30. We waddled down the hall toward the bathroom, her hair dripping.

"Here, go on. Hurry up."

"Don't stand by the door. My mom always said . . ."

"Alright, alright. Just go."

She finally came out and I returned her to the dryer.

"I'll come back and check on you in a minute, okay?"

"Okay". She replied softly.

After ten minutes, she screamed.

"What's wrong?!"

"It burns! Ouuuchhhh! It burns! I want my momma!"

A fellow stylist ran over to Candace and rushed her over to the shampoo station. "We gotta get this stuff outta her hair." I turned on the water and we pushed Candace under the hose. All I could think was my styling days were over. Hopefully I wouldn't get in trouble for this. I was so nervous. The cream, which I thought was leave in conditioner, was actually relaxer cream. It slowly rinsed from her hair, along with a few patches of her hair. Once we were finished, her scalp was as red as a tomato, her mom, angrily stood looking at us.
"I can't believe you did this to my baby!"

"I swear I thought it was conditioner. I didn't know it was Motions super strength relaxer." I lifted my hand over my face. "I'm so sorry."

"Yes you are," she said as she swung her big pocketbook at me. It thudded into my forearms. "Where's the manager? You shouldn't be working with people. Where's the manager?"

"We'll give you your money back," I told her. "Besides," she took another swat at me while I pointed to our sign, "at your risk, we are student in training."

"Yeah, training for IDIOTS! You're paying her doctor's bill!" By now, the stylist who helped me, dried Candace's hair a bit. The mother put her arm around her daughter. "C'mon baby, let's get you outta here."

Candace turned and looked at me with tears streaming down her face. I felt so badly. After her mother was refunded her money, they left.

Over time, I became more skilled and even had returning customers. My success gave me a small taste of what I could achieve in the hair industry. Still, I felt it wasn't enough money to make me want to give up selling dope. I decided I would do both. I'd do finger waves in the morning and sell dime bags in the evening. I even sold dime bags of weed to the girls in school. The game didn't stop just because I was trying to do something positive with my life. I had grown addicted to making money. I wanted hair relaxer money and coke money.

One day before the school opened, I was sitting in my chair stroking my beard, the little bit of hair that I did have anyway. What little there was sort of nappy. One stylist's boyfriend came in the salon. As he sat and waited for his girlfriend, he started rubbing his nappy beard. I glanced at him, then looked back at myself, an interesting idea came to mind. *Hmmmm.. what if I could develop a straightener for men? For our beards, that is.* Many more ideas filled my head. I thought, *yeah, I could add skin ointment to prevent breakouts. Yes! I can do this.* I was always told that when I was younger, I constantly searched for get rich schemes but no one ever gave me credit for being an idealist. Entrepreneurism was what I was born to do. It was how I was wired. People like me would get a bad reputation of being lazy or being dreamers, but I wasn't chasing dreams, I was chasing a secure and stable lifestyle.

By the time I got home that day, I had worked out all my plans. First, though, I had to create my wonder cream. In cosmetology school, we learned a bit of chemistry. I pulled out all of my products, put them on the kitchen table and started reading labels. Since relaxers burn, or so I'd heard, I knew my blend needed to be toned down a bit. So, I began to experiment on myself. At the end of three weeks, my beard had unnapped and uncurled enough to notice a difference. Not to mention it didn't peel the outer layer of skin off my face. I had found my perfect formula.

The next night I was up late watching TV when an infomercial about "selling your invention" came on. *This can't be a coincidence*, I thought, and called the number on the screen. The guy I spoke with was nice, he said he'd send the necessary paperwork the next day. Days later, I received the paperwork. Looking at the form, the first line read "Name of Product." I hadn't quite come up with the perfect name at that point, I even spent most of the day trying to think of one: *Straight Beard, Curl Away, Simple Beard,* even *Nappy Be Gone* came to mind. I finally settled on *B-Complex*.

Using my own results from the experiment, I gathered some before and after pictures of my beard, sent them in with the forms to the North Carolina based company and waited. A week later, they called.

"I think you have a great product," the man said. "Need to change the name though. How about Complex Beard?"

"No, that sounds stupid. Let's keep the name I came up with." I tried to sound cool, but my heart was pounding with excitement. "Now what?"

"First, we'll check it out. If it's good to go, you can fly down and do an infomercial."

"Man, that's cool."

"We like it that much," he told me. I could hear him shuffling papers. "Pretty soon, you'll get a contract. When we get it back, we'll be ready."

Just as he said, the paperwork arrived that weekend. Though I struggled reading all of the legal jargon, I searched for the magic number that would be my "cut" in all of this.

"What? Ten percent?" I said aloud. I showed it to my friends.

"Don't let them take your idea, Diamond," they insisted. "White people always trying to take our ideas and get rich off of them.

"Yeah, no kidding." What I failed to grasp was that I had spent a grand total of three weeks, maybe a month on my discovery, so it wasn't like I had invested a great deal of time in this. I called the company and tried to negotiate a better percentage. The man on the phone was understanding. "I know, Mr. Hummons, it doesn't seem like much."

"That's because it's not."

"But, you have to understand. We do all the marketing and production. You just sit back and collect royalties."

"And it says here," I continued, "that I have to send you a hundred dollars for handling my case."

"Just to make sure you have a reason to keep your part of the deal, and that you're honest. Besides, you'll make that back in one day."

"Me? Honest? I could be asking the same thing. I want forty percent."

"That's right. Don't let them cheat you." My supportive friends chanted.

The man half-laughed, "Forty percent? We'd never make a dime."

"Well, those are my terms."

"Sorry, Mr. Hummons, we can't do business." He hung up. I never heard from him again. I thought I had fought a good fight against "the man" but by the end of it, I wasn't sure who had actually won this round. Needless to say, my beard and lots of others are still nappy. I still wanted to run my own business, so I just invested in what I knew what was a sure thing—the streets.

Chapter 9

Six and a half years in prison
November 1994- May 2000

Shortly after I left cosmetology school (for the second time), I caught another case. One night I was out, spending time with a girl I'd been dating. I received a text message that read "911, come home quick!" I dropped my girl off and rushed to the building where my working girls were. When I arrived, the door was kicked in. I asked them if they knew who had done it, they said some guy and his girlfriend were banging on my door, assumed they wanted drugs. Realizing that I was not home, the guy kicked in the door. I was enraged. *Who in the hell would be bold enough to try to rob me?* I thought. I quickly changed into a long t-shirt, so that it would cover my pistol. I remained calm, cool and collective, I never let anyone see me sweat. While I appeared unbothered, there was a war inside my head. I had to find these assholes and make them pay.

I spotted the couple on the street, I tucked my 9mm in my back pocket, so they wouldn't suspect confrontation. But before I could even approach them, Gold, my main girl, hurled a 40 ounce bottle filled with hot water past my shoulder, aiming it at the two of them. It wasn't long after, that all of my girls joined in, attacking the couple. The guy pulled out a knife, so I pulled out my piece and started shooting. Leaving the woman, he ran for his life. The girlfriend was left to fend for herself. Needless to say, she was already getting jumped and beat up by all my girls anyway. After breaking up the scuffle, I gathered my gun, dope and money. Once I secured my girls' safety, I drove to the west side of town, to my girlfriend's house.

Amber, the girl who got her ass whipped by my girls, went to the police. She told them about the gun and how I sold dope and pimped girls out of the building. By the time I returned to the building, the cops had surrounded the entire block. I knew they were looking for me. Once the cops left the scene, or so I thought, I snuck inside the building and into my apartment to sort things out. I had barely tossed my keys on the table when I heard loud banging on the door. *Boom! Boom! Boom!* I looked through the peephole, and saw a silver gun barrel. I couldn't tell if it was the guy that I shot at wanting revenge, or if it were the police. Whoever it was, I didn't want to get caught with drugs. I quickly wrapped the half ounce I had in pocket in a napkin and stuck it in a glass, half-filled with water on the counter. When I opened the door, the cops came shoving in, asking me about the gun and the drugs.

"I don't have any guns or drugs," I said. The cops searched everywhere, but there was no gun. The dope was right in front of their faces, though. They literally stood right over it with a flashlight pouring all over the countertop. The flashlight scanned the glass at least three times, and still the cops didn't think to touch the napkin. Then I saw a twenty cent piece of crack right next to the glass. it must have dropped out of the bag when I wrapped the rest of the dope in the napkin. Still, they didn't see it and I was off the hook, or so I thought. They still handcuffed me, took me outside, stood me in front of the building. Amber came crawling out the back seat of the cop car, that's when they asked if I was the man who attacked her and her boyfriend. She nodded her head, then she spit on the ground right in front of my feet. "Yeah, he's the one who tried to kill my boyfriend." Before I could say anything, they shoved me in the back seat. Once we got to the JC (Justice Center), I was charged with felonious assault. I couldn't believe it. The good thing was they didn't find any drugs. I was still on probation for a gun case, so they wouldn't let me bond out.

With being stuck in jail, I needed a new plan for my girls. I plotted a scheme that would make us a quick $7,000. A new opportunity came along. There was this young attorney who had just passed the bar and landed a job down at a firm, located on the corner of 13th and Walnut - the same location I started where I started pimping my girls. He was at least twenty seven years old, but he was very ambitious and in love with black girls. It was funny because white guys from the suburbs did more crime in the hood than we did; only difference was they could escape to their plush homes and cozy neighborhoods while we were thrown in jail. His love for black women was going to cost him $7,000. I told Gold to go give him a treat since she was his favorite - I told her to take Red with her too and tell him the extra girl was on the house. Red took a small camera with her to his Downtown apartment on 4th and Plum. It needed to be small enough to fit in her panties. His treat was a night of threesomes, liquor, and drugs. I told her to get as many shots as possible of him doing all type of sexual positions with Gold and join in to make it more interesting. Red was a pro. She waited until his face was buried deep in between Gold's legs and started snapping pic after pic. He had gotten so drunk and high that he never realized what was going on. After Gold and Red had the film developed, they came to visit me. They held up the pics to the window so I could see them. With the way these pictures turned out, I knew we had him.

The next part of the plan was to go to him and let him know that the photos would be blown up to poster size and would mysteriously appear in the atrium of his law firm if he didn't deliver $15,000 in seven days. When they met and showed him the pictures he freaked out and became emotional.

"But Gold, I thought you loved me". He said.

"Ain't no love in this...you better charge that shit to the game. Just get us that bread ASAP or someone will be paying a visit to your job with these pics." Gold replied.

He wasn't able to come up with all of the money, but as I said, his love for black women cost him $7,000. That was the most he could come up with. I almost laughed at the irony of the whole situation. After spending another thirty days in jail, my attorney was able to get the charges dropped since the "victims" never showed up to court. I was a free man once again.

I took a trip to Chicago to pick up a pack of dope - I needed to get back on track. When I came back home I bagged up a couple of grams and took a walk through the hood. I was walking down John Street on the westside of Downtown when I saw this girl with the coldest body and prettiest smile I'd ever seen. She had a Nia Long haircut but had a body like Trina. She was perfectly thick with no stomach and all ass and hips. We caught eyes and couldn't stop looking at each other. Finally I crossed the street and approached her.

"Hi."

"Hey" She replied.

"My name is Diamond, what's yours?"

"Patrice."

From the sound of her voice I could tell she wasn't from around there. She had suburban girl written all over her. I could tell she was a good girl, trying to be bad. She was in the one of the roughest neighborhoods in Cincinnati, walking through the hood like she was at home.

"What are you doing down in this part of town? You look outta place. You better be careful before you get kidnapped" I laughed but I was dead serious. This girl was too fine not to have a man with her. "What's your plans for later? We should go out to dinner."

"I'm down for that." She replied.

"Cool, here's my number. Call me later and let's make some plans."

"Ok."

I watched her walk away and it was like she was walking in slow motion. That ass was so right that it seemed to slowly move side to side like a stripper booty. She called that evening and gave me her address to pick her up. She wasn't from Cincinnati so she was staying with her cousin Tangy. I can't lie, I was excited about dinner but I was more excited about after dinner plans.

"So why do they call you Diamond?" She asked.

"Because I'm priceless". I responded. "Why do they call you

Patrice?"

"Because that's what my momma named me."

"So do you have a boyfriend?"

"Something like that."

I thought to myself, *Oh shit, here we go*. "What's something like that? Either you do or you don't."

"We're broken up right now because he put his hands on me and I can't deal with it anymore." "You should leave dude alone and roll with me. I promise you he would never mess with you again if you were my girl."

"He's crazy though. I don't wanna get you in the middle of my drama."

What Patrice didn't know was that I loved that type of drama, especially if it would get me closer to her. I let it go though.

We spent so much time together that you would have thought she was my girl. I would pick her up whenever I went to Indianapolis to pick up some work (dope). She was so cool, she didn't even mind some of my girls riding with us. We made our usual stops at the truck stops and even worked the hotels when we got there. She was, as we called in the streets, my bottom bitch. She had my back and was cool with everything I did. One night I had to go to Walnut Hills to pick up some money from this guy I fronted some dope to. When we got there he didn't show up. Three weeks went by and this guy never showed his face. One night while I was taking her home I saw him walking down the street, so I pulled up on him and pistol whipped him. "What's up with my bread homie?" He tried to run but I was on his ass like the police.

"I got you bruh, I swear. I got robbed and I'm trying to get back now."

"Man fuck that shit, get yo ass in the car."

I drove him far out, pistol whipped him and left him out there. I know I shouldn't have been doing all that around Patrice, but she seemed to love this street stuff. When we would ride around she would hide packs on her body for me, tuck my pistol under her seat, and even watched my back when I was on the block. She had a dude or whatever but she was my ride or die chick when we were together. I decided to put some distance between us for a while when she got pregnant by that lame she was with. I was mad as hell. *How the hell this cornball ass nigga put a baby in my ride or die bitch?* Anyway, I had to fallback.

To add to my list of schemes, kidnapping became a normal way of life for me. My team and I weren't killers, but we did what we had to do to get money and respect. I was Diamond, fully integrated. I didn't know how to separate the real from the fake. It was all real to me and as long as I could keep people believing that Diamond was real and not some character. One day while counting money, rolling up thousand dollar stacks in rubber bands and putting them in shoe boxes, I miscounted a couple of rolls. I counted them over and over, one box had room in it and I knew there should have been a couple more stacks. The only people around was my dude Hank - I knew he wouldn't steal from me because we got money together - my girl from Chicago - she was a Vice Lord gang member - she was too real to steal from me - and another one of my homies that I had been friends with for years. Everybody except for my friend Donny. I instantly assumed he must've stolen the money. "Let's go get that nigga." Hank said. He didn't waste any time or play no games - I can't lie, his do or die attitude juiced me up. "Shit it's whatever. Let's show this nigga how we get down." I said

We rode all though Downtown looking for Donny. We finally caught up with him in the business district. In broad daylight, we kidnapped him and took him back to my apartment in Over the Rhine. When we got upstairs I made him take off his socks, shoes, and every item of clothing and turn it inside out. I'm disappointed to say he didn't have it. I found out my little gangster bitch from Chicago was the one who stiffed me and used the money to get a bus ticket to go back home. I felt so bad about what I had done to Donny but I had to be sure I could trust the people around me.

Since things were getting hot for my team, Hank thought we should do a dry run to Chicago, to check the pulse on the streets. After an hour into the trip, we got pulled over by State Troopers State with guns drawn.

"PUT YOUR FUCKIN HANDS ON THE DASHBOARD!" One officer shouted.

We weren't worried because we didn't have anything on us - no guns, no dope, no prostitutes, nothing. Once we were out of the car, they separated us by putting us in different squad cars so that they could play their little "good cop, bad cop" game.

An officer asked, "So where is the dope?"

"Man I don't know what the hell you talking about. We just riding to Chicago to visit some family."

"You can make this a lot easier son if you just comply. You can be honest with me, you weren't driving the car so you won't get in any trouble, it will be all on your buddy."

He thought I was stupid or something. I knew if they had found any drugs, we both would have gone down. He got out the car and went to other car to talk to Hank. After he talked to Hank, he said something to the other cop and came back to where I was.

"Son I hate to tell you this but your friend is saying it's all on you and if we do find any dope he says he has nothing to do with it and you must have planted it in his car."

"Hahaha, you guys are funny. I don't have anything else to say. If y'all taking us down, then let's roll."

Cops use that trick so much that it was played out, I knew Hank was no snitch.

After the police tore the seats and cleared everything out of the glove compartment, they bought in the dogs. They were sure they would find something under the hood or under the car, but there wasn't a trace of anything. Finally, after hours of keeping us handcuffed in the back of the car, they released us. Being detained like that did something to me. It made me realize that I was either going to be dead or in prison if I didn't change my ways. When we got to Chicago, I stayed at a lady friend's house on the Eastside. I was tired. This life had taken a toll on me and I didn't want it anymore. I took a hot shower, put my head in the water and let it run down my face and back and I cried. I was so empty inside. All of the women, money, and popularity that Diamond had built were meaningless. Those things only temporarily filled voids that I had since birth. The thing about filling emotional voids is we usually only fill them with dissolvable ingredients. If your value is stored up in achievements, possessions and identity, once they have dissolved, you're left with same hole you started with, except it's bigger. I tried to fill my voids with relationships. I just needed to feel loved even it was the unhealthy kind.

I thought about Patrice a lot on the ride back to Cincinnati. All I could think about was her beautiful smile and incredible body. I called her as soon as I got back in the city.
"Hello?"
"Hey Patrice, it's Diamond."
"Oh, hey Diamond. I've missed you. How have you been?" She replied.
"I'm doing ok. Honestly I'm a little depressed. My life is a mess and I'm ready for a change. I was thinking maybe me and you should connect, but permanently this time."
"Uh, yeah about that. I'm seeing someone right now."
"Is it serious?" I asked.
"Kinda. It's the guy I was with when me and you first started messing around." I learned later that he was still putting his hands on her.

Our reunion brought about so much drama. Drama I definitely didn't need in my life. I almost got myself put back in jail. This dude thought he was a real tough guy. The abuse got worse after he found out about me. I told her, one day, he's going to hurt you, bad. I encouraged her to leave him alone and put him out, but she said she was afraid of what he'd do to her. She even suggested he might kill her. I told her that if he put his hands on her one more time that I was going to kick his ass.

Then one day she called me in tears, saying he smacked her so hard she hit her head on the door. I was sick with a cold and running a fever but I was fed up with this guy. I hurried over there in my flip-flops, pajama pants, and tank top. On the way there I called him.

"What up cuz?"

"Who dis?" He responded.

"This Diamond nigga. What's up with you putting your hands on Patrice? She told me you just slapped the shit outta her and I told her last time you put yo hands on her I was going to see you." I replied.

"Bruh, what this got to do with you?" He asked.

"Oh, you a tough guy huh? Well tough guy, come downstairs and put your hands on me."

"You downstairs!?" He asked.

"Bring yo bitch ass down here and see me."

I hung up and stepped out in the middle of the street to make sure I would have some traction fighting in Justice Center shower shoes. I waited for almost twenty minutes and he never came down. Finally, I saw the hallway door opening. I thought it was him coming out, but it was Patrice. This lame sent his girl downstairs to talk to me and convince me to leave. When I saw it was her, I ran to the door to catch it before it closed. I wanted to hurt this dude badly. He was a fake thug, wanna-be tough guy when it came to Patrice, but when a real man confronted him, he was as soft as a marshmallow.

"Patrice open up this door and let me up in there. I told you what I was going to do to him if he'd ever put his hands on you again."

"He's not coming out that apartment. I have never seen him scared like this before. He is so terrified that he said if you left he would take his stuff and leave and never come back."

The funny thing was I really wasn't a tough guy either. I liked to call myself a sweet gentle butterfly with the temper of a lion and strength of a bear. I didn't even like to fight but it if you took me there it I was going to show you how beige niggas got down. I left and gave him the chance to escape from the building. We dumped most of his belongings on the street and we went to get new keys made. It wasn't too long before Patrice and I moved in together.

Our relationship was cool for the first few months. She even encouraged me to finish cosmetology school. We had a nice apartment, nice cars, and a little bit of cash—we weren't living in Indian Hill, but we were comfortable. Then Patrice decided she didn't want to work anymore and our cash was getting low. "I know you said you were done with the dope game but money ain't coming like it used to. I mean, would it hurt to move a couple bricks real quick and then get out?"
She suggested I go back to the streets so we could quickly build up our cash flow. I hit up my connection and told him I needed some work. The life I had been living came at a cost and I was about to pay a huge price. We were in New York almost every weekend, shopping and handling business. We were together but it was a complicated relationship. I was from the streets and she grew up in Florence, in a middle class working family. She really wasn't about that life but she caught feelings.

I was away a lot trying to get at the money. I had some homeboys in Dayton that I would hang out it with on the weekends. Dayton was a small city, north of Cincinnati. Dayton and Cincinnati boys clashed all the time since we were so close in proximity. We used to ride from Cincinnati through Dayton, going to Detroit or Canton, Ohio to drop off packs of dope. We would rob them or they would rob us but it was always bad blood. One weekend, my cousin Bud and I went to club Majestics in Dayton. Majestics was a place with a reputation that somebody was going to get killed - somebody died every week, but we Cincinnati boys didn't care, we was still going up in there if that's what we wanted to do. We wanted to meet some Dayton girls and turn them out. Bud and I were playing pool when these two chocolate girls walked in.
"Aye bruh, what's that over there?" I asked my cousin.
"Dammmn cuz, they both hot." He replied.

"I want the short chocolate one." I said. I claimed the one I wanted A.S.A.P before my cousin tried to work his hand. I needed some information on her first though. I didn't know if her boyfriend or baby daddy was up in the club so I asked my homeboy what was up with her. Tyrone was my homie who was throwing the banging party at the club.

"T, who is shorty right there?" I asked.

"You talking about the short thick one in the jeans?" He replied.

"Yeah. She sexy as hell." I said.

"That's Dee. She cool as hell. Most of these girls you gotta be careful with because they'll set you up to get robbed but she cool. Let me introduce y'all. "Hey Dee, this my dude Diamond from Cincinnati. Diamond this is Dee. I gotta go get some more bottles so ya'll two cool from here?"

"Yeah we good." "So what's the Dee short for?" I asked her.

"Deidre." She answered.

She had a real sweet voice and a soft personality. We talked all night long. After the club closed I tried to convince her to let me come back to her house.

"I hope you don't think we're having sex." She said. Of course I agreed.

"We don't have to have sex. We can just talk and get to know each other."

In the back of my mind I'm thinking, *whatever, WE FUCKIN*. We got back to her house and watched some T.V for a little while.

"Let me go slip into something more comfortable. I'll be right back." She said.

She came back in a red see through nightgown and sat back on the couch.

"I'm ready to lay it down, how about you?" I asked her.

"Yeah but you gon have to sleep on the couch. We just met and I don't want you to think I'm easy."

I looked at her like she was crazy. Now my "Tupac" side had to come out.

"Bitch it's 3am and you come out half naked. Oh we smashin

tonight so chill with all that. All she could say was, "Okay daddy." We spent the rest of the weekend together, but then I had to drive home back to Cincinnati. As I drove away, I decided then and there this would be my Dayton boo. I went back and forth from Cincinnati to Dayton every other weekend. When I got calls from some of my young homies in Dayton for work (dope) I would stay in Dayton over Dee's house.

    As the weeks wore on, Patrice and I continued to argue. She accused me of sleeping with other women, lying to her, and staying out all night —until I couldn't take it anymore. I had to go to Chicago to pick up a pack, not knowing it would be my last dope run. After I picked up the dope I went to Dayton to see Diana. I still had the drugs packed under the truck so I knew I couldn't stay there long. As I prepared to leave Dayton to head back to Cincinnati, Dee started acting really strange. She was holding on to me and grabbing me real tight.

"Diamond don't go, stay here in Dayton. I got a bad feeling for some reason. I think you should stay here for a few days."
What she didn't know was that I had my truck packed with coke and guns and I needed to get back to the city.
"Babe I gotta get back to the city. I'll be ok." I replied.
"I may not be here when you get back. I'm going to North Carolina and I don't plan on coming back."

    Even though things were rocky between us, Patrice was still my girl and I needed to make sure everything was good before I made any moves. When I got back to Cincinnati, Patrice wasn't at the apartment. I called her phone but it kept going straight to voicemail. Thing was, even though she didn't trust me there was a part of me that didn't trust her either. Even though she was from the suburbs, she was the type of chick that you couldn't sleep on, in other words, don't underestimate her. As fine as she was, she had a side that you didn't want to see. I think that's what I loved about her.

    I was awakened from by a loud slam.
"Where the fuck you been?" Patrice screamed at me.
"You know where I been. I had to go pick up a pack." I replied.

"You went to go see that bitch again didn't you? You know what, fuck you and that bitch. You two can have each other." She was furious.

We argued for about an hour before she left. I didn't think anything else about it. We've argued plenty of times but we always ended the day on a good note, that time felt different though. I kept thinking about what Dee said about moving and not going back.

After I fixed something to eat, I was headed to unload the dope. When I reached for my keys on the speaker, they were gone. You'd thought I was a psychic because right then and there I knew what was up. I ran downstairs to see an empty parking space. My truck, dope, and guns were gone. I called Patrice.

"Trice where are you?" I asked calmly. She was crying so hysterically I couldn't understand her. "Patrice it's cool, just bring my truck back and we can work this out. I'm sorry and I promise to leave ole girl in Dayton alone. Please come back home and let's talk…." Silence. "BITCH BRING MY TRUCK BACK OR ME AND YOU GONNA HAVE A PROBLEM!" She hung up on me. I put the kidnap plan in motion.

That was the beginning of my downward spiral. That was one of those moments that my irrational thinking got me so caught up. I had done some stupid things in my life and made so many bad choices but this had to be the dumbest. I kidnapped three people, shot one, and threatened to kill the others. Irrational thinking always has a price and I was about to pay a major one. As I was acting all this out I never took a second to think about the consequences. I never weighed the outcome of my choices in the moment. I was in such deep rage that I couldn't separate my emotions from my reality at that time. All I could think about was how I was offended and my actions were justified by my prideful thinking. There's a scripture in the Bible that says that pride comes before the fall and man I was about to fall flat on my face.

The police came after me like I was Nino Brown from New Jack City. I was at my mom's when they found me. I looked out the front window and saw cop cars up and down the street. I tried to escape out the back to find out they had the whole block surrounded. I thought somebody had died and they were coming after me with murder charges. I couldn't understand why the police were coming after me so deep. I didn't plan on spending the rest of my life in prison. I would have rather died before I let them take me. I ran down in the basement to hide. I heard the cops creeping down the steps.

"Mr. Hummons come out with your hands up!!"

I wasn't going out without a fight but I didn't have my gun me so I pulled out my black flip cell phone and bent it halfway so that it looked like a gun. It was dark in the basement so I figured if I jumped out and surprised them they would shoot me. They yelled for me to come out again but I didn't move a muscle. I wanted them to be completely surprised when I jumped out on them. All I could think about was spending the rest of my life in prison. I couldn't go to jail for murder. I felt I had no choice. Once I heard the cops feet hit the bottom step, I jumped out and pointed the cell phone at them. To my surprise the just yelled "FREEZE!!" and then they handcuffed me. After they put me in the police car I asked what was I being charged with and they wouldn't tell me. I thought maybe things were turning in my favor. The cops drove me around for forty-five minutes before they got a call on the official charges. Kidnapping, felonious assault, and attempted murder. I knew I would never see the light of day with these charges. In the Justice Center, the nightmare of my first prison experience came back, and my heart raced with anxiety. I couldn't do time again, I thought. I have to get out of here. I was willing to do whatever it took. Plus, I knew I could be facing so many years I would probably die in prison.

After three days in the Justice Center, I decided to reach out to Patrice. I asked my lawyer to call her and tell her that I wanted her to visit me. My lawyer told me I was facing forty-four and a half years in prison so I needed to make peace with this girl.

"Hummons, you gotta visit." The CO said. I get up to the visiting area and to my surprise.

"What are you doing here?" I asked. It was Dee.

"I came to see you and make sure you're alright." She replied.

"Hell naw I'm not alright. I'm facing life in here, that's why you have to leave. I need to make things right with Patrice and she's coming to see me today and I can only have one visit at a time." I told her.

"So what are you saying?" She asked.

"I'm saying I gotta deny this visit so that when she gets here they will let her come up here. Right now I need you to fall back so I can try to save my life and hopefully get outta here."

Dee wasn't happy but she understood. She left crying and within minutes of her leaving, Patrice showed up. She had seen Deidre's name in the registry book and knew she had come to me.

"So you still messing with that bitch huh?"

"No. I didn't tell her to come down here to see me. You see I denied the visit or you wouldn't be here." I replied. I was facing too much time to play hard so I had to come correct.

"They said I'm facing almost fifty years in prison. I need you to tell them the truth about what went down and get me the hell outta here."

"You think I'm stupid don't you? I'm supposed to help you get outta here just so you can go back to your Dayton bitch, nigga please." She said.

"You must not have gotten my message from my lawyer Patrice. I love you and I want to make things work with us."

"So we're going to be together? She asked me. "Yeah babe. It's going to be you and me when I get out." I told her. She didn't believe me. She had good reason to though. Under the circumstances, I was honestly prepared to say anything to get her to help me. Some of the charges got dropped, which helped to get a lower bond.

After getting out on a $40,000 bond, I went to the Justice of The Peace with Patrice and we got married. I thought going back in front of the judge with Patrice as my wife would definitely secure my freedom. After much pleading with the judge and the prosecutor, my lawyer was out of options.

"Ronald they are not budging on our motion to dismiss. They are offering you a plea deal. It may be your only shot at seeing the streets again as a young man." My lawyer said.

"But they have no witnesses and the main witness is my wife now so how do they have a case?" I asked.

"They have the police reports signed by the witnesses and I can't cross examine a police report. Ronald take the deal and I'll do everything to get you home before you're thirtieth birthday."

I had planned on going to the Waffle house after court, then back to Dayton, but instead I was headed to the penitentiary with almost a seven year sentence.

I had to go to CRC initially where I spent 23 hours a day in a hot cell. Then I was sent off to Ross Correctional Institution in Ross, Ohio. They locked me up in Cellblock C. I hated that place. I felt like I was in a concrete hell. I was surprised when I saw tough guys I knew from the streets messing with other men. On the weekends we could go to the movies. The prison had a theater just like the ones on the outside, only a little smaller. This was date night for some of these guys.

Another time I was coming down the steps of the library. I heard a pounding type of noise, and there was some guys punching and beating the hell out of another young black guy. He was getting the hell punched out of his head and face. He had big lumps all over his head from the beating. After the guys were finished they hugged the smaller guy and said, "Much love." The other guys shook his hand and hugged him back and they went on outside. This was the first time I had ever saw a gang beating before. I guess to have someone beat the hell out of you and then tell you afterwards how much they loved you was something I had to get used to.

In my free time, which I had lots of, I drew pictures of clothes and shoe designs. Since I only had state blues to wear I would draw pictures of outfits that I could see myself wearing. Another inmate named Chris saw my drawings and was really impressed by them. "Man, you should start your own clothing line," he said over and over. I had never really thought much about my drawings; I was just trying to pass the time and stay out of trouble.

Then, one day, some guy came up to me in the yard—his name was Sam—and asked if I knew what a prophet was. I was on edge when he first stepped to me. You don't walk up to a guy in prison talking about I'm a prophet.

I said, "Sure, those guys from the Bible that predicts the future, right?" I answered.

"Yeah, but they aren't always guys from the Bible" he said.

At first I shrugged him off, but then he said, "They call you Diamond on the streets don't they?" I said yeah. He went on to say, "God told me to tell you that when He's through with you that you *will be* a diamond. He started telling me how God came to him in a vision and said that I would be a successful businessman and I would be very wealthy. He also told me I would be on the cover of national magazines. You're going to create programs that will have a huge impact on people and your name will be known all over the world. For days, I prayed about the "prophet's" words. "God, if this idea is from you, then give me a sign." The next day I opened my Bible and read a passage from John 15:5: "We are the branches; he is the vine." The name Grapevine came into my heart, so I designed my logo by intertwining a G and a V. After I had my logo, I sketched furiously and the designs began to flow. But this time I drew a shoe—a high top with a thin sole and an alligator-embossed design on the front of it. I wrote the words "lambskin," "trimmed in suede" and "pink" next to the drawing. I scribbled and erased and sketched until I had the exact design I wanted. "You are beautiful, baby," I said when I was finished. I kissed that piece of notebook paper and smiled at my artwork. That shoe was hot! For the first time I felt a sense of purpose. I had a feeling I'd never felt before. It was a feeling of hope. Hope can give you life even in the desert. I never realized how powerful having vision was. The Bible says people perish from lack of vision. The word Sam just gave me set me up with a different outlook on life. No longer was I just an inmate doing time, now I had purpose.

Still, I wanted to be sure this was from God, so I prayed for confirmation. "Let me hear the name you gave me for this company Grapevine three times today, and then I'll know this vision's from you." And don't you know that day, walking through the chow hall, I heard some guys talking and they said, "Man, did you hear Marvin Gaye last night singing 'I heard it through the Grapevine'?" Then I sat down to go eat, and guys were talking to each other, saying, "I heard it through the grapevine that Davenport got paid at his parole hearing. You know what I mean. Man, oh man." That was two times I heard the word "grapevine." All I needed was to hear it one more time and I would know. Later on, I was watching the Tonight Show, and they were talking about those old California raisin commercials with those goofy raisins singing "I heard it through the Grapevine." At that point I knew God was talking to me. That was it. Even though I didn't have any education about business or clothing lines, I believed that if God was in it that he would make provisions.

About six months before I went home, I got into a big fight with a couple of homeboys against some guys from up North. After the C.O's broke it up they made some racist comments. "We should've let you niggas kill each other." One of them said. I tried to let it go because my attorney said that, if I stayed out of trouble, I could get out early. I tried to walk away, but another inmate said, "Man, fuck you." The C.O's thought I said it and I got put in the hole.

They put me in a cell where there were no bars or windows, no working lights, no air circulating, in the middle of summertime. That damn near broke me. After three months there, when I got out and looked in the mirror, I didn't recognize myself. I had a full beard and an afro. I came out looking like I had been on a desert island.

A few weeks later, someone yelled for me. "Hummons! The sergeant needs you!"

"What's he want?" I asked.

"I dunno. Go to the front desk."

I turned to one of my buddies, "I hope it's an early release."

"Chaplain needs to see you," the sergeant told me.

Oh no, I thought. The only time the chaplain needs you is when someone has died. My mind raced to think who it could be. I tried to remember who was really old in my family and didn't look well the last time I saw them. The walk down the hall seemed like forever and my stomach knotted. When I pushed open the door, the chaplain looked up at me over his glasses. He put his pen down in slow motion while he gathered his words.

"Have a seat, Ronald," he said quietly.

"What's wrong?"

"There's been an accident," he started. "There's no easy way to tell you, but your father was killed."

The words hit me like a fist to the chest. I bent over and put my head in my hands and cried. It hurt more than I ever would have imagined,

After the chaplain consoled me for a few minutes, I was allowed to make one phone call. I called Patrice—she was my wife and I trusted she would tell me the truth about my father.

"What do you know about my father dying?" I asked her.

"They found him dead in the hallway of his building."

"Do they know how he died?" Every word made me realize how removed from the outside world I was.

"Word is someone put traces of moth balls in his heroin. I don't know if they'll do an autopsy. I suppose they will." She said it so matter-of-factly but I instantly pictured my father on a cold slab.

"Bad dope," I whispered.

"I can't believe someone would do that." She hesitated and then continued, "I'm sorry, Ronald. I really am." Her voice trailed off.

"I know. When's the funeral?"

"Couple days; Wednesday, I think. Will they let you out to go?" She asked

"I hope so."

"Are you going to be ok Ronald."

"Sure," I said and hung up.

I walked back to the yard. I ran into Chris, and he saw the tears in my eyes. He asked me what was wrong. After I told him about my father, he said he would keep me in his prayers. I couldn't tell him it was more than just the death of my father. I couldn't tell him that there was now a major part of my life that would never be resolved, demons that I feared would now never sleep. He told me again to be strong.

After I washed my face, I put in a request to see the warden. Later that night in his office, I asked if I could attend my father's funeral. If inmates had the money and good behavior they were granted this type of request and I figured my case wouldn't be any different. He said he would get back to me. The next morning, the C.O told me I couldn't go.

"Why not?"

"Something about no father's name on your birth certificate," he said without looking at me.

"But he's my dad. I gotta go." I sat down on a bench and my shoulders slumped.
"There's no way?" I looked at the guard so intensely he had to look in my direction.

"I don't think so," he said. I remember him opening his mouth to speak and then he stopped. As I was walked away he said, "I'm sorry, Hummons. I really am." When I turned around, he had walked away from his desk.

The ironic thing was, I had only a few weeks earlier tried to call my dad. I had thought that if I was going to make a fresh start on the outside, a good place to start was my relationship with my dad. I called him, several times. But he never answered any of my calls. I grabbed some paper and a pen and wrote him a letter. I started with something I thought was funny; *I know you don't like for me to call you Dad but no one is around and they won't hear.* I think I said something about feeling like . . . *this is the last time in here for me.* The letter went on to say how, when I was young, I thought it would be so great to be with my real dad, especially with the way Walter treated me. How all I wanted was for him to tell me he loved me, and how angry I was – still am – that he couldn't do even that for me. But as I was writing the letter, I suddenly realized that the look in my father's eyes was my own. We were both looking for the same thing. I am so glad I wrote . . . *I wanted you to know that I love you. No matter how you feel toward me, I will, from this day on, love you.* Then I told him I had started drawing again and hoped we could get together once I got out. I asked him to write back. He never did.

As I walked away from the C.O's desk, I didn't hear the normal commotion in the corridors. The clanging of steel doors, the television turned up too loud and the pointless arguments—it was all muted. Back in the yard, the tears in my eyes made it difficult to recognize anyone; they were just men sitting on benches, lifting weights, leaning against fences. Yet, somehow, I could see, or perhaps *sense* is a better word, their faces. I could see their sweat and the stains it left upon them, I could see their scars and the stories behind them, and I could see the children they once were. It was like I was in a dream. I sat down alone, watching the inmates while they marked the minutes. One man, his hair gray, was gesturing with his hands as his friends listened. Those listening had become a smeared painting but the man's creased face and sparkling eyes were in perfect focus. I tried to read his lips; his words jumped into my head like he was right next to me. *A man should not be judged by the color of his skin but by the content of his character.* And then he looked in my direction. It startled me and I turned away from his glare. My eyes met another face and he was staring directly at me. I thought he saw something behind me so I looked over my shoulder but there was nothing to see. As I turned back around, another voice, slow and maybe southern, said, *Before I can live with others, I've got to live with myself.* The words were so close I felt that someone had walked up without my seeing him. I was alone. I looked around the prison yard and saw generations of dark eyes and dark faces looking back. I knew it had to be a dream but it felt so real; all the beatings, stealing, pimping, dealing, prison and my father's death, it all swirled in my head. Then more voices came and I put my hands to my ears. *You're killing people, you know.* "Yes, I know," I said out loud. *Nobody needs to wait a single moment before starting to improve the world.* This time it was a gentle, feminine voice. The voices wouldn't stop. *You must be the change you wish to see in the world.* I couldn't stand it. Walter was pulling his hand back, I winced, I was crying while my daddy beat a man with a club, "No, Paul, no!" I could see a man being raped in prison. I turned away. "Here, take this. It's the best dope around." She's getting into the car; it's her first time. I never saw her again. "She's only fifteen," someone was screaming. "Guilty! Guilty! Guilty!" It was me screaming. *The time is always right to do what is right.* And then the voices stopped. I lifted my head and everyone was doing what they always do, which was not much. I don't really know what happened that day but I had enough sense not to forget. I was ready to move on.

I found out that after my father died, the police went to his apartment to piece together what may have happened to him. I'm sure they were looking for drugs since they knew he was an addict. They did discover a little cocaine and a little bit of money stashed in a drawer. On his bedside table, there was a letter. It was my letter, and it was opened. I feel so sad that he died alone like that but I thank God that I wrote that letter. He knew that I loved him, that someone did. Maybe I could put that demon to rest, after all. My grandmother says that in death one is set free. Maybe Paul has been set free; maybe he regrets what he did to me, to my mom. Maybe he regrets his years of using. What did he think of my mama's comments when she faced the congregation from the pulpit? I lay down on my cot and listened for his voice to echo inside of me.

Chapter 10

Free at last, Free at last
April- December 2001

The afternoon I left prison, the deputy sheriff picked me up and drove me down to the Justice Center in Cincinnati. I spent the night in the HCJC, and the next morning I went back in front of the judge and he released me from my incarceration. My mother and my little brother—he was 13 at the time—were outside the Center waiting for me. As soon as she saw me, my mother started crying.

"Oh, my baby, my baby. It's so good to have you back with us, Ronald." She hugged me tightly, and as she did, I looked over her shoulder expecting to see Patrice walk up any minute but she was nowhere around.

"She didn't come with us, Ron," my mother said, as she gently let me go. She had a hard time looking at me.

"Why not? Something happened to her? I tried to call her about my release. I left her several messages, but she never answered."

My mom's face turned into stone.

Instead of a joyous homecoming dinner, it was a tense occasion. My mom and brother tried to cheer me up, but their laughter and talk all seemed forced, like they were keeping something from me. Later, at my mother's house I found out why Patrice didn't want to be around me or my family.

My mother took me aside and told me that she and my little brother saw Patrice kissing some dude at a local grocery store. She paraded all over the city with this man, and she had been doing this for almost the entire time I was in prison. Man, I was steamed.

"Why didn't you tell me?! You just let me believe everything was okay, the whole time?"

My mother tried to put her arm around me, but I pulled

away.

"I didn't tell you because I didn't want your prison time to be any harder than what it was. I'm sorry, baby."

"That's okay, mama. It's not your fault."

I tried calling Patrice on her cell phone, but she wouldn't answer. She told me during one of her visits that when I came home, she would cook me all my favorite foods, including my favorite dessert, chocolate cake. Finally, at one o'clock in the morning I went to her apartment. The door was locked and my truck was gone. I was determined to find her and get some answers. Walking away, I felt a knot in my stomach, and my eyes swelled with hot tears. When I got back to my mother's house, I took off my wedding ring and flung it into the street. Then I hit the pavement looking for her. I walked from my mother's house in Golf Manor, to Patrice's grandmother's house in Pleasant Ridge, a distance of about five miles. She wasn't there. Then I backtracked three miles to her aunt's house and sure enough, there it was - my green truck.

"Patrice, get your ass out here!" I yelled at the house. I was so enraged, I didn't care if I woke up everybody in the house. "I know you're in there!" I continued. "I'm not leaving till you get out here and talk to me!"

Her aunt and her three grown sons came out of the house. "Go home, Ron," her aunt said. "It's not a good time. Patrice is sleep." Her cousins stood behind their mom with their arms folded.

"I don't have a problem with you, ma'am," I said. "I just want to talk to my wife, and I know she's not sleep."

"Get outta here or we're calling the police." one of her sons said. "You ain't even been out a day, and you're causing trouble."

"I'm not going anywhere until I see Patrice. I don't give a damn if you call the police."

The three dudes came down off the porch and walked towards me, but they were cautious. They must have thought I had a gun but I wasn't going anywhere. "Patrice isn't going to talk to you tonight. Maybe you can call her in the morning," one of the guys said. "We don't have any problems with you we just don't want any drama at our mom's."

"I'm not leaving till she comes out. I need to see my wife!"

I stood there hollering until I heard sirens and the flashing lights of a police car. I explained to the cop that I was locked out of my house and needed to get the key from my wife.

"Why don't I give you a ride, son. You have somewhere you want me to take you?"

I thought about arguing with him, but he seemed nice enough. I didn't want to go back to my mother's so I had him drive me to our apartment. After the cop dropped me off, I broke a window and climbed into the apartment. There was no food in the refrigerator. My first day home from prison turned out to be a bust.

The next morning, I cleaned up the apartment. Between taking out the garbage and doing the dishes, I called Patrice over and over. She finally answered.

"Hey, Ron." She acted like nothing happened.

"Hey Ron? What the hell you mean hey Ron? I thought I was gonna come home to a hot bath and a good meal. What happened?"

"I'm sorry. I broke my arm and I came to my aunt's house so she could take care of me. I wanted to be there when you came home but I had to work."

"I hear you been doing more than just working."

"What's that supposed to mean?"

"Why don't you come over here and we can talk about it."

She came over to the apartment later that evening, and at first she denied that she cheated on me. But she could only lie for so long

"You want to go over to my mom's house? Maybe she saw your twin, is that it?"

She finally admitted that she had been dating this other

guy. She said she was sorry, that she was lonely with me gone so long and that this guy didn't mean anything to her. I accepted her apology; it wasn't that big a deal. I couldn't expect her to do something I couldn't do. We look for ways to not let the outside life affect us during our prison bid.

We attempted to work on our relationship. We argued all the time, even though I tried to keep things civil between us but Patrice used my fear of going back to prison against me. She would try to provoke me, knowing that I wouldn't dare touch her. I put my hands up and out of the way, every time she approached me. If I tried to leave the house to get away from her, she would block the door, and dare me to touch her. When she got too out of control, I would go into the bedroom and climb out the window. I didn't want to give her any ammunition to put me back in the joint.

I picked up work by delivering newspapers for the Cincinnati Enquirer. I was gone all the time, from midnight until six in the morning. One day I came home early from work, and saw a guy driving creeping down our street. He had his head sticking out the window, staring at our apartment building. He had long braids and looked just the way my mother and little brother described Patrice's lover. We lived on a dead end street so there was only one way off the street. I turned my car long ways so that the only way you could drive off the street was drive up on the sidewalk. I walked over to his car.

"What's good homie?"

"Who are you." He replied"

"Bruh I know who you are and after fucking my wife you got some big balls showing up at my house."

I stuck my head in his car window and grabbed him around the collar and started punching him in the head. "I'm her husband bitch."

He was reaching for the gear shift trying to put the car in drive while I was trying to yank him out the car. I pulled out of his car just in time as he sped off, driving up on the sidewalk trying to get away.

Things finally settled down with Patrice and I, we decided to go to couples' counseling to see if there was anything salvageable in our relationship. We were constantly at each other's throats, usually about money. I did odd jobs but I wasn't able to land a regular job and I was determined I wasn't going back to the streets. I had made an oath to God that if he'd bless me to make entrepreneurism work for me then I would never return to the street life.

Patrice wasn't thrilled this new idea I had to start my own business. I understand It's difficult to see someone else's vision when they don't have the resources to actually make it happen. But I had faith, I didn't need anything else. Entrepreneurism was it for me. If I was going to see success it was going to be from my creating it.

Patrice shook her head. "You're crazy. You can't start a business with just some sketches on notebook paper. You are always dreaming. You ain't changed a bit. Look, Ron. I know you think this is a good idea, but it's not. Do you know how many people have dreams of owning their own business? People who have business degrees have a hard time making it, and here you are with no training, money, or education thinking you can start a clothing line? You need to get real."

I found an organization in Cincinnati called Smart Money. I thought they'd be impressed with my ideas and could help. My drawings were simple pencil drawings but they were clear and presentable. The representatives looked at me and saw a guy with no money, no business experience, and some pencil drawings on a professional art pad. When I told the associate I wanted to start my own clothing line, he looked at me like he thought I was crazy.

"You have any experience with design? Any education? You think we're going to hand you money because you draw a shoe on a piece of paper? I don't think so. You need a business plan."

"A business plan?" I asked.

"Yes, you really need to have one. I'd be glad to help

you out with it."

"That's okay. Let me work on it first. If I need any help, I'll get back to you."

"Sounds like a plan. Thanks for stopping by, Mr. Hummons."

Patrice was on my case day in and day out. What hurt the most was that she didn't believe in me. I could take all the rest, but that really cut to the core. But I had married her, so I felt obligated to make things work. I went to the library to figure out how to write a business plan. Most nights I stayed in the library until it closed. I never got home before 9 o'clock.

I didn't know anything about business or what direction to go in—all I had were my drawings and my logo. At the library, I flipped through books in the business section: *The McGraw Hill Guide to Writing a High Impact Business Plan: A Proven Blueprint for First Time Entrepreneurs, The Business of Making and Selling Fashion, Principles of Fashion, Ernst & Young Business Plan Guide, and Built to Last: Successful Habits of Visionary Companies* were just a few of the books I pulled off the shelf. After I practically memorized these, I read articles about *FUBU* and how they started. I studied Dada, and read about their first design and how they marketed it. Pretty soon, every evening was spent in the library reading everything I could about design. I did this several hours a night for months.

Patrice's lack of support really hurt. I knew the idea seemed farfetched that I would actually make this work but a little support from her would've carried me a long way. Suddenly, I felt hopeless. I was in a marriage I didn't want to be in, I had a dead-end job and my dream of Grapevine seemed like a foolish fantasy. I stared at Patrice's angry red eyes, her disappointed face looking at me and thought *what am I doing? This shit will never work. Who was I fooling to think I could actually accomplish this?* There was only one way out for me: Death.

The next day I asked a friend for some pills to help me

sleep. That night after another argument with Patrice, I lost all sense of hope, I was even angry at God for all the hell I suffered. So, I swallowed the entire bottle of pills, lay down in my bed, pulled the covers over my head and prepared to die. As I was dozing off, I kept telling God, I'm coming to see you face to face to ask you why You made my life a living hell. I slept a day and a half, before Patrice realized something was wrong. She started shaking me to wake me up. When I came to, I opened up my eyes but I couldn't see anything. I tried to turn over, but I couldn't move. I couldn't even talk. After I threw up on myself, Patrice called 911 and the ambulance took me to Jewish Hospital. The doctors thought for sure I was going to die. They tested my liver to make sure it wasn't shut down. Later, I was told that I swallowed enough pills to kill a three hundred pound man, but by some miracle, I survived.

I was totally paralyzed from head to toe. I stayed in bed for a week after I came home. That meant no work and no money. All I had was my thoughts. I lay there confused as to why I wasn't successful at ending my owning life. Apparently this life had nothing good for me. I felt I would be doing the world a favor if I wasn't here anymore. I was miserable lying there all day. Patrice was resentful that I tried to take my life; she wouldn't talk to me when she fed me. Over time, I managed to fend for myself and scrape together meals whenever I wasn't too dizzy to stand.

As I grew stronger, I realized how stupid I was to try to kill myself. I still had my vision and having just missed death, I was even more determined to make my dream work. I told Patrice that I was going to make something happen for us and to just be patient. Her frustrations grew as our money problems grew.

"Seven dollars? On copies? You tell me to sacrifice, and you go out and waste money on this? For something that'll never pay off? You're wasting your time, and mine on this fashion shit!" She screamed.

I couldn't take any more of her degrading taunts, so I

went into the bedroom, shut the door and sat on the bed. Seconds later, Patrice came in after me. I stared at the wall.

"That's it; just walk away when I'm talking to you. That's what you always do anyway. Walk away from me, all the time. I took care of you when you were sick, and then you go out and spend our hard-earned money on stupid copies!"

I held my face in my hands. On and on she ranted. After a while, I didn't hear a word she said. Her screaming turned into an incoherent squawk, much like the "Waaah, Waaah" of the teacher from the cartoon Charlie Brown.

"You don't make enough money to support a business, much less a home!" With those words, she jerked me out of my trance.

"I'm done," I told her. "I can't do this with you anymore. I want a divorce."

"Divorce? I'll leave you with nothing if you divorce me." Patrice screamed.

"You want my car? Fine, get your keys, and we'll go down to the title department right now. You can have both of the cars. I just want out."

We drove in silence. Once there, we sat down with a clerk who helped us transfer the car titles to Patrice. As soon as I signed, I was out of there. No money in my pocket, my bag of hair clippers, my Bible, my designs and the clothes on my back. Luckily I had grabbed my jacket before leaving. It was the last day of October, Halloween and it was starting to get cold. I walked down Liberty and Main, where store windows displayed lit pumpkins with frozen grins and ghoulish masks of werewolves and vampires. I angled across Liberty and crossed down 13th Street and found a park bench right behind the Elm Street Clinic. I collapsed on the bench and watched the blurred clouds slide by. I didn't sleep well that night—the bench was hard and the wind cold. When I was finally able to find a comfortable position and closed my eyes, a dope fiend tried to steal my clippers.

"Hey! What the hell are you doing?" I jumped up and

grabbed the guy's shirt. "You touch any of my stuff?" I searched under the bench for my clippers and sketchpad and to my relief, they were still there.

"I was just looking for some change," he said. "You got a couple dollars? I'm just trying to get something to eat." The lights from the clinic shined in his yellowed eyes. His hands shook, but not from the cold.

The next morning a cop woke me up. "People will be coming to work soon son. You're going to have to pack it up." I grabbed my things and headed into town.

I was so hungry. I remember this feeling as I kid and now as an adult I was back to being homeless and hungry again. With no place to go, and without a shower or a change of clothes, I took my Bible, clippers and designs and sat outside the library until it opened at nine.

Now homeless and no job, I had no choice but to make this business stuff work, or probably end up back in prison. As soon as the library opened, I sat for hours studying on how to write business plans and formulating my own. At night, I would hide my Bible, clippers and notes under my beat-up coat so they wouldn't be stolen while I slept. I snoozed with my sketchpad in my arms though; there was no way I was going to let go of that. My sketches were my life, my hope, my chance at a future. The next morning, I would walk down Liberty Street to the Free Store where I would get a little food, a change of clothes and toiletries. My afternoons and evenings were spent in the library; when the library closed I was back on the bench. If it got too cold at night I would sleep in the alley next to the heating duct. Some days, I went to the Drop-in Center and talked to the guys there. A lot of them were just like me—homeless and jobless ex-cons estranged from their families. Men filled the ugly green benches covering the first floor of the square brick building. Many of them sat for hours, some for days, waiting to talk to a social worker or a job counselor, a rest from their endless wanderings. Some, like me, hoped to get a shower and shave and a haircut. It was there that I took out my clippers again and gave myself a cut and shave. Other guys saw me and begged me to cut their hair, and soon I found myself giving free cuts to guys that needed a little help grooming themselves. As I cut the guys' hair they would share their stories with me, "We paid for our crimes in prison," a weathered old man told me. His hands reflected years of hard work. "Why do we have to keep paying when we get out? No one will hire us because of our records. We're condemned for the rest of our lives. Sometimes I wish I was still in prison."

"What'd we have in prison?" another asked. "Nasty food, mice, and roaches. How's that better?"

"It ain't worse."

"Well, we didn't freeze our asses off in the winter."

"You weren't in the same prison I was."

"All I want is a chance. I got skills but no place to use them."

"What skills you got?"

"I can build things. I used to build houses."

"Why do you have to wait for someone to hire you?" I said. "Start your own company."

"Oh, yeah." The man put his finger against his forehead. "Now, why didn't I think of that?" The others laughed. "Tomorrow, I'm going down to the bank and borrow a few thousand."

I ignored his response. "You need a business plan. Look," I gripped my folder, "I'm working on one."

"He's young," one old guy said. "He still believes in the American Dream."

"Ronald Hummons," a big guy with a beard announced my name.

"Over here," I said, packing up my gear. I followed him up a short flight of stairs to the second floor. He opened a door with a glass pane and held out his hand for me to enter.

"How's it going?" He asked me. "My name's James."

"Things are alright, I guess. Probably could be better. I left my wife. She took everything, so I'm on the streets."

"You working?"

"I've put in so many applications but employers haven't been willing to give me a chance, not with my record"

"We might be able to place you somewhere around here." He replied

"It's tough out there. That's why I want to start my own business."

"Doing what? We might be able to give you some help."

"Fashion design called Grapevine Collection."

"Those your designs in that book?" James asked, pointing to my sketchpad.

"Yeah, I've been working on casual stuff, like sweat suits and jeans. Here's a few of my drawings." I opened the book and handed it to him.

He turned the sketches around and held them up. "These are real nice. I'd wear these. These are real good, man."

"Thanks," I said as he gave me the book back.

"Listen, we need to get you off the streets. I know someone who may be able to help.
You heard of the Lord's Gym?"

"Yeah, I've seen it."

"The manager's a guy named Jerry Dubose. He could help you."

"How's he gonna help me?"

"They work with men like you that are trying to better their lives."

"I'm not taking charity."

"Lose the pride son. It's okay to need help sometimes." When you go meet with Jerry, tell him James Johnson sent you. He'll help you out." He shook my hand. "I don't what it is about you but I have a good feeling you're going to be okay. Good luck son."

"Thanks Mr. Johnson."

Instead of going to the library that afternoon, I went back to my bench. My eyes were burning so badly. My insomnia was now chronic and nothing helped me rest. I knew I couldn't do any reading. I stuck my clipper case and sketchpad under the bench, tucked my Bible under my jacket, intending to just rest my eyes for a few minutes and surprisingly I fell into a deep sleep. When I woke up, my belongings were gone. I couldn't believe it. The one time I didn't guard my things, they disappears. "I can't believe this!" I yelled, my hands waving at the sky. "I hate this city! I hate my life!" I paced back and forth like a furious cat, and then I saw it. My clipper case had been tossed over the short chain-linked fence in front of the clinic. "Thank god," I cried. Looking over my shoulder to see who might be watching me, I jumped the fence and retrieved the case.

I sat on the curb and held my head in my hands and prayed, "God, I don't understand what's going on. I gave my life to you and I know that this entrepreneur journey I'm on is your will but my faith is shaky right now. If this is your will please help." I didn't expect things to be this difficult. Honestly I thought since I had committed my life to God that things would just fall into place and doors would open, but what did I really expect? Living on the streets, I was lucky to be alive. *What else can happen to me?* I thought. Tears of frustration running down my face,

"Ronald Hummons, is that you?" a female voice asked, interrupting my stare. "It's been a long time."

The sun was in my eyes, so I didn't make out who it was at first. Then I recognized her, Tawana Sanders, she was an old friend from the suburbs - I remembered that she likes bad boys. She and her friends used to come to the hood and hang. She knew me when I had money and now she's seeing me homeless.

"Hey, babe, what's going on?" She asked.

"I could ask you the same, you see what I'm up to."

"Yeah. I heard you were out of prison"

"Yeah, I've been out for several months now"
. "So, where you living now?"

I tapped the seat of the bench. "Right here, home seat home. I've been sleeping here for a few days."

"No way—can't you stay with your mama?"

"I have to find my own way out here. I'm a grown man

and I need to pave my own way and make a life for me and my kids."

"You making any money?"

"I bring in some from cutting hair, but the job hunt has been a dead end."

"You can stay with me if you want. My boyfriend moved out and I could use someone to help around the house."

"I ain't got much." I replied.

"The money isn't important. We can think of other ways for you to help out. I've got an extra bedroom and everything. I have a real nice computer my ex left and never came back to get it, so now it's mine….so, you coming or not?" She asked.

"Are you kidding? It'd sure feel good to sleep in a nice, soft bed again.

Our arrangement worked out great at first. She worked at one of the department stores Downtown, and her hours were from 9 to 9. That gave me plenty of time alone to work on my designs and business plan. I didn't have to tell her where I was going or when I came home. My time in the library was filled with intense studying, since I didn't have to think about where I was going to sleep at night. It was great. Sometimes Tawana and I would hang out together and watch TV and talk about our day. I was cutting enough hair to give her a few dollars and put a few groceries in the apartment. I felt good about how things were going. I was really trying to do what I needed to do to make a better life for me and my kids. In the back of my mind, I knew eventually she would want to have sex with me.

One night when I came home from the library, Tawana tried to get close.
She had just come home from hanging out with her girlfriends, and I could tell she'd had a few drinks.

"Ron, do you think I'm cute?"

"Yeah, you cool. Why"

"So, why haven't you ever tried anything with me?"

"We're friends. Plus, you know what I just went through

with Patrice. I'm just trying not to get involved with anybody right now. I have to stay focused"

She pushed her bottom lip out. "Why'd you move in then?"

"I didn't have anywhere to go."

"Nothing else?" She asked.

She wrapped her arms around me and tried to kiss me. "Don't act like you don't want it."

"What're you doing?" I gently pushed her away.

"Boy come here."

"You trippin. I'm cool on all that right now. Maybe I should leave." I walked towards the door.

Tawana crossed her arms. "Alright, then. Go! You'll be back."

She screamed at me the whole time I got my stuff together and she continued screaming as I walked out the door. It wasn't that I didn't want her but I knew I would be successful and I didn't want any women trying to take credit for my hard work.

Later, on the streets when I got cold, I had second thoughts. *Maybe I should have slept with her. Was that too big a price to pay for a warm place to sleep?* But the days of using women were over for me. I wanted to make it on my own.

The next day I wandered into a place called The Lord's Gym. It was the week before Christmas. I thought, maybe some of the guys might want a haircut. That's when I met Jerry Dubose.

Chapter 11

The Lord's Gym and the Cincinnati Riots
December – April 2001

I had walked by The Lord's Gym several times and saw the guys pumping iron and hanging out. The Gym, located at the corner of Liberty and Walnut within the fractured shadows of Over-the-Rhine, offered a variety of weight-lifting equipment and a running club. The building had the seasoned aura of an old dry goods store with large storefront windows. Since its opening in 1993, it helped, or tried to help, at least 400 guys a month. The gym was famous for getting men in rehabilitation programs and leading men and women to the Lord. But I didn't know any of this at the time and didn't think this place could offer me much—mainly because I knew myself well enough to know that I'm not too good at asking for help.

But I was desperate and tired. I was only twenty-six, but I felt like I had been through enough pain for a hundred lifetimes. When I pushed open the wooden door of the gym, a thin man, maybe fifty or sixty, greeted me at the check-in desk.

"Welcome, brother," he said. "My name's Jerry Dubose—I'm the manager here. You come to lift weights or to find the Lord, or both?"

"Honestly I don't know why I'm here. I'm just trying to find some answers."

"What's your name?"

"I'm Ronald."

"Well Ronald God always gives us the answers but we have to be ready to receive them."

"How do you get ready? I ask God every day for direction and it feels like my prayers go up to the ceiling and fall back to the ground."

"Son, God does things in his timing and even though your journey right now may be difficult doesn't mean God isn't in it with you. You didn't walk through these doors for no reason.

God led you in for a reason.

I snuck a look around the room. Guys were pushing weights and doing curls. Several, with towels draped over their shoulders talked quietly while they cooled off. In the far corner of the room, a man with a beard leaned against a stationary bike while sketching the t-shirt designs. "Yeah, it's been hard," I finally said, avoiding both of their faces. I felt awkward and ashamed. I didn't know what to do. My eyes darted towards the door. I thought about just leaving.

As if he could read my mind, Jerry stood directly in front of me, blocking any move I might have made. I stayed for bible study and his message on faith was just what I needed to hear.

"Sometimes we have to work our faith before it works for us." He said fiercely. His words felt like they could move mountains and where I was in my life, his words helped build my faith. After Bible study he asked me where have I been sleeping.

"Mr. Dubose I'm homeless right now and have been sleeping on the streets off and on for the last couple of months."

"We have rooms for guys to stay in until they get on their feet, Jerry replied. They ain't much, but it's a place for you to sleep without worrying about getting cold." Jerry flipped through a tattered notebook. "Looks like we have a room."

"What'll I have to do for it?"

"Just give a few haircuts to the guys sometimes, help clean the gym and come to Bible study from time to time. If you work out here, you'll be forced to listen to my preaching, but that's about it. You been to the Lord's Pantry?"

"No. What's that?"

"It's our outreach center where we give out food and clothing. You can get a meal there during the day when they're open"

As we walked into the Lord's Pantry a woman shook her head, like she was coming out of a fog. "You need to listen to him, brother. Last month, I was living in the pit of human despair; I was in a prison without bars. Then God reached down and lifted me out, with the help of this angel." She smiled widely revealing crooked yellow teeth.

"She used to be a hooker," Jerry said. "She never missed a day of getting high for ten years. Crack and heroin. She sold her soul for her addictions."

I flinched inside while he continued.

"Hunger brought her here—and she listened to the word of the Lord. She heard a voice ask her how she wanted to spend the rest of her life and she knew she didn't want to be a hooker anymore."

"Our Bible meeting's starting in about an hour." We headed back to the gym.

"I haven't lifted since I been home. I need to get back right again."

"Help yourself, brother." Jerry said. "You just got out of the joint, right?"

"About a year and a half ago. Does it show?"

"Prison is an occupational hazard for guys who live on the streets. I served time myself. I had a deficit inside me, but then I filled it up with the Lord. Most of us end up on drugs or in prison because we don't know that Jesus set us free on Calvary. We're a tire with a slow leak, and no amount of air's going to keep that tire from going flat. Small or big, we all have a leak. If we don't fix it, we get thrown away for good. Jesus can patch you up, son."

He reached for something behind his desk—it was a 4x6 postcard with the Lord's prayer written on it.

"Keep this in your pocket and use it as a weapon every day. When you read this focus on the part that says Thy kingdom come, Your will be done. God has a plan for your life and sometimes God has to take you through the fire to get you prepared for the purpose He has for our lives."

He picked up a folding chair and took it over to the front of the gym, away from the workout equipment. Six men followed him, unfolding their chairs before they formed a semi-circle. I didn't make a move to join them but watched for a minute. Then I lay down my clippers and sat at one of the machines and adjusted the weight. As I lay on my back lifting weights, I listened to Jerry read from his time-worn Bible. He read a section from Isaiah about the suffering servant, a quote I was very familiar with. My mother had read it to me when I was in prison and preachers often read the quote on Good Fridays.

"'He is despised and rejected of men; a man of sorrows and acquainted with grief: and we hid as it were our faces from him; he was despised, and we esteemed him not," Jerry read. "'Surely, he hath borne our griefs, and carried our sorrows: yet we did esteem him stricken, smitten of God, and afflicted. But he was wounded for our transgressions, he was bruised for our iniquities; the chastisement of our peace was upon him; and with his stripes we are healed. All we like sheep have gone astray; we have turned everyone to his own way; and the Lord hath laid on him the iniquity of us all. He was oppressed, and he was afflicted, yet he opened not his mouth; he is brought as a lamb to the slaughter, as a sheep before her shearers is dumb, so he opened not his mouth."

Jerry paused when he finished and stared at the men in the circle. When he spoke, his voice was raspy.

"You guys in here who feel sorry for yourselves, because you ain't got nowhere to go, or your suffering because you're trying to get off crack and it hurts real bad, or you did time and it was hard, well, what you went through was nothing compared to what Jesus suffered for you. Jesus showed us the way—if He can suffer the sins of the world—the world, mind you, not just the few of you sitting in this circle, then you can put up with some hardships that come your way. Some of you sin day after day because you can't stand a little suffering. You drink the booze and forget about your families; you rob stores to support your habits—but with Christ on your side, you don't have to walk the hard road alone. He'll help you get through the bad times and find a better way."

"Amen," a few responded and the rest nodded. "Jesus will show us the way," another prayed.

"Now, I know once you're hooked on sin it's hard to get

the barb out. That's where the Lord comes in. And prayer," Jerry said.

"I had a real bad night yesterday—I was so depressed and almost relapsed. One of my friends was smoking and offered me some but by the grace of God I was able to walk away," the man in front confessed.

"Some friend," a young guy said.

"Yeah, no kidding. But I'd been clean for sixteen months, and I thought 'if I had one hit, what would it hurt.' The devil was tempting me real bad, but then God reminded me of what I did to my family, and to myself on that stuff. I told my friend, former friend, to back off."

"We're proud of you, man. It ain't easy, but you did it."

"One day at a time, brother. One day at a time."

His eyes red, his voice quivered. "God's blessed me with you all, man. It's hard talking about all this."

His testimony was followed by the testimonies of others, and after about an hour the guys picked up their chairs and put them back.

My arms ached from the weights, but my spirits were lifted. I didn't realize how lonely I'd been until I walked into the gym and heard Jerry speak. I'd missed hanging out, having somebody to talk to.

"Hey!" I yelled. "I'm giving free haircuts if anyone's interested. Of course if you have any extra cash for a tip, I'd appreciate it."

A few guys came over and I cut their hair. We set up shop, newspaper on the floor, metal chair by the front window. Then a few more came, and I had a steady flow for almost two hours. The guys gave me what they could afford and I ended up with twenty dollars in my pocket.

When I finally had some down time, Jerry came over and placed his hand on my shoulder. "Didn't I tell you? The Lord always provides. Trust in the Lord, son."

"The Lord hasn't been much help lately."

"The Lord suffered for you Ronald. He loves you. Open up your heart and he'll guide you. C'mon let's get something to eat."

"Thanks, Jerry," I said, devouring a chicken sandwich. "You saved my life."

"No, son, God did. And you did."

That afternoon I moved into a small room with a bed and a hot plate. To get to my room, I had to ring a buzzer next to a green metal door on the outside of a four story building. The buzzer was attached to an intercom system into which I spoke my name. The stairway leading up to the rooms was dimly lit, and the hallways were dark and damp. My room was on the third floor—Jerry lived directly above me—and I shared a bathroom with my hallmates. The room was plain. It looked a lot like my old cell, except for one thing – I could walk out of it when I wanted to.

After a few days of hanging out with Jerry, I told him about my dream for Grapevine.

"What avenues have you taken to bring this idea into fruition? Jerry asked.

"I go to the library every day. I spend hours there reading books on business plans, financing and different corporations.

"Get the librarian to help you find names of organizations and businessmen who might want to invest in young entrepreneurs."

"I've tried that already. I sent out at least fifty letters about Grapevine. I used my mom's address and still haven't heard a word."

"Well try again, man. You just need to find the right ones."

I went back to the library and again the librarians took the time to search the stacks for business books. They found listings of local angel investors and free entrepreneur organizations, and with the Lord's help, I sent out ten letters a day until I had almost 100 letters in the mail. I was pumped—I felt good about the letters and good about life. God had a path for me and I was following it.

It was April of 2001 and I was out of prison for a year

when on April 7th, my city would be turned upside down. It was a Saturday afternoon, the week before Easter. Timothy Thomas, a 19-year old African American, wanted for minor traffic offenses, led policemen on a chase through the alleys of Over-the-Rhine. According to reports, Thomas was spotted by two Cincinnati police officers. When the officers became suspicious, they started chasing him through the back streets. Officer Steve Roach, hearing a radio alert about the fleeing suspect, joined the pursuit and abruptly came face-to-face with the 19-year-old in a dimly lit alley. Roach shot him once in the chest. Two days after the Thomas shooting, Monday April 9th, hundreds of angry black and white residents stormed city hall, including Thomas 'mother and her attorney Kenneth Lawson. The Council meeting spun out of control so the crowd left City Hall. Swelling to over 1,000 along the way, headed toward the Cincinnati police headquarters, protesting the deaths of fifteen black men—a tally of suspects killed by the Cincinnati police since 1995.

Over the next three days, crowds would march through Cincinnati's Over the Rhine. On Thursday afternoon following the shooting, a bullet hit a cop, grazing off his belt buckle. Mayor Charles Luken imposed an 8 PM curfew and announced a state of emergency.

I couldn't believe what was happening. The city was in chaos—the division between black and whites was growing wider, and here I was, a black ex-con asking investors, mostly white, to help me. My chances of finding investors in the middle of all this turmoil and confusion seemed slim indeed, and I watched the city spin out of control as I walked to and from the library. I made the decision to stay clear of the riots since I was still on parole from my early release. I had no doubt the police used force against black men, since I had been victim of such discrimination many times. But after being in prison I didn't want to do anything that would land me back there. For me, the best way to fight discrimination and police brutality was by making something of myself. Then I would have the voice to speak up and make a change. I could play my part as an effective leader and healer. No one wants to listen to an ex-con who lives on the streets, but an ex-con who works within the system and wins, now there's a person to reckon with and I wanted to be that person.

The riots finally played themselves out, and after a few months the city quieted down, but the tension was thick and people were nervous. I continued working on perfecting my business plan, cutting hair, hanging with the guys at the Gym and searching for work. But when a month passed and I hadn't received a single response from any of my letters, I became anxious and a little disappointed. Jerry kept telling me it takes time; the riots might have slowed the mail, and above all, trust in the Lord. Finally the responses started coming in. All rejections. I didn't have any experience, no college degree in design, and a felony record was the most common reasons; some gave no reasons. I was bummed and fell into a deep depression. I stayed in my little room for two days—I didn't come out to eat or bother to change my clothes. Jerry noticed my absence and came up to check on me.

"Ronald, you there?" He banged on the door. "We missed you at the gym. Some of the guys were asking about you. Ronald, come on, I know things seem dark right now but you gotta continue to fight. The devil wants you down and depressed so he can keep you from the future God has for you."

I dragged myself out of bed, and walked to the door. "It's a mess in here," I said when Jerry walked into the room.

"You got that right, man." He waved his hand in front of his face. "It smells like somebody in here. You need some Tums or something?"

His comment made me smile a little. "Nah, man, but I could use some grub."

"Look, get showered, change clothes and we'll go out and get something."

"Alright," I said, relieved that maybe Jerry would give me a word from God.

Jerry was waiting for me when I got to his cluttered office – it was almost noon and my stomach ached for a good meal. "I could eat a dozen eggs," I told him.

"There's a First Watch on Walnut—they serve great breakfast food and we can walk there."

After we settled into our booth by the large windows, Jerry asked me why I hadn't been coming around.

"Nothing's working," I said. "I spent all that time in the library, wrote all those letters—fifty—and nothing. Nobody wants to invest in me. I feel like a big loser." I put my head in my hands.

A waitress came by. "You ready to order?"

"What you want, Ron?" Jerry asked.

"Let me have a stack of panacakes and some orange juice."

"Panacakes? Don't you mean pancakes?" Jerry asked.

"My grandma called them panacakes so that's what they are, panackaes." I replied.

"Panacakes, coming right up." The waitress replied laughing. "You can get them with blueberries, you know."

"That's alright. Coffee too."

"What about you?" she asked Jerry.

"I'll have two eggs, sunny side up, and an order of sausage. Do I get hash browns and toast with that?"

"Yep."

"And no juice, but coffee. Black." The waitress smiled and put her pen in her pocket. She left to take orders from an adjacent table.

Jerry spread his napkin in his lap.

"So, you can't find any investors. Maybe you ain't ready for 'em yet. You have to wait for God's timing. Keep your eyes open and you'll find someone who believes in you. I know one thing," he paused, and watched the people walking by the restaurant, "what do you have to gain by giving up? You only lose if you don't persevere. God can turn things around for you at any time, you just have to submit to the process He's taking you through. When the pain of staying the same is greater than the pain to change then you'll start to notice a shift in your circumstances."

Hearing that word, "change", jolted me awake better than any cup of coffee.

"I feel like all I do is work on change and that I'm getting nowhere. I spend all this time reading my Bible and praying— how do I know it will even work out?"

"You don't. But you have to believe God wants you to share what He's doing in your life with the world. You're so used to the dark side of things, you don't even know how the other side works.

The waitress sat a pot of fresh coffee in front of us.

"Thank you," Jerry said. I nodded. "Things on the dark side come easy—you don't have to work very hard for your highs. But the highs are artificial and they don't last, because they aren't real. But on God's side, the highs take a lot of hard work. Years sometimes. But those are real and they last forever."

"I guess…but I don't have years… I need to get on my feet and find my own place."

"We can find odd jobs out there—didn't you say you worked construction and landscaping? I'll talk to a friend to see if he can help find you some work. Being an entrepreneur doesn't come as fast as other careers. Look at this as college. It takes four years to get through college, so give yourself four years—at least to get your company off the ground."

"So, do I send out another 100 letters?"

"If that's what it takes. You just have to have faith and not quit."

"Excuse me." The waitress spread plates of food on our table. "Can I get you anything else?" she asked, shifting her eyes right and left.

"No, ma'am," I said. "This looks just fine."

We didn't speak much after that. We both focused on eating our food. Seemed Jerry was just as famished as I was.

Chapter 12

Daybreak
January 2002- March 2003

     With Jerry's words of encouragement and a place to live in the shelter, I continued cutting hair and working on my business plan. I rode the bus to see my kids several times a week, the little bit of time I spent with them helped. Everything I did was done with my kids' best interest at heart. I wanted to give them a much better life than I had. I wanted them to be better than me and to achieve more than I ever could. I had read every book in the library studying everything I could find on business. I had finally finished writing a business plan but I needed it typed and formatted in a way that made it look professional. Gwenn was the secretary for the shelter I was staying in and she had a heart for young entrepreneurs. One day when I was leaving I had dropped my sketchpad on the steps right in front of her.

     "You're serious about this design business, aren't you?" She asked

     "Yes I am. I'm not stopping until see this thing come to fruition."

     "How far have you gotten on your business plan?"

     "I'm finished. I just need it typed."

     "Okay then, get your plan together and I'll type it up for you. We'll make it look real nice."

     I leaned over and hugged her. "Thank you," I said. She was Heaven sent.

     I worked hard at getting my business plan perfected, but I had trouble with the financial section. I wasn't sure what the right protocol for that was. I only had drawings. My vision had not manifested yet, and I didn't have any finances to put down. I gave it to Gwenn to type up. She did my financials in EXCEL and put the finishing touches on it for me. I re-submitted my plan to Smart Money. After a few weeks, I received a letter from one of the members of the review team. She said my plan was incomplete and that I needed more information about the marketing. So back to the library I went to study more about marketing.

The next time I saw Gwenn I told her what the lady at Smart Money said about my business plan. "It was better than the last one. One step at a time," I said.

"You know, Ronald," she said, "I think you should go to church with me this Sunday. I know some people there you might need to meet."

Jerry's words echoed in my mind. "Open up your heart to the Lord."

"Yeah, it's been a while since we went to church together."

That Sunday I met the pastor, Rob. After service, he listened intently to my ideas. I told him what I had already learned about business and manufacturing.

"I'm impressed. You know more about business than some college grads I know." He scribbled on a notepad. "I have a friend who might be interested in you. Here's his number. I'll tell him you're going to call."

The next day, I called Dennis. He seemed excited to hear from me.

"I was waiting for your call. Can you meet me at my house later this week—say, Thursday evening?"

"I'll be there," I said.

I arranged for Pastor Rob to take me out to Dennis' house in an area where you don't see many faces like mine - a high-end suburban neighborhood. On the way there, the pastor and I talked about my dreams and designs. He told me God was leading me. "Nothing is a coincidence, Ronald. It's all in God's plans. When the time is right, your dream will come true."

There it was again—that message: "Keep an open heart." In prison, I was bitter because of my past and everyone that hurt me or caused me hurt but as I began to see God moving me into my destiny, the bitterness didn't affect me as much. Having hope is like receiving a heart transplant. Hope will take you from a feeling of death and despair to life and confidence.

I was so nervous during the ride to Dennis' house. We rang the doorbell of a two-story brick colonial with large pillars out front—at the time I thought I had entered a mansion. Dennis answered the door. "Good to meet you Ronald.... Reverend. Let's talk in my study. You want something to drink?"

"No thanks," we both said, as we followed our host.

The pastor and I sat on brown leather chairs facing Dennis' desk. Dennis leaned across his desk; papers scattered everywhere, and smiled.

"Tell me about yourself, Mr. Hummons."

"Call me Ron," I said. "Well, my life has been a story of pain and perseverance. I was incarcerated and until recently I was homeless. In prison I had a vision of creating my own design company, Grapevine. I need some investors to help me get it off the ground. The last six months I've spent studying in the library learning all about business plans and manufacturing. Rob thought that maybe you could help me."

I shifted in my chair, Dennis rocked back in his. Before he spoke, he gripped the edge of his desktop. I could only see the ends of his fingers.

"I'm in the manufacturing business and have many contacts overseas. And just so you know, it costs thousands to get samples made. It doesn't sound like you have access to that kind of money."

"No sir, I don't. All I have is this." I opened my notebook and showed him several drawings of my shoe. In the back of the folder was my first sketch. "Here's what I drew while I was in prison."

He held the ragged notebook page in his hand. "Hmmm. Good, real good."

"That was the beginning of my dream. I've come a long way since then."

"This is good, Ronald. Talent is definitely here." He

handed the paper back to me. "Maybe I can do something for you." He talked about his manufacturers overseas and explained the whole process to me. I listened as intently as I could.

Silent for most of the meeting, the Reverend spoke. "Be specific, Dennis. How can you help Ronald?"

Dennis thought for a minute. "Tell you what, Ronald. I'll send your drawings to my manufacturers in China and get some prices for you. Then you'll be able to be specific about the amount of money you need when you approach investors."

"That'd be great. How long do you think it'll take?"

"Shouldn't be too long. A couple weeks at the most. Are these your only copies?"

"I have a few more in my sketchbook. You can have these." I handed him my best drawings. "Thanks for all your help, Dennis."

"Glad to do it." He reached across the desk and shook hands with both of us. We let ourselves out.

On the ride home, I shared my excitement with Pastor, but he was not as optimistic.

"He's nice, but be careful. Business is about making money. He sees something good in it for him—which is fine, just make sure it's just as good for you."

Dennis' manufacturers did make the samples for me, but they weren't much of a facsimile of my designs. They changed my shoe design hoping I would go along with any design they chose as long as I could put my name on it. After a few rounds of sample making, they finally made the shoe exactly the way I wanted it. Two months later, the sample came back. It was perfect.

But then, Dennis told me we needed to find investors for the clothing line. I had made him a partner in my company. I felt as if he wanted me to bring the creativeness to the table and he would run things the way he saw fit. I wanted Dennis to be a part of this company, I knew he was more business savvy, but I wanted the chance to run my own company. Grapevine was my baby and I wanted to raise it myself. I offered to give him a percentage of stock in the company, but he declined. He said he was doing this to help me and he didn't want to have any contracts drawn up just yet.

Dennis was a businessman. He had some shrewd ways about him, but I guess that's what made him so successful. After getting back the finished samples, it was now time to get stores to give me orders. I just of went along with the flow of things. I wasn't comfortable with not having any contract, but I trusted God to help me make the right decisions concerning my business.

I arranged a photoshoot with a friend Scott. He also worked at The Lord's Gym with Jerry and he had a very giving heart. He did the photoshoot for free. I was still living in the shelter at the Lord's Gym, but he believed in my vision and devoted his time. I used the photos to advertise to the stores I was interested in. I had color postcards, posters, and a website made. I was now ready to go see the buyer at the local stores. The first store I went to was Deveroes, one of Cincinnati's largest chain stores. They had an interest in my line but were skeptical because I wasn't branded yet. When I went to the meeting with the buyer I was very nervous. I didn't know what to expect. This was my first buyer meeting so I took Dennis along to help with negotiating.

When I handed the guy my light blue sample shoe, he stared at it for a minute, turned it upside down, then handed it back to me. I told him he couldn't go wrong with this product and it would be the hottest thing to hit the market. He said "is that so, well walk into the warehouse with a pair on without saying anything to draw attention to the shoes and see what happens." So I did, and to his surprise everybody I walked past asked where I got them from. We went back into his office and talked numbers. Then the big question came; are the shoes ready to be delivered? That's when my stomach dropped. I hoped they would like the shoe so much they would help pay for the initial shipment. Man was I wrong. If I would have already been big time they would have put some money up front. But they wanted me to bear the expense of the first order. I left the meeting with mixed feelings. Part of me was sad because I hoped to get that big breakthrough I worked so hard for and the other part was happy because someone as big as Deveroes showed interest in my line. It costed over $150,000 to get my first order paid for and I didn't have the slightest clue where I would get that kind of money. My journey for cash begins.

      After the disappointment with Deveroes, I read in the paper about a company sponsored by the University of Cincinnati called Small Business Development Center. A wonderful woman there named Gloria Parke, along with my accountant Candice Tolbert, helped me perfect my business plan. Gloria and Candice were very patient with me. I know I must've gotten on their nerves at times, but they hung in there with me. I took advantage of every free entrepreneurial resource available. I was also referred to the SCORE program; an organization of retired business men and women. They referred me to a guy named Ralph, a mentor who believed that if you wanted something, you have to do your own research, he was not going to do the work for you. I worked the plans he gave me and stayed dedicated to making things happen.

      I didn't have to wait long. In late March, Jerry told me about the pool tournament the Lord's Gym has every year in the spring. It's a way to have some fun, win prizes and build relationships inside and outside the community. An organization called Jobs Plus put the event on. We used to have 3-on-3 basketball challenges, but guys like the pool tourneys better.

      Now this sounded like something I could get into - I was able to perfect my pool game in prison. "Where's it being held?"

      "Right down the street at the Westminster Billiard Club—1120 Main. Can you break some sticks?"

      "Man, can I? That's all I did in prison. There's not much else to do for fun except lift weights. Better tell the guys to watch that first prize, because I got a real good game going on."

The pool tournament was held a few weeks later, and even though I didn't win first prize—I came in second—I met two men who would be pivotal in my life—Abe Woolfolk and Burr Robinson. Abe was the Job Placement Director at Jobs Plus and Burr its Executive Director. Jobs Plus, a non-profit organization, helps people in Over-the-Rhine find jobs. The organization exists for people in low-income communities who want to break the cycles of poverty and dependence. Since opening its doors in 1994, Jobs Plus has provided many individuals with the support, encouragement and training they needed to find and keep a job—and to succeed in life.

Abe Woolfolk came over and congratulated me after the tournament "Good shooting. Too bad you scratched, you were better than the guy who won."

"Thanks, man," I humbly replied. I held out my hand, "Ronald Hummons."

"I'm Abe, I work over at Jobs Plus. You need any help finding a job, give me a call. You know where our offices are?"

Another man walked over, skinnier than Abe, and white. He put his hand on my back. "You giving lessons? You know how to shoot." He held out his hand. "Burr Robinson. I work with this big fellow here."

"Nice to meet you," I said shaking his hand. "I'm Ronald. Do you guys have any barber jobs available? I've been cutting hair all my life and I'm pretty good."

"Why don't you drop over Monday and you can cut my hair." Abe suggested.

Monday morning I showed up at Abe's office with my clipper case in hand. We chatted while I trimmed his hair into a fade.

"So, you a full time barber, Ron?" he asked.

"No, I do other things. But mainly, I'm working on launching my own business," I said.

Then I told him all about my shoes, my dream of having my own clothing line and Grapevine.

"You ought to talk to my boss Burr, the guy who founded Jobs Plus. He knows a lot about business. He used to work for Proctor and Gamble."

"How do I get a meeting with him?"

"I'll take you to his office after you finish."

The next time I cut Abe's hair, I asked him about Burr. "You talk to him about me?"

"Yeah, he said for you to stop in his office sometime. He's here today, why don't you see if he has some time for you."

I gathered my nerve and knocked on the open door. He was on the phone, but waved me in.

"You're the young man from the pool tournament," Burr said, hanging up the phone. "Abe's been talking about you. Is there something in particular I can help you with?"

I leaned forward in my chair. "Abe tells me you're great with business and marketing and thought maybe you could help me with my business."

"Perhaps next week. I have meetings all this week with new clients." He looked at his watch. "In fact, I have one starting in a few minutes. Why don't you stop by the middle of next week. Wednesday or Thursday, and maybe we can talk."

"I'll be there Wednesday," I said.

He was tied up Wednesday as well. So, I drifted over to Abe's office.

"You look like you lost your best friend," Abe said.

"Burr was too busy to talk to me. Do you think he's really interested in helping me? Maybe he doesn't take me seriously because I'm an aspiring entrepreneur. If this doesn't work do you think you could help me get a job?" I asked Abe.

I knew most of the clients with Jobs Plus came from referrals—mainly churches and social services.

"I don't know. It could be tough," said Abe. "I checked your record - with the violent history, it makes it difficult. Most of our employers will barely look at anyone with a record, much less one that involves violence."

"Are you telling me there's no hope for me?"

"Nah, there's hope for everybody. Didn't you say you had some designs?"

"Yeah, but so what?"

Abe glanced away and then fixed his eyes on mine. "I didn't figure you for a quitter. Bring 'em over tomorrow and let me take a look."

"Sure." I put my business plan in my gym bag and walked down the street to my room at the Lord's Gym shelter. When I got there, I just lay on my bed. I didn't even turn on the light.

A few days later, I showed Abe the samples. He thought they were good, and said he would definitely tell Burr about my designs. He thought Burr might be able to help me financially, but even after Abe talked to him, he said he brushed the idea off. I guess he thought I wasn't serious. An African American, with a felony record, I couldn't even get a job. My imagination took over and I dreamt up all sorts of reasons he didn't want to see me. Here I was cutting hair, trying to make a little money, what kind of business sense does that show, I thought. I had no college degree and no experience, why would anyone want to invest in me?

That's when the Lord's Gym saved me again.

Every year the Lord's Gym has a fundraiser - a breakfast at the Sharonville Convention Center hosted by FOCUS, the Foundation of Compassionate American Samaritans. They invite business people from all over Cincinnati to come to their breakfast—businesses donate money to participate, and the funds help support the Gym for the rest of the year. The breakfast features inspiring videos and testimonials about how the gym's spiritual programs changed the lives of desperate men and women.

"You're in our slideshow," Jerry said one morning as I prepared to set up shop. It was already the middle of September and I had been living in the Lord's Gym for over six months—it was starting to be more than I could take. My business plan was done, but I had no one who cared to see it. I needed some good news. Dennis was still around, but he was tapped out on money. I didn't see how all of this would come together but I was open to anything at this point.

"Tell me more about this slideshow" I said to Jerry.

"Every year we have a fundraiser and we give a slide show of all the different events going on through the year. We also show the people that come in and out of here. Scott Bowers snapped a photo of you holding your tennis shoe and your business plan so we're putting it in the show."

"Fine with me," I said.

"And, Ronald, there'll be businessmen there from all over. I thought you might like to speak at the breakfast."

"Me?" I said. "About what?"

"About your life, your vision…your shoe. Most importantly how you've changed your life since you got out of prison."

"My life's not been all that great lately."

"But the fact that you're still trusting God in the middle of your storm and pursuing your dream is a great testimony." Jerry said. "So, you'll be one of our speakers then?"

"Just give me the time and the place."

When I arrived at the hotel ballroom, there was already a crowd. Men and women in business attire drank coffee and waited for the program to begin. At first, the big audience was intimidating and I was very nervous. But then I thought about why they were there. *These people are here because they want to help*, I told myself. When I saw it that way, it gave me the self-confidence to relax and share my story. Maybe if these business people, the vast majority were white, and entrepreneurs heard my story, they would see that those of us who have made mistakes in our lives can and want to change. Maybe my story would bring a better understanding of the struggles of the poor in the inner cities. At least I'd hope.

Right before I was to speak, Bob Clark, one of the gym's founders, displayed a slide of me holding my shoe. He explained how I had just recently been released from prison, and how finding God had changed my life. He briefly mentioned my vision and my determination to make it as a fashion designer.

"This young man has spent hours in the library studying fashion design and business plans. He could have gone back on the streets and made easy money selling drugs, but with God's help, Ron decided to live in the light. He is determined to succeed by education and persistence, but I'll let Ron tell you all his vision for the future. Ladies and gentlemen, Mr. Ronald Hummons."

As I stared out into a sea of dark suits and black and white faces, my knees began to buckle, but then I looked behind me and there was a full picture of my tennis shoe I designed while in prison—nothing else, just the shoe. I turned toward the audience and smiled. After introducing myself, I spoke for about five minutes discussing my ideas, my business plan and my designs. Point by point I stated how everything was going to work, where I was going with my design business and how my clothing line was going to be successful. Then I spoke about my childhood - my father, my time in prison and how God led Jerry Dubose and the Lord's Gym to help save me in my darkest hour. When I finished, the audience applauded. It was very exciting. Then, one by one, rows at a time, people began to stand up until the whole auditorium was standing. My eyes filled with tears as I left the stage, I feared they would run down my cheeks. I needed to get myself together from the emotional speech, so I scurried off to the restroom to put water on my face.

Scott Bowers, the guy in charge of fundraisers for the gym and part time photographer – put the slide show together. He told me that Burr Robertson came up to him after my speech. "That guy with the pink shoe who talked about his designs and business... I've seen him at Jobs Plus. I think he cuts one of my employee's hair. What else do you know about him?"

Scott told him how I had come a long way and was trying to start my own business. Then Burr asked him for my contact information. Funny how I had been trying to meet with him for weeks, and when I walked past his office he barely even spoke to me. Now all of a sudden, he's interested. The next time I went in to cut Abe's hair, I ran into Burr in the hallway.

"Mr. Hummons, isn't it?"

"Yes, that's me," I said.

"Good to meet you, again. I saw you in the slide show at the breakfast the other day. What's going on with your business?"

"Right now, I'm looking for serious investors. I've been sending out more proposals to people referred to me."

"Do you have a minute?" he asked.

"I'm on my way to cut Abe's hair, but I can spare a few minutes."

He waved me into his office. "What kind of financial backing do you have so far?"

"Not much. There's a guy here in Cincinnati who has helped me with some samples but I need way more than what he's offered to get my business off the ground."

"I'm really interested in your business. I'd like to talk more about being an investor. I'm tied up today, but can we meet tomorrow morning, around 8 to go over your business plans?"

"That'd be great, sir. You really liked the shoe?"

"I probably wouldn't wear it but I'm sure the young folk would love it. You sounded like you've done your homework."

I held out my hand. "Thanks, Mr. Roberson. If he's available, would you mind if I brought in Dennis, the guy who helped me get my first samples made? He shook my hand.

"Not at all. I'd like to get his input, and by the way, call me Burr."

"See you in the morning, Burr."

Later that evening, I called Dennis and told him I had a meeting with a potential investor, and he rearranged his plans to free up his morning At the meeting I showed Burr my business plans.

Dennis handed him invoices from the manufacturing team. "These guys did the samples. The pink and blue shoe," he told Burr.

Burr scanned the business plan and the designs, along with the manufacturers' paperwork. "This feels good, like something I want to be a part of. I'll look over everything and let you know."

We talked a while longer. As Dennis and I were leaving, Burr firmly grasped my hand

"I'll call you at the shelter in a couple days, Ronald." And he did.

"I'm in," he said as soon as I picked up the phone.

I clinched my fist and smacked an invisible punching bag as he continued.

"We need to talk about my part -investment, that is. You're the shoe guy, not me."

In the beginning his investment was small, just enough to help make more samples and build capital to pay my attorney fees and salary, so I could concentrate on my business. But I was able to move into my own apartment and buy a used car—things were beginning to look up for me.

Unfortunately, I began to have problems with Dennis. His attorney drew up an agreement saying in so many words that I was giving total control to Dennis. Needless to say, that didn't sit well with me. Sure, he was a successful businessman with plenty of experience, and I'm sure he only saw me as a young guy who was in over his head. I confronted Dennis about the contract. "It's just a formality, don't worry," he said. But I had enough sense to know that once I signed, I would basically be working for him - not owning my own business. This led to a lot of distrust between Dennis and me. I trusted Burr - I knew his motives were right. Yes, he hoped to gain by investing in my business, but he did not want to steal my ideas or my company.

Even though I never signed my name on the dotted line, I continued to work with Dennis and Burr for a few more months. But, the more I worked with Dennis, the more he tried to control the business. Since I wouldn't sign the first contract, he had his lawyer draw up another one. This contract stated that he would own 51% of the business. Initially, the impression was that he wanted to split the business fifty-fifty, but my attorney detected the truth in the legalese. After that, things got worse between us.

I wanted nothing more to do with Dennis. I did keep in contact with Burr though - he was always honest and upfront about how much he thought each of us should have in the business. But, at that time, even Burr didn't think I should own more than half of the endeavor. He said that all of us should have an equal share. If they were going to put up the money, then their opinions should count for something. In one of the most difficult decisions I ever had to make, I dissolved our partnership. Burr and Dennis didn't say much when I walked out of the meeting that day. I guess there wasn't really anything to say. Burr told me when I got more organized to give him a call. I respected that. I knew there was a lot more work I needed to do.

As I drove away from Burr's office, I felt I was back to where I started. I slipped into depression again. Once again, reminding of my status - ex-con, no money, no college education, potentially homeless again and worst of all, alone. I moved through the next few weeks in a trance. Every morning, in those moments of waking up when a dream and reality mixed together, the pain would be hidden. Then, all that happened in the last few weeks, the last years, would rush into my thoughts. Without my faith, it would've been easy to fall back into my old ways. So very easy. Even with the business dealings not working out, I had learned so much about the world outside of Over-the-Rhine, I knew that moving forward would keep me out of prison. So, life went on.

I pulled into the lot of Kroger. As I got out of the car, I saw this good looking woman roll up with her cart full of groceries, she was parked next to me.

"Have we met somewhere before?" I asked. "You look really familiar."

She scanned me from head to toe. "I don't think so." She hesitated for a moment, as if she wanted to say more. "Excuse me," she finally said, pushing the cart closer to her car. After fumbling in her purse for a few minutes, she pulled out her keys.

"Need some help?" I asked. It was hot and humid. A typical Cincinnati day in August.

She smiled a gentle smile. "No, I'm fine."

"Ok then, I'll just stand here and stare at you until you finish."

She laughed. "Okay, you can grab the drinks from the bottom."

I reached under the basket for a case of Pepsi and put it in the trunk. Looking in, I saw a large sweatshirt and some used tennis shoes.

"Live with your brother?"

"No, Mr. Nosy. It's my ex-boyfriend."

In tense silence, we continued loading the groceries into her car. She shut the trunk and turned to me. "Thanks. See ya"

"Hey, wait a minute, what's your name?"

"And why do you want to know?

"So I don't call you 'hey' again." I said jokingly.

Her shoulders relaxed. "My name's Erica….and you are?"

"Ronald, but my friends call me Ron."

"Well, Ron thanks for helping me with my groceries. Sorry if I seemed mean. It's just been a stressful day….week."

"Work?"

"School… I'm studying to be a nurse. I'm in my senior year at U.C."

"What else has you stressed? Issues with your ex?" I asked.

"That's just the half of it. The breakup is not quite official yet but we're almost there."

"Well you know he has just been preserving you for me right?"

"That's a new one." She laughed. I hate to be in a rush but I have to go. My ice cream's probably already melted. Thanks for listening though." She walked to the car door and grabbed the handle. Then she let her fingers slide off of it. She glanced back at me and hesitated, her hand barely touching the door. Her eyes grasped mine. "You always come here trying to pick up helpless women?" She asked hesitantly.

"No, but there was something about you that made me wanna speak to you. You know, you should smile more. You have a nice smile."

"People say that all the time."

"That you have a nice smile?" I inquired.

"Well yes and that I should smile more."

"I won't keep you, I know you have to go but it was nice meeting you Erica. Maybe I'll see you around."

"Maybe. Bye."

What she didn't know was I was actually doing bootleg trips with a busted up car I was able to purchase with the help of my church. Glad I didn't have a trip when I saw her.

Chapter 13

New Beginnings

I didn't see Erica again for several weeks. I swore if I did see her again, I was going to ask for her number. Another day, at the same Kroger, I locked my keys in my car. I was busy digging a coat hanger in between the doorframe and the glass when she walked up behind me.

"Ronald?"

I spun around. "Erica, how are you doing?"

"Is that your car?" She tilted her head and raised her eyebrows.

"You think anyone would try to steal this?"

"Yeah, no kidding." She replied jokingly. "Can't get in, huh?"

"Oh, I'm fine." I held up the hanger. I pried it just a little further until I was able to pull the latch. "Got it! I'm so embarrassed. This is not the impression I wanted to make when we crossed paths again." I said.

"Ron it's ok. I've locked my keys in the car a dozen times. You gotta pen?" She asked.

"Yeah, why?"

"So I can write my number down." She replied.

I gave her a pen and a piece of paper ASAP.

"Call me later."

"You can hold me to that." I told her.

Even though Erica was still having issues with her ex-boyfriend I called her up and invited her to go to out with me. We went to BW3's to shoot some pool. She claimed she couldn't shoot but I suspected she was a pool shark.

"You wanna break?" I asked her.

"Sure." Smack!

She hit the balls so hard, three went in off the break.

"What the...? I thought you said you couldn't play."

"That was a lucky shot." She said laughing. After the break she was dropping balls left and right.

"Now you know if you make this shot there won't be a second right?"

I was joking but she must have thought I was serious because she missed a shot she could've easily made.

"Now you know you could have made that shot. Now I hope you don't expect me to give you any mercy. I play to win." I spoke too soon because I had the eight ball right where I wanted it - an easy shot I hit over and over again in prison. "What the hell?" I missed it. To make it worse, I set the eight ball right up in front of the hole.

"The no mercy rule right?" She said sarcastically.

"Eight ball in the left corner." She called. Smack! "Game time."

"Good game. I see now you're a hustler though."

"No. I just got lucky." She said with her eyes slanted.

"You wanna get one more game in? I know you let me win." She handed me a cue stick. "Your break."

"Yes ma'am." To break the tension in my shoulders, I moved my neck back and forth. "Stand back, girl. Watch me bust this up." I bent over and sighted the target, the yellow one-ball staring back at me. With a surge of strength, I wanted to more than break, I wanted to shatter the triangle of pool balls. As I surged my arm forward, I pulled my head up. The chalk of the stick barely touched the cue ball and I lurched off balance. The white ball with its blue smudge rolled so slowly you could count the rotations; once, twice, down the table it trickled. When it finally got to the other end of the table, a slick "click" sounded when it touched the front ball. None of the others rolled away from their spot. I didn't look up. Erica said nothing. After a few seconds, she bursted own laughing.

I couldn't help but smile and when I turned to look at her, her eyes were wet, tears of repressed laughter rolled down her face. "Seriously Ronald? That did not look like the shot of a big time prison pool hustler." She said with tears rolling down her face.

I was glad I could entertain her. I placed my cue back on its stand, waving at people nearby. "I don't think I can top that." I turned to her. "You ready to go?"

"Sure, I need to get home."

In the car she told me how much fun she had and how she enjoyed my company.

I wondered what it would be like to have her with me all the time. I was so mesmerized by her sweet manner. "Erica," I said, "you are a gorgeous woman."

"You trying to get you some?" with a huge smile on her face. "You're sweet. Thank you."

"Does that mean you'll go out with me again?" I asked.

"You haven't asked me yet."

"Would you go out with me tomorrow night?"

"It's a date Ronald." She responded.

I didn't have any money so for our next date, so we went for a walk down on the riverfront - Sawyer Point in Downtown Cincinnati. A nice, quiet spot where we could sit, talk and get to know each other better.

"So Ronald, tell me everything I need to know about you. I wanna know the good, the bad and the ugly," she said. I shared with her my ambitions of entrepreneurism and the steps I was taking to pursue them.

"I've been educating myself on everything to do with business. All I do is study and apply. One day I will be the next Russell Simmons or Puff Daddy." I told her.

"What kind of business do you want to start?" She asked.

"I'm going to start my own clothing line. I have sketches of a lot of clothing designs including a really hot shoe design. I call it the Grapevine Collection." She leaned forward and listened intently. We sipped on hot chocolate as I told her more about my goals and dreams. I hesitantly showed her my drawings - nervous about what she would think of them.

"You designed these? They're amazing. You're really talented. Did you go to college for design?" She asked

"No. Just a God given talent I guess."

"Well you definitely have the talent to make this into a huge success Ronald."

"You asked about the good, the bad and the ugly right? Well here is the bad and ugly, I designed all of them in the penitentiary. I was locked up for nearly seven years, it was there that God gave me the vision to start my own business."

"Wow, you wouldn't even know by looking at you that you've been to prison. You're really smart for a hood dude who's been to prison and never been to college."

"I may have not been to college but I went through a different educational system, life. I have a lot of life experience that helps me achieve what I want to do. I don't need to go to college to get an education with a world of knowledge at the library. I spent hundreds of hours there studying books on business plans, business development, the clothing line business and graphic arts. Can you believe that when I came home I didn't even know what an email was?" I said laughing. "A nice librarian actually had to help me set up an email account. I felt so much like a fish out of water trying to educate myself on business and the basic communication of the multimedia world. It was very discouraging. It still is. Don't have a car, money, or a place of my own but I got this vision and I believe God is going to provide me with everything I need to see it manifest. So there you have it, the bad and the ugly."

"You have an amazing story Ms. Hummons. I don't know what it is about you but I believe you're going to do everything you say you will do." She replied.

I appreciated her words of encouragement. They were just the confidence booster I needed. She didn't know, but her sweet words sunk into my heart and gave me fuel to continue on my entrepreneurial journey.

Erica had a daughter, they lived in a neighborhood called Mt. Auburn. After hearing of all of the drama she experienced with her ex-boyfriend and the heartache he put her through, I knew she was guarded. The one thing I didn't tell her during my good, bad, and ugly story was that I was still married to Patrice. We were legally separated but our divorce wasn't final yet and I wasn't sure how Erica would take that so I kept that little secret to myself until....

"Hello. Is this Erica?"

"Yeah, who is this?"

"This is Patrice, Ronald's wife." Patrice replied.

"His wife? Well look here wife. Don't call my fuckin phone again. If that's your husband then you need to be checking him not calling my damn phone."

Erica called me with so much anger, she made me nervous.

"I got a surprise phone call today from a woman that claims to be your wife. You got something you wanna tell me?"

"First I just wanna apologize. I should have told you in the beginning. She's not lying, we are still married but we are legally separated, but that doesn't justify me not telling you." I responded.

"How did she get my number?" Erica asked.

"She must have gotten into my phone records. I'll talk to her and make sure that never happens again."

I thought Erica was done with me at that point but luckily, we were able to move past it.

Over the next three months we lived apart and even though I wanted to be with her all the time, I stayed in the shelter until 2001, about six months after we met. We finally moved in together - that gave me the stability I needed to really put my plan into action. I appreciated everything Dick, Bob, Jerry, and Scott did for me at the Lord's Gym shelter, but I needed to move on and make my own way. Things between Erica and I seemed to progress really fast. Even though neither of us were quite ready for a relationship we were determined to make it work. Truthfully we seemed so unbalanced. It was hard to make ends meet, with it being her last year of nursing school and me with nothing but a visionless dream. Day after day, I was confronted by people from my past, they wanted me to come back to the street life. I was offered guns, drugs, even saw some of my old girls who said they wanted to get back to work for me. The idea was tempting, but I didn't want to risk my freedom and most of all, my peace of mind.

"Things will work out" Erica told me many times. "Just hold on, when your big break comes, it will have made the struggle worth it."

A few weeks later, I proposed to Erica. I didn't have much money, but I managed to get enough to get a really nice ring from the pawn shop. I arranged for her daughter to spend the night with her grandmother, and then I drove Erica to Sawyer Point, where we had our second date. We walked until I found a remote, grassy area where I spread a blanket on the ground and took a candle, champagne and a couple of glasses out of a paper bag. After lighting the candle and pouring the champagne, I told Erica how much she meant to me. I remember her eyes were shining in the moonlight.

I knelt down on one knee. "Erica, baby, I love you more than anyone in this world. You have been my inspiration, my savior and my gentle conscience. Will you do me the honor of being my wife?"

"Oh, Ronald," she said, when she saw the ring. "Oh, baby, I would love to marry you. I will marry you! Oh, Ronald, you are the most romantic man I have ever met!"

"Put the ring on, so you don't go changing your mind."

With the ring on her finger, Erica's eyes brightened even more than usual and she put her hand over her mouth to suppress her laughter. For a split second I felt like the biggest fool in the world. Then she threw her arms around me and kissed me all over my face. "Ronald, it's beautiful. I love you so much."

She called her mom and shared the news with her. For the next several months, they spent all of their time making wedding plans.

"You're going look too so good in a tux," Erica said one day. "All the women in my family are going to be so jealous."

Our wedding day, March 29, 2003, was the highlight of my life; we had an elegant, intimate ceremony at our church in Mason. We had an evening reception with dinner, flowers, music and an endless array of photographs. Erica was pregnant with our son, Tierre - with the glow of pregnancy she looked as fine as a woman could look in her long white gown and veil. Her beauty took my breath away, so much so that I stumbled over my vows like a schoolboy. On July 14th, two days after my birthday, she gave me a son - the greatest gift she could've ever given me. Holding my child in my arms for the first time, it was impossible for me to comprehend doing anything less than my best for him... or for Erica.

With my renewed confidence, I had planned on paying a visit to Smart Money, the organization that previously declined my application for a loan. By this time, I had learned a great deal during my entrepreneurial journey - much more than I did when I first came home from prison. Looking back, I remember how I thought I was so smart, *I'll never let anyone get the best of me*, I'd say. In actuality, I knew nothing. If I had figured that out a lot sooner, I'd be better off. Some of us have to learn most things the hard way, and I definitely fit *that* profile.

One of the things Burr taught me, was that presentation meant everything. "You only get one first impression, Ron. Be organized, whether it's a lecture or just a casual meeting."

With that in mind, I prepared for my visit to Smart Money. My first clothing catalogue was ready, my business plan was in tip top shape, and I had a clear vision as to where I was going and how I could get there. I also had media coverage to show them. After my speech at the breakfast, a reporter for the

Cincinnati Post wrote a great story on me, which led to a TV interview on Cincinnati Matters. I told my story about being an ex-con who believed enough in his talent to pursue a dream. The response was great but kind words didn't get me what I needed: the money to keep the endeavor alive.

"Can you press my pants?" I yelled to Erica.

"I already have. C'mon, you gotta go in a little bit. What time's your meeting?"

"Ten."

A few minutes later, I walked out of the bedroom. Crisp jacket, creased pants, portfolio under my arm, I was as ready as I could be. "How's this?"

Erica smiled and nodded. "You look great. Like a banker. You look sooo good." She walked over to me and started to put her arms around me.

"Don't get me wrinkled," I said with a laugh. "You can hug me all you want when I get home."

"Okay, okay." She kissed me on the cheek. "Good luck."

Half an hour later, I pulled open the door at the bank. The secretary told me to wait until the loan officer was ready, so I sat down and watched people come in - making deposits, signing checks and making withdrawals.

"Ms. Abernathy can see you now."

All right, here we go.

"Thank you." I walked in.

"Have a seat here. Mr. Hummons" She looked at me and narrowed her eyes. "Do I know you?"

"No. but I came here a while back asking for help trying to get funding for my design company, 'Grapevine.'"

Her eyes widened. "I remember discussing you with Mr. Simms!"

I opened my portfolio, showed her my designs and the overall business plan. It took a good thirty minutes to discuss everything.

"Very nice. How much money are you looking for?"

"I think three thousand would be great."

"I need to talk about this with my manager, Mr. Simms. Hopefully we can work something out." She got up and went into the office next to her's.

Within a few minutes, she came back. "He likes what you're trying to do, but a three person committee makes the final decision. We'll be in touch."

We shook hands and I drove home wondering if this would be another case where people would tell me one thing but would do another. I didn't have any collateral and no credit to speak of but I thought my plan was a good one. My letter to investors was great, they told me. All I could do was wait. The next morning, the phone rang.

"Mr. Hummons, this is Ms. Abernathy at Smart Money."

My heart jumped. "Hey. Any news?"

"Yes. With the initiative you've shown, we're thrilled to help."

"So the loan went through?"

"Yes. But there's one change."

Oh no.

"The loan is approved for five thousand. You need to come down and sign the papers. Do you have time today?"

"I'll be there by noon." Maintaining my composure, I said, "Thanks so much."

After I hung up, I turned to Erica. When she had heard me on the phone, she came and stood in the kitchen doorway.

"Baby, we got it!"

She ran to my arms. I'd never gotten a better kiss.

An afternoon or two later, I ran into my uncle in Over-the-Rhine.

"Nephew. What's going on with you, I heard you're trying to start your own business?"

"Yeah, something like that. I designed a shoe and some clothes. I 'm not *trying* to do anything, I'm *doing it*. I don't have too many options, now that I'm a felon."

"Well let's talk about it tomorrow over lunch. I'd like to

hear more about it."

"I could meet you at Sugar and Spice for breakfast."

"That'll do. See you at nine."

I brought one of my prototypes to our breakfast meeting, I wanted to show my uncle just how serious I was and how far I'd come with my business plan.

I sat a pink and blue tennis shoe on the table.

"Man that is *too* cool."

"You think so? If I can get them out there, I could sell thousands."

Sitting next to us, a man with glasses and scruffy gray hair scooted his chair over. "A pink shoe?" he asked.

I looked at him, his eyes were youthful. "It's my new shoe line."

"Interesting. I like it. Where can I buy them?"

"No place yet," I told him "I only have samples now." I handed him the shoe, he studied it in amazement.
He gave the shoe back to me, then extended his hand. "My name's Gordon Baer."

We three sat and talked for a bit, Gordon mostly asked me questions about my life and how I came about designing the shoe. I told him about my prison bid and how I grew up in Over-the-Rhine. He seemed sincerely interested and I sensed that there was more to this man than a quiet voice and well-worn jeans.

Gordon stood up and pulled out his wallet. "Hate to leave, but I have to get some work done. Very nice to meet you," he said us.

"Same here," I replied.

"Can I get a picture before I go?"

"I suppose. Why?"

Gordon took a small disposable camera from his nylon jacket. He checked to see that the film was ready. "Oh, I don't know. I just like to document interesting people I meet."

"That's cool." With the little I had told him about the loan, the shoe and my life, I could see how he might feel that way. My uncle and I leaned across the table toward each other.

Gordon snapped the picture. "One more," he said and thumbed the film ahead. The flash went off again.

"So, Gordon, what do you do?"

"I'm a photographer."

I raised my eyebrows. "You're kidding? That's your camera?"

"One of 'em."

"Do you ever sell any photos?" I couldn't imagine the Enquirer buying pictures from a three-dollar camera, but it didn't hurt to be nice.

"I've sold a few."

"To who? Local papers?"

"Yeah and National Geographic. People magazine. Essence. A few others."

My mouth fell open. Over the next months, he became a good friend and supporter. Through his connections - a writer for City Beat, a local Cincinnati paper, did another story on me.

The article was great; it told of my prison experience and all about the clothing line. Then, Cincinnati Magazine called. They wanted to promote the pink shoe in their spring issue. I said yes because I thought it might lead to an investor and it did. When Leon decided to invest a whole lot of money, I couldn't believe it.

"I'm just the investor, Ronald. You handle all the day to day and I'll cut the checks," he told me. At that point I felt as if I had some leverage with the media focusing on my story, so I used it to raise as much money as possible. Candice, my accountant, told me about one of her clients she thought would be able to invest. She gave me his number and told me to call him. His name was Keith and he owned a successful construction company. Keith also did time in prison and managed to gain success. When I went to meet with him, he didn't appear to be a successful business man. He had a rough beard, well-worn clothes and seriously beat up work boots. Little did I know - this guy was loaded. He asked me a lot of questions about my plans for Grapevine. I told him I was still in the preliminary stages and

I needed a lot more money to get to the next stage. "Ok Ronald" Keith said "give me a couple of days and I'll give you a call and let you know what I can do for you."

Two weeks went by with no call. I asked Candice if she heard anything and she told me he wanted to see how hungry I was. Luckily for me, "showing and proving" is my specialty. I rounded up some models, male and female, and dressed them in Grapevine gear, grabbed a boom box and went to his office without notice. When I walked in he was in a meeting and looked very surprised. I didn't care if he was meeting with the president of the United States, he was going to see me. I walked in, sat the radio on the floor, pushed play and the sound of the song, "I heard it through the grapevine" queued the models' entrance. We did a fashion show right in the middle of his office. He was so impressed that he gave me a few thousand dollars in cash. He told me he didn't have all the money I needed but he wanted to give me something right then and there. It wasn't much, but it was a little something to add to the pot.

With Keith on board, I was able to move to the next level. A new piece of the puzzle dropped into my lap. God kept placing the right people in my path. I was on my cell phone, talking to a friend about which material and colors he thought might look good on a shoe to make it hot.

When I hung up, an attractive lady next to me caught my attention.

"You sell shoes?" she asked.

"Yes," I responded. "I'm an apparel designer."

"Is that one of your designs?" Her accent was British with a gentle Scottish brogue, her skin light, hair auburn.

"Yes they are. I'm in the process of making them. It's very complicated."

"Oh, yes. Very." Something in her voice spoke of experience, more than mere observation.

"Do you design?" I asked, extending my hand. "I'm Ronald."

Palm down, she placed her hand in mine.

"Margie. Nice to meet you, Ronald."

Fifteen minutes later, I had learned that Margie had connections in Indonesia. She was an import/ export agent. For years, she bought various items there for own shop. She knew the inner workings and the people who make things happen in that part of the world. That knowledge included the mass production of shoes. I would've spent months, if not years, developing a network of contacts in Jakarta but now, with this one person, was an instant Rolodex.

As we finished talking and exchanging information, I suddenly felt a hand on my shoulder. When I looked, no one was there but I knew who it was. I turned back to Margie, pulled a finger across my chin, and asked, "Are you really going to help me."

"Trust me Ronald. I've got your back.

Those words would come back to bite me later.

Margie became my agent, liaison, and good friend. Even when she learned of my background, her trust was unwavering. The money part of the venture was incentive for her; international investing is so different from investments here in the U.S. Even with Keith on board, I was about a couple hundred thousand dollars short. I asked Burr again to invest, and after thinking it over for a few days, he agreed. I was honored by his faith in me. Coming from him, it meant a lot. The journey of educating myself and being consistent was finally going to pay off. Keith, Burr and I worked it out so that I would be the major shareholder in my company, while Burr and Keith would split the other forty-five per cent. I was already taking orders for Grapevine clothes; all I needed now were the shoes, all six thousand pairs of them. Margie told me that her suppliers in Indonesia had a minimum order quantity of 6,000 pairs and the total price of that order would come close to $300,000. I figured that was much doable compared to Dennis' China manufacturers, who had a M.O.Q of 15,000 pairs. Margie invited me to her home in Amberley Village. She had a beautiful home. It was the type of home I would have loved to raise a family in.

"Welcome Ronald. Come on in and meet my family."
She said after answering the door.

"Meet my husband Ronald and my son Scott."
I thought it was cool that her husband and I shared the same name. We sat on her Victorian style couch and discussed the details of how she runs her outsourcing business and the process of how the manufacturers would work with us. I was so excited that I ignored all the red flags. I figured this middle aged, successful white business woman wouldn't scam me. She looked and sounded trustworthy and she had to be sent by God. I later learned she was sent but it surely wasn't by God.

"Well Ronald, since you already have a prototype, you already know something about the business. My suppliers are in Jakarta and I have a great relationship with them, that's how I was able to get you really low minimum order quantities My manufacturers can duplicate your design from one of your prototypes once we send it to them."

"I only have 2 samples of the design - these prototypes mean a lot to me since they are perfectly made. Will I get these samples back?" I asked.

"Yes. They will need them so they can make a mockup...if/when you're happy with the product, you'll sign off on it and they will produce the full order of 6,500 pairs. Trust me Ronald, my guys in Jakarta do the best work in the manufacturing business."
There she goes with that trust word again, I thought silently.

"Ok so where do we go from here to get started?" I asked.
"Once you sign the contract." She replied.

I read the contract over and over but I still didn't quite understand it. All I really understood was the total: $255,000. Damn, that was a lot of money. I didn't understand why the price was so high per pair since I was buying so many. Something didn't seem right about this. I know she said she worked out a deal for a lower M.O.Q but even with only 6,500 pairs, that should have been enough to drop the price. With

Dennis out of the picture, I felt I had no choice. I signed the contract and gave Margie the down payment to get the prototype process started.

"Here's the contract signed and notarized, and here is check for $10,000."

"Great Ronald. You won't be disappointed. I'll wire the money overseas ASAP and we will get things rolling." She said excitedly.

I went back Downtown - I walked the streets to clear my head. It felt like a large weight had been lifted, like the clouds had spread and the warmth of sunlight had finally dawned on my face. This feeling was one I'd never felt before. *This was really happening for me.* I've been waiting for this my whole life. Manifestation of the better life I knew I always deserved. As I walked, I noticed the same slumping shoulders and look of hopelessness of the men that survived there. The dampness chills me a little, but when I sat on that bench I once used as a bed, I watched the window, waiting for my dad to come home. I feel Walter's belt sting my legs, and the cramps of my hunger, and I bow my head at the despair of loneliness. Always, it's the loneliness that hurts the most. And as much as I wish those days away, I must *never* forget them. They bind me to those who are labeled hopeless, because I know they're not. And to those who are called ignorant because I know they're not, I used to be them. And to those who are unloved because without love, life is not worth living.

The disparity of the faces of men and women in the communities I grew up in are driving forces for me. Their faces tell me I have to make it - for them, my family and myself.

Chapter 15

The Process
March 2003

Erica and I bought our first apartment building in Avondale and rented it out to tenants. I knew how to do construction work and some carpentry, so I spent a few weeks renovating the building - we wanted to rent the apartments out for six to eight hundred dollars a month. I made sure all of the tenants were on Section 8, a government assistance program to help low-income residents get affordable housing. Renting to people on Section 8 guaranteed payment on the first of the month, the system always pays on time.

One Friday afternoon in March, right before an article was to come out about my clothing line in *Cincinnati Magazine*, I had to go to the apartment building on Forest Avenue. I had hired some maintenance men to do some work, and I drove over there to let them in. As I pulled up, I noticed there were two police cars and an ambulance parked at the corner, and several policemen were standing out on the street. I asked the contractors what had happened and they said somebody had gotten attacked, and it was pretty serious. I didn't think much about it and we went up to the third floor apartment. I showed the guys the work that needed to be done and then went back downstairs. Two of the workers followed me down to get some tools, and as soon as I reached the doorway to the street, a police officer yelled for me to put my hands above my head.

It happened so fast, I was a shocked. I put my hands up and the two maintenance men stayed behind the door. Later, they told me they thought the police were going to shoot me. One of the three officers, a tall skinny guy, waved his gun in my face and repeatedly yelled for me to put my hands up. He was very fidgety and nervous, even more nervous than I was. That made me anxious, so I yelled back at him, "My hands *are* up!" Then he told me to put my hands on the wrought iron rail right outside the vestibule door. After seeing all the black guys who got shot without a weapon, all I needed was to touch that rail—I didn't want to because any movement would give the police an excuse to shoot me. If I bent down to grab the rail, the policeman could say he thought I was reaching for a gun and had no choice but to shoot me. (I was glad I didn't take my toolbox down with me. Since my drill was too big, I would've had my toolbox in one hand and the drill in the other. As I approached the doorway, I easily could have been shot on sight.) I kept my hands in the air and said as calmly as I could under the circumstances, "I own the building." The contractors stood behind the doorway defending me. "He's the owner. Don't shoot. He's the owner!"

Finally, another officer, an older guy, came on the scene and I told him I was the landlord. He told the other officers to lower their guns, but I kept my hands up anyway. "Go look around upstairs while I question him," he said. He wanted to know about my tenants, how long I owned the property, who the workers were, and whether or not I lived in the building. He still didn't believe I was the owner, and after he frisked me, he made me take him around to the different apartments. When we reached the second floor, I saw that the door of an apartment had been kicked in and the doorframe was split. Evidently, while the older officer was questioning me, his buddies went upstairs and let themselves in. The lock was broken and even the back window had been kicked out. A single woman with three kids, a good church going woman, lives there. Her door now dangling by a bolt.

"What the hell? You just bash in here? Are you going to pay for this?" I asked. I couldn't believe how they kicked the door in. I at least wanted to get the lock on the door fixed before my tenant and her kids came home.

The older officer, I found out later he was a sergeant, said the city might pay for the damage, but he couldn't be certain of it. I told him I was an innocent victim of police harassment, and they needed to fix my property. The sergeant got all red and said the police have the right to enter any areas that look suspicious and they don't have to spend a dime on repair.

"Man," I said to the sergeant. "How do I look suspicious entering my own building?"

"There were four of you."

"So, four black men entering a building in a black neighborhood looks suspicious? If we were four white guys, I'd understand."

"There were some other things going on. The officers thought you were part of a gang we've been surveilling."

"How many gang members wear tool belts? And Jimmy's almost sixty."

"Well, they thought it looked suspicious."

I ignored his statement. "So, what are you going to do about my door? It's going to cost me a bundle, you know   and for what? Cause we looked *suspicious*? And, that skinny dude, he's got a problem. He was ready to blow off my head."

I looked at my watch—1:40. It was my turn to pick up my daughter from school. Her school was only five minutes away, but she expected me at 1:45. "I have to leave," I said. "But first, let me take down your names real quick."

"You're not going anywhere, buddy," the sergeant said. "I'm not done questioning you."

"My daughter's waiting on me. I can't leave her sitting out in front of the school."

"We can't let you go just yet. I have to do a report."

I checked my watch again. "My daughter is standing outside waiting on me. I've got to go!"

The sergeant put his hand on his holster and the other officers stood next to him.

"Your daughter will have to wait. We need to ask you some more questions."

"You don't understand. She's a little girl; she's not in high school. She'll be real scared if I don't leave now." I was really steamed—the cops almost shot me, tore up my apartment, and now my daughter has to stand alone in front of her school. I clenched my hands into fists and struck at the air. "Damn! Damn!" I hissed.

Then one of the officers, a big white boy, got in my face. "We don't know what happened and we're just trying to find out. We checked your records, Mr. Hummons, and you ain't so innocent. You just recently came home from prison right? You better watch it or you'll be headed back."

"I'm not trying to be smart, but I've got a little girl that is probably bawling her eyes out right now because I'm not there."

"We're gonna let you go," said the sergeant. "We just need to get a report and you'll be on your way."

"Are you gonna pay for repairs?" I said right before I opened my car door.

They all just laughed.

I rolled my window down. "How many doors you kick down in Indian Hills lately?" I drove off, careful not to speed.

I wasn't sure what my rights were, but the guy they were looking for was a thin dark-skinned man with two women. There were no women in sight, my skin is fairly light and I'm stocky; no one but a blind man would describe me as thin. They were looking for a black man, and to them, any shade of African-American skin is black. It's ironic for the cops to go to a black neighborhood looking only for a black man. We *don't* all look alike. Nor do we all act or think alike.

When I arrived at my daughter's school, there she was sitting on the steps, her face with a small frown. As soon as she saw my car, she picked up her books and stormed over to me. "You're late. I thought you forgot. All the other kids left, and I'm all by myself. My teacher even asked if I needed a ride home." She tried to fight back the tears, but they came anyway.

"Sorry, honey. Something really bad happened. I promise, I won't be late again."

She refused to speak to me and stared out the window.

"You want to stop at Wendy's?" I asked. "Mmmm, I have a taste for a chocolate Frosty."

She still didn't respond, but she moved her left shoulder closer to me. Just like her mama, I thought. "Well, I guess if you don't want any, I'll drive right past. Your mother wouldn't like it if she knew we were having ice cream before dinner anyway."

Kiva cut me a sideways glance. "She wouldn't care."

"You want to stop?"

Kiva shook her head up and down.

As we pulled into Wendy's, I spotted another police car right around the corner. My heart sank. I thought about turning around and going to McDonald's but then I stopped. *What am I doing?* I said to myself. *Why should I be afraid? I haven't done anything.*

"Let's go inside," I said. "Daddy needs a little rest."

Kiva took her time with her Frosty, stirring it with her straw. As I watched her, I couldn't stop thinking about the cops and what they did. The broken door frame, the lock, the windows, their attitude, someone needs to draw a line somewhere. How can they go around tearing up people's property and blame it on suspicion? I decided to file a complaint at City Hall. Maybe I would get reimbursed for the door, but probably not. I hoped I didn't have to go through hell trying to get someone to listen to me. Maybe it would be a waste of time, but it was the principle of the matter. I couldn't even walk around my own property without the cops coming after me. I was so angry but I didn't want to explode in front of my daughter.

That following week I got the call I'd been waiting for. "Hey, Ronald? This is Margy. I was calling to tell you the first round of samples are in. When can you come so we can view them together?"

"I can come this evening if that's okay." I replied.

"Great, I'll see you then."

"YES!!" I excitedly yelled. Finally it was my time to shine."

I ran into the kitchen where Erica was cooking and gave her a big kiss.

"What's that for?" Erica asked.

"They're finally here! The prototypes are here! I'm going over to see them this evening. I just hope and pray they're done right."

When I got to Margie's house she pulled out a big cardboard box. When she pulled out the prototypes of my shoe design, my mouth dropped. I was not happy.
"Ugghhhh, what the hell is this?" I asked her.
"This is just the first round Ronald. They're going to continue until they make your designs look exactly like the shoe your China supplier made. Sometimes they get it right on the first try and sometimes they don't. It's all part of the process." She said.
"But this doesn't look anything like my design. It's not even the right material. This is terrible. My spec sheet and prototype was perfect and if they just follow the directions I sent, it shouldn't be that difficult."

I was so disappointed. When I say it wasn't even close I mean not even a little bit. They used a completely different mold for the sole and the material was fake leather. There was supposed to be an alligator embossed on the leather that looked more like bubble popper wrapping. It was terrible. Margie and her husband guaranteed that the prototype process wouldn't stop until they made it perfectly. I was somewhat comforted.

Margie called a week later and told me that she spoke with the manufacturers and explained what my issues were. They guaranteed to fix the problem, but they wanted to be sure they would get the final order once they finished. She told me I needed to make a $50,000 down payment to secure my manufacturing spot. My suspicion returned.

"50,000? I just gave you $10,000. I need the samples to come back right and then I'll give you the rest of the money."

"I thought you had backing. When we met you told me about Burr and Leon." She responded

"Leon made a small investment but it was only enough to do research and development, and Burr is on board but we need finished prototypes."

So much time has passed and I was at the point that I

would do anything to bring Grapevine into fruition. Margie's manufactures were having a hard time perfecting the samples. After the separation between Dennis and I, his suppliers wouldn't deal with me without an agent. The manufacturers said they would work with me on the price, but they clearly were trying to stiff me, and Margie included. I didn't have an additional $175,000 just lying around. I wasn't quick to let it be known and I acted as if getting the money wasn't a problem.

Early one morning I got a phone call from Margie.

"Hello Ronald "she said in her British accent. "It's on its way."

What's on its way? I asked.

"The order of shoe samples" she replied.

My heart dropped. They started on another round of samples, even though I hadn't paid the extra money yet. Of course I was happy, but there was something I hadn't told Margie - **I didn't have all of the money.** *Oh my God. What was I going to do?* I had to think fast. Suddenly I had an idea: I'll flip some of my investment money and double it up. I had some New York connections on Timberland boots and Air Force One sneakers. The process was the same as the dope game. I would take a trip up to N.Y, get a couple boxes of Timberlands, come back and sell them for 30% more than what they cost in the store. Everybody from the hood loved Timberland boots but the ones I had were knock offs but no one could tell the real from the fake. Once my homie Frank and I built a reputation on the streets as the shoe guys, people all over the city wanted shoes. They were calling and putting in orders all day and night.

I know what you're thinking, "why not just tell Margie the truth" right? Telling the truth would've been the easier route but Ronald Hummons, better yet Diamond was a man with pride. He (I) didn't know how to admit that I didn't have my shit together yet

Taking trips back and forth to New York caused me to lose focus and not make good use of my time. Instead of saving the money I made to pay my debt with the manufacturers, I used it to pay bills and everyday expenses. The money was decent but it was a dangerous job, riding around all day, going from neighborhood to neighborhood, but a man is going to do what it takes to feed his family.

I definitely was not selling enough shoes to pay a $200,000 dollar bill. I had to come up with a plan, and fast. Margie called me every day and I spent most of those days screening her calls. I knew that wasn't fair to her but I did what I felt I had to do until I got my hands on some real money. I was beyond stressed - entrepreneurism was more difficult than I imagined. I wanted to pack up my family, leave Cincinnati and never look back. I figured maybe I could go somewhere and start over, find a cozy little job, maybe get back into the hair business and forget all about this business stuff. Instead, I called up my buddy Chris Rob for some brotherly love and support.

"Chris, hey man what's up? I'm in a serious dilemma and I could really use some Godly advice. I need $200,000 in less than two weeks." I said.

"Damn man, $200,000? You don't need Godly advice bro, you need bank robbery advice. How the hell you gon come up with that kinda cash in a short amount of time? He asked.

"I don't have the slightest clue. Just do me a favor" I said. "Just please pray for me because as you can see, right now things are rocky. Some days I wake up not sure if I can, or even want to make it through the day."

"No problem bro, you know I got you. Keep ya head up man, things will pan out" he said.

There is a practice in the Christian faith called fasting. It means to deny your "flesh" or natural state (body) of food, while instead feeding your spirit through prayer and studying the Bible. It's purpose is to quiet the mind and spirit, so that one can hear more clearly from God. It's during prayer and fasting that one's spiritual nature is heightened and communication with God is at its zenith. I felt I needed to fast, it was in my darkest time that I needed God the most. I knew the solution was within reach, I just needed him to help me grasp it.

One early morning, it was still dark out, I woke up to a noise but I didn't know where it came from. I couldn't go back to sleep so I went into my study to pray. While I was praying I kept seeing images of a previous investor in my mind, Burr. The last words he uttered to me kept ringing in my ears, "when you get more organized call me." I believe that message was given to me divinely. There it was - the solution. I knew then I had to reach out to Burr. But how? What would I say? How would I ask for $200,000? I'd figured it was the time to have a conversation with Margie, who was very frustrated at that point. I called and told her I knew where the money would come from, but I needed her help. After sharing my plan, she eagerly agreed to help.

I called Burr at his office and asked if he had some time, would it be okay if I stopped by his office. He responded "come see me tomorrow Ron." "Thank you Burr." I replied. Margie and I met him at his office the next morning. He and I were able to catch each other up on our lives, since it had been over a year since we last saw each other. Shortly after, he, Margie and I got down to the nitty gritty - it was time to reveal the real reason we were there. I told him all about how I'd finally created a business plan, scored some investors and became connected with manufactures. I told him about the samples and the new problem I had encountered with having to pay for new ones. He asked me "Great, so what do you need from me?"
Reluctantly I said "$200,000."
He sat in deep thought, then he finally replied, "If I do this, I'm only willing to invest $125,000, no more."
Gratefully, I said "Aww man, that would be great, it would really help me out a lot. I'm sure I can come up with the rest."
Luckily, I had a few thousand put away.
He said, "I'm not saying yes for sure, but I'll consider it."
Weeks went by and I didn't hear from him. I started to doubt he

would actually give me the money. I guess Margie started to worry too because she started calling everyday like she had before. And once again I dodged all of her calls. Finally after three weeks, he called.

"Ron, praise the lord brother."

"Hey Burr, it's good to hear from you." I politely replied.

"I decided to invest, but I need you to come down to my office so we can discuss the specifics." Burr was one of the kindest hearted and God fearing men I knew. I was so thankful that he was willing to take a chance on me. All I could do was cry and thank God for making provision for the vision.

We were still in the prototype phase and things were getting closer to being complete, but the manufacturer still hadn't developed a perfect match.

"Ronald, I spoke to the suppliers and they guaranteed me that they will continue until they get it right." Margie said. "They're so close to being perfect and I don't want us to lose momentum. Now that you have the rest of the money, let's go ahead and pay for the order in advance and once they get your approval on the final sample run, they can go straight into production."

"I'm not sending any more money until we get the samples right." I replied.

"Ronald you're going to slow things down. Wouldn't you like to get the ball rolling so that you can fill your orders and as you say, 'get that money?' " she asked.

"Um, for one thing, watch your step on quoting me because you will get cussed the hell out. Two - I don't really trust you or your people in Jakarta. I dont'care how long it takes, I wanna see the finished product before I send any more money."

Margie wasn't happy with my response so she went behind my back and contacted Burr. She knew with her being a white wealthy "Christian" woman, she could put on her charm and make me out to be the bad guy. Their conversation probably went something like:

"Hi Burr, this is Margie. Do you have a minute to talk?"

"Sure Margie what's going on?"

"Well Ronald is holding things up overseas. My team has been working so hard for you guys and Ronald just doesn't seem to appreciate that. They are one step away from producing the order and he refuses to pay them. If they put the order off then all the money you spent will go to waste."

"Ok Margie, I'll talk to him." Burr replied.

I got a call from Burr asking to meet at Starbucks. When I got there I could tell by the look on his face there was something wrong. "

Ron I got a call from Margie saying you're holding things up. What's going on?" He asked.

"Did she tell you that they haven't given us a finished prototype yet, or that she wants me to pay the whole amount by wire transfer? I wanna see what we're paying for first. I don't trust her word."

"I don't think Margie has any bad intentions. I think it'll be ok Ron. You're not in the streets anymore and Margie seems to be an outstanding woman." Burr replied.

We may not have been in the streets, but the same principles applied as far as I was concerned. "Okay man. I'll head to the bank tomorrow and have it transferred."

The manufacturers were paid and the shoes were shipped. Instead of producing more prototypes, they accepted over $200,000 and instead produced 6,500 pairs of a flawed design.

After waiting four weeks, I finally got a call that the shoes had arrived from Indonesia and could be picked up the next morning. I was overwhelmed with excitement. My partner Frank and I went to pick them up. I couldn't believe I was actually getting ready to see my vision, a vision revealed in prison, become a reality. This is the day I've been waiting for all my life. This was the day I dreamed of since I was a boy. I was on such a high that I could hardly breathe. I opened the boxes and was terribly disappointed. I was looking at 6,500 pairs of complete bullshit - every pair was defective. I just knew in my heart of hearts that we should not have sent that much money overseas. "I've been scammed!" I yelled to Frank. I didn't know what I was going to do. The orders I had were for the perfect sample made in China. I needed to get to Jakarta A.S.A.P.

I didn't know quite how to deal with foreign manufacturers but I wasn't willing to just take such a huge of a loss. They agreed to meet with me. After venting my frustration, they were confused. They told me that they were given permission to produce the full order based off the last sample.

"Permission from who? I didn't sign off on any approvals." I said angrily.

"Margie said you gave her power of attorney as your import/export agent."

I put my hand over my head as if I had suddenly got a headache. Apparently she paid the manufacturer part of the money and she kept $100,000 for herself. My suspicions of her were right, she had been playing me the whole time.

There was nothing I could do legally so I had to put on my hustle man hat and find a way to sell the defective shoes. I met with a guy named Rodney who owned an upscale store in the mall. He sold furs, leathers and expensive clothes. His store was one where I would want my merchandise sold. After negotiating with him about prices, we finally came to an agreement: Amp clothing store would carry the Grapevine line. The manufacturer was able to get the correct mold and shape of the shoe the way I wanted it, but the alligator embossing looked so fake. The colors were vibrant though.

"That's a trip man, just three years ago we was sittin on a park bench talking about you starting your own line of clothes and now you've accomplished that. If anybody can make this work I know you can." Frank was very optimistic even with the defects.

"Let's go bruh before I get emotional" I replied.

The next morning I got a phone call from Regina Russo, a local reporter from channel 19 news. She said she wanted to do a story of how I came to create my own line of clothing. She would be at the store for an interview within the next couple of days. I hurried and delivered the first order to the store. On the day of coverage, my models were prepared and I was dressed head to toe in Grapevine gear - a silver button up shirt, white pleated slacks and a crispy white derby to complete the look. When I arrived to the store, I was surprised to see Grapevine gear in the front display window and various other displays throughout. I couldn't believe my eyes. Rodney outdid himself on this one. I was at a loss for words.

"What time do you have Rodney? I asked anxiously.

"Its 11:00 a.m." he said.

The news team was late. I started to get nervous. Negative thoughts ran through my head. *What if they changed their mind or forgot about me?*

"Ronald?" someone said in a high pitch voice. I turned to see Regina and her camera crew.

"You had me worried for a minute, I wasn't sure you were coming." I said nervously.

Pointing toward the display, she asked "Is this it?

"This is it." I said proudly. "All of this it is hand- made. Alligator screen with an alligator appliqué trimming the high density screen. There was a lot of work put into these pieces." I led her to the other display. We even have clothing designed for women, pointing at the merchandise. This is my exclusive women's line called Grapevine Dimepiece."

Smiling at her, I said "This might be more your speed."

Smiling back, she said "Let's go ahead and get started with the interview."

3...2...1...ACTION! "You don't have to go to New York to find the newest and hottest clothing line to hit the market. You can find it right here on WHAT'S HOT!"

"I really appreciate you doing this for us Regina."

"It was my pleasure. I imagine how hard you must've worked to get your own clothing off the ground. I just wanted to help make this day memorable for you." she replied.

After the news team left, I stood outside the store and

looked into the glass case of what was now the birth of my vision. This was something I created. The process wasn't perfect, but it was my perfect process and I decided to embrace it as such. As I stared into the glass, I caught a glimpse of my reflection. I said to myself, "you did it...with God's help you actually did it. You're not a failure, you're a winner." I felt accomplished and content, but that was just the beginning.

Chapter 16

Profits, Pain, and Purpose
2007-20014

Even though I had officially launched my Grapevine shoe and clothing line I still wasn't fully satisfied - I felt there was something missing. I had made a little money but not much. My clothing line didn't sell at the rate I hoped. I marketed the shoe to professional ball players and other popular people in the city but I was still sitting on thousands of pairs of shoes. I could feel my depression and anxiety resurfacing and in flooded negative thoughts. I once again felt like a failure. I didn't know how I was going to explain the lack of sales to my investors. I had sunken into a really low, dark space. I isolated myself from everyone including my wife and kids. How could I be so stupid to trust Margie? I felt like I let everyone down, especially myself. My thoughts were all over the place.

"Ronald, where are you going with that knife?" Erica asked.

"I'm going to see Margie and Ronald." In the streets, if somebody robs you for that kind of cash there's a price to pay and I wasn't going to let them get away with it. "That bitch robbed me for hundreds of thousands of dollars. I can't retaliate legally but I sure can get my point across physically." I replied.

I was so angry. I was angry at Margie and her husband but more than that I was angry at God. I worked so hard to get to where I was and I had devoted my life to what I thought was my purpose. I did it to make a better life for me and my family. This bitch had to pay. I couldn't even think straight. I was in such an irrational state that I couldn't think of anything but hurting the thieves that took almost everything I had.

"Ronald please don't go over there! Do you wanna go

back to jail and be away from your children and me?"

"Move Erica. I gotta do what I gotta do right now!" I yelled.

I hopped in my truck and drove to Margie's house. My face - red, my breathing - heavy, and my heart - pounding and beating fast. I pulled into the driveway.

Knock, Knock, Knock! I banged on the door as hard as I could. I had the knife hidden in my sleeve. As the door slowly opened, I let the knife slide down my sleeve.

"Yes, how can I help you young man?" an old Jewish man asked.

"Is Margie or Ron home sir?" I asked.

"Son they moved to Scotland months ago. My wife and I bought this house several months ago."

"I'm sorry to bother you sir." I said.

"It's okay son. If you don't mind me asking, what were your dealings with them?" He asked.

"They scammed for almost $300,000. I came to get answers and hopefully some closure." I lied.

"Is that why you have a knife in your sleeve?"
I hadn't realized he saw the knife. Filled with emotion and unsettled rage, I started to cry. Right in front of the nice older Jewish man, I bore my soul.

"Sir if you knew my story you would understand why I'm so angry right now. I have a family to provide for - they took almost everything I have."

"Son, attacking them wouldn't bring you closure. It would close the prison doors behind you but that's about it. You're willing to throw your life away over money? What do you value more, freedom and being with your family or money and proving you're the man?

"Well, since you put it that way, I guess I would have to say my freedom and my family." I replied.

"My advice: forgive them son. Forgive them for you, not for them. God knows what they did and he will deal with them. Whatever you did to achieve your success once, trust me, you can do it again. Don't let your story end with getting your revenge against them, let it start with your forgiveness of them. Then you'll have to grace to do bigger and better than you did before." The old man said.

His words sunk deep in my heart. It was like God was talking directly to me through him. Forgiving was going to be difficult. I hated them so much that the thought was impossible.

I prayed, "God, thank you for not letting Margie and her husband be there. I ask that you forgive me for my intentions towards them. I'm lost and I don't know what to do. Please help me. I say with my mouth that I forgive them but help me to forgive in my heart. In Jesus' name I pray, Amen."

When I got home, Erica put her arms around me. She was relieved that I didn't carry out my plan to harm Margie and her husband. After the failure of Grapevine I went into a deep depression for months. I spent all my time in my basement studying software books about Photoshop and Illustrator. I was determined not to let anyone get the best of me regarding business dealings again. I learned how to do all my designs digitally. I buried myself in creating designs. I knew I had to come with something that would lead me back to success.

"Hunny Bunny, why don't you take a break for a while and go to the park with me and the kids...." Her eyebrows raised, "we're getting ice cream." She knew I loved ice cream.

"That's actually a good idea." I needed a break from hours of staring at the computer screen. "I'll call and see if Jelisa and Tre can come too." I said.

Spending time my kids was difficult at that time. I can't say I was the best dad but I really tried to be the best I could be at that time. I was getting buried in child support and income was slow from the clothing line. I was getting disconnection notices back to back. Entrepreneurism was not an easy life. It was really scary at times. When money was coming in, it was good but in this profession, steady income was never guaranteed.

One day I got a phone call from Erica.

"Hello?" I answered.

"Babe the lights are off. I thought you took care of the bill?" Erica asked in frustration.

"I paid something on it but not the whole amount. I'll take care of it I promise." I told her.

"God, what is this? I know I don't do everything right but you know my heart. Please help me, help us. I'm just trying to take care of my family and it seems like everything is coming against me. I don't understand why my struggle is so difficult but I pray that you give me the strength to face these storms in my life. Please remind me that You are for me, not against me. Amen."

The next day, I called Duke Energy. I gave them my checking account number and paid the bill but my account had no money in it. Power was restored in the house but I knew I needed to get the money quickly before the electronic check was to go though. I couldn't afford for the electricity to be cut off again. I prepared three big bags of my expensive clothes and shoes and took them to Platos Closet to see how how much I could get for them.

"Eighty-nine dollars? Are you serious? These jeans cost me $250 alone."

"Sir this is all we're willing to offer you." The young cashier replied."

"That's fine." I had no choice to accept the offer. At that point, I needed $150 more to cover the bill and I knew just how I would get it.

Frank was a guy who I could always depend on - we go way back. He traveled the country with me doing trade shows and meeting with merchandisers. I had a warehouse full of shoes and I knew he would help me sell them.

"What up bruh, I gotta plan. Since the Africans took over selling Timberlands and Jordans, let's sell them the defective shoes from the warehouse."

"You know I'm down." Frank replied.

We loaded a bunch of cases into my SUV and headed to see the Africans. We were able to sell them several cases. Next, we went to gas stations owned by Arabs, yard sales and wholesalers. We moved the product like we were back in the streets. I can laugh now but looking back, I really portrayed myself in a way like I had it going on. Those on the outside looking in had no idea of my struggles. I based my value on my appearance and achievements so if it didn't look I was doing it big and could show that I was successful, my self-esteem was super low. I based my worth on material things. When I was steadily making money, my self-esteem was high but when I was wasn't, my insecurities would show. One of my ex-girlfriends used to say I was narcissistic, maybe I was. Even with success, I still hid behind a mask. My insecurities were fueled by other people's perceptions of me. I drove expensive cars with only $5 to put in my gas tank at times. They could never tell by looking at me that I was struggling. People would say all the time how I don't look like what I've been through. I would quote my favorite tagline: **I just make fucked up look good.**

No matter who or what it was I always had a card up my sleeve that would trump anybody else that made me feel or look inadequate. I couldn't figure out what it would take to heighten my self-esteem so I just continued to add value by creating businesses.

I went to Atlanta for the yearly Birthday Bash they give that draws thousands. Fraternities and sororities from all over the country would come to promote their organizations. There were concerts, parties and food festivals to compliment the event. I had 100 shirts printed that read, "I'm Jetti." Jetti is a Cincinnati word that we used to describe someone who goes hard sexually. I figured people wouldn't know what it meant so I decided to introduce Jetti to the ATL. While waiting in line to get into Gladys Knight's Chicken and Waffle restaurant, a girl walked up, tugging at my chin and rubbing on my chest.

"What up boo?" She asked.

"Chillin, what's good with you?"

"You hopefully. Where you from?"

"Cincinnati." I replied.

"What hotel you staying at?" She asked me.

"Damn, why you wanna know all that and why you all in my face?"

"I'm trying to chill with you tonight." She replied.

"Damn babe, you jetti as hell." My homeboy laughed and agreed.

"Jetti, what's that mean?" She asked.

Realizing she didn't know what it meant, I responded in a way that she wouldn't know we were actually talking about her in a negative way.

"Jetti is a Cincinnati word we use for 'she fine as hell'" I told her.

"Oh that's what's up. Well I'm definitely jetti." She replied.

My homie and I laughed at her.

"Bruh we gon have everybody in the south talking about they jetti."

While driving back from Atlanta, a song by Alicia Keys came on the radio, "I'm ready." Damn! Another great idea had come to me. I called up a producer buddy and asked him to put a beat together that sounded like the song, with a little twist. I then called my friend Chris Rob and told him about the song and asked him to write a hook with the words, "I'm Jetti" in place of the words "I'm ready." When I got back to Cincinnati, I gathered some friends to put the song together - Chris, Janara, Drama Queen, Black Jack, and Skee - we went to the studio and laid a hot track. The song became a hit in the city but it wasn't enough.

While doing some research of the market analysis for a business plan I was writing, I came across some data, reporting that the beverage and sex industry were two of the highest grossing industries, with a combined a profit of 120,000,000,000 a year. I was amazed. *Damn, how can I get a piece of that?* I thought. After a few of days of pondering I came up with the idea to combine the two - an energy drink with an aphrodisiac. I named the beverage Jetti Juice. I didn't know much about the beverage industry but I knew I could gather plenty of information from the library. I learned that I needed to contact a formulation company to put the formula together. After calling several companies, they all told me that they did not have the experience of combining a drink containing ingredients for both energy and an aphrodisiac. I kept searching. I finally found a company in Louisville called Flavorman. I reached out to the company and after explaining my idea, they were excited to work with me to put the formula together. Only thing is, it would cost $25,000 for research and development. I knew the cost would be high, but *damn, $25,000?* I decided to call my friend Adrienne in Nashville to see if she was still interested in getting into the entrepreneur game.

"Aye, what up?"

"Nothing, headed to work. What's going on?" She asked.

"I have a great idea that I think could be big. Imagine an energy drink combined with an arousal booster. I'm calling it Jetti Juice. It would be the perfect nightlife beverage."

"I think you're right. I'm in what do you need from me though. I don't know anything about the beverage business."

"It's going to run around $50,000 to get it started. I have to pay for R&D to get the formula together and some marketing dollars. If you can put half I can give the other half."

"Where am I going to get $25,000 from?" She asked.

I knew Adrienne had access to some cash, she just needed some influence and Jetti Juice was just the push she needed.

"Let me see what I can do and I'll let you know in a couple of days." She replied.

Two days later, she called.

"I got the money." She said.

"Let's make it happen then."

We scheduled a meeting with Flavorman and discussed how I wanted the drink to taste, the effect I wanted it to have and most importantly how I wanted it to differ from Red Bull.

After we paid the research and development fee they assigned to chemist to the project. I went back and forth to

Louisville for a year tasting samples of different versions they had produced. After so many trips they finally did it. I tasted the drink and it was perfect.

I knew I had to get it to market A.S.A.P. I had already designed a label for the can. After I put in for the first order, I gave a rooftop sampling party. It was a big hit. Everyone there loved it. Cash Butta, a local rap artist wrote a song called Jetti Juice and performed it live. That night's success was definitely one highlight of my career. *I'm a beverage owner now.* I was one among the few black males to own a clothing line in Ohio and one of the only to own an energy drink. I felt like I was on top of the world.

I had made another huge accomplishment but I was still missing something. Business was steady and I loved making money but after meeting with one of Cincinnati's wealthiest entrepreneurs, I felt I had to change my direction. He said "profits should follow purpose, not the other way around." I gotten so caught up in making money and trying to be "the man" that I had forgotten about purpose. I took some time off to do a self-diagnosis of my life and the results were disturbing. I had been through hell since my conception. I experienced so much pain and heartache in my life. I was conceived by rape, abused, dropped out of school, went to prison and came home to end up homeless - yet I've started businesses, traveled the world and fluent in other languages. This had to be a sign that God was with me and that he had a great purpose for me. From then on, I wanted to live in that purpose. I never enjoyed the word "ministry" because it always reminded me of preaching, but I quickly learned that what God was calling me to was ministry. I didn't know where I would start but a phone call quickly changed that.

"Ron? Hi, this is Les Gaines. I hope I didn't reach you at a bad time but I heard you help people with writing business plans."

Les was the son of one the most successful lawyers and judges in Cincinnati. I couldn't believe he was calling me for help with a business plan. We met up and talked about how I could help. Honestly, I didn't understand why he would reach out to me, he was smart enough on his own and had countless resources available to him. However, I do believe the meeting was part of a much bigger plan, ordained by God.

"Hey Les, I have an idea but I'll need some help. I want to start a program called Vision Caretakers Inc, (V.C.I) and launch it in the prisons."

"That's a great idea Ron. Count me in. What help do you need from me?" Les asked.

"I need help putting the curriculum together. I want to teach inmates everything that I know." I replied. Then Les said something that made everything so simple.

"Ron let's just recreate the Ronald Hummons experience. Your journey to become a successful entrepreneur should be the blueprint."

That was it. My first lesson was learning to write business plans. Writing a plan was the most important piece of starting a business. You need a map to help you stay on course. The next step was business development. You need to know how to implement the plan once it's finished. Last, character development. The slogan I use when I have speaking engagements is, "Good character can take you places money and education won't."

Now that we had a full curriculum how would we get it in the prisons? I went to the one person I knew had the answers, God.

"Dear God, I know in my heart this is your plan and I know I'm your servant, here to do your will. I don't know what to do with this program we've created but I pray that if this is Your will that you'll open the door for it to move forward. Amen."

The very next day I got a booking to speak at a big conference in London, Ohio for Ohio Department of Corrections. They wanted a speaker who served time in prison but who had also had success as an entrepreneur. Since I was popular and had media coverage of my success, they booked me for the event. I began the speech with talk about my experience of becoming an entrepreneur and my closing ending with this statement:

"I've created a program called Vision Caretakers Inc. It's an entrepreneurial training program for inmates. The program is called the R.H experience."

By the time I got back to Cincinnati, I had already received three voicemails from the Ohio Department of Corrections asking to meet with me about the program that following Thursday.

I went to meet with the director to lay out the plan.

"Mr. Hummons we want to participate in your program. We've had groups with much more money and business experience come to us with programs, but we turned them down. We feel you have what it takes to teach inmates how to become job creators. These inmates need someone they can relate to and we feel you're the man for the job. Can we launch A.S.A.P?"

"I'm ready to start whenever you are." I wasn't quite as prepared as I seemed, I hadn't even written a plan down on actual paper. Once I got home, Les and I started to write it out and after about a week, we had a full, carefully written and detailed program. When we first launched, we had no idea the impact we would have.

"You ready bro?" I asked Les. This was his first time visiting a prison so I figured he might be a little nervous. "Man I'm ready. I think we're going to change the world with this Ron. Giving these guys hope in a place so deprived of life is an amazing opportunity and I'm thankful you brought me in." Les responded.

"Honestly bro I don't think I could've done it without you."

When we walked into the prison, a feeling of heaviness came over me. It's hard to explain but I felt like a dark spirit was present. It was a suffocating feeling. Old memories flooded my mind, the scent in the air smelled like death. When I went to the bathroom to put water on my face, I could smell the odor of the lye soap and water that smelled like metal residue. It had been so long since I'd been there. Tyra, the program coordinator and close friend knocked on the bathroom door.

"You alright in there. Don't be coming up in here bringing no heebee geebees." She was the comedian of the group.

"Yeah I'm good lil sis. Give me a minute."
I prayed. "God please let these men be able to receive what Les and I have put together for them and I pray that this program blesses their life, Amen."

We covered a whole range of topics. Les taught half of the curriculum and I taught the other half. It was as if we had brought life into those prison walls. I didn't realize how an infusion of love could bring restoration to a person. Every time we would leave from the prison I would drive as fast as I could with the windows down trying to shake the feeling of darkness I felt when we entered.

V.C.I. had become such a huge success that we were given a Vision Caretakers Day in the city of Cincinnati. Guys were coming home and starting their own businesses, thanks to the program. There were given hope they wouldn't have otherwise had. One day while I was grocery shopping a guy walked up.

"Mr. Hummons, its Brandon. I graduated from your V.C.I program two years ago,"

"Oh yeah, I remember you. How you been?" I asked.

"I'm great. I started a carpet cleaning business, thanks to your program. I even got married, life is good." He said with a sincere smile on his face.

I walked away from that brother seeing the fruit of the seed that I sowed. I learned a lesson about seeds from that experience - when we sow seeds we don't always see the fruit right away. Sometimes we never see fruition. The weird part about it is a lot of times when we sow seeds we're not even the ones who nurture the seeds for them to grow. God will use us to sow the seeds but He is the one that nourishes, water, and care for the seed to bring about the fruit.

Seeing the brightness in Brandon's eyes and how happy he looked when he talked about his business and his family made me realize that businesses were not the only thing we were creating through our V.C.I program, we were giving hope. Hope is a powerful thing. It can bring life into the most deserted situations. There is a scripture in Proverbs that says, "Hope deferred makes the heart sick but when it is fulfilled it's a tree of life." Hope is so important but what I found to be just as important was vision. In prison you will hear some of the greatest ideas but when they come home most guys never move on those ideas. That's why I named the program Vision Caretakers. People would always say it sounds like a hospital, I'd say "it's a hospital for visions." One day while I was walking the prison grounds a young kid walked up and asked me how he could participate in my program.

"How much time are you serving?" I asked him

"Thirty-four years." He replied.

My heart broke when he told me that. He was only 20 years old.

"I'm sorry little bro but you have to be within two years of release to be eligible for my program."

"Damn, I swear if I would 'a took a second to think about the consequences I wouldn't be here right now." He said.

"What made you say that?" I asked him.

"This shit ain't no joke in here big bro. You served time so you know what I'm talking about. Every day I wake up wondering if it will be my last day on earth. Sometimes I hope it is so that I don't have to see this place anymore."

I walked away feeling a sense of obligation. I felt like there was a new burden on my shoulders. I knew God was letting me feel this kid's pain.

The whole drive home, I felt a longing in my heart telling me I had to do something to bring about change. I heard T.D. Jakes say once that if God gives you a burden for something that's where he's calling you to affect change, but what could I do? I couldn't get this kid out any sooner and I couldn't promise he wouldn't get killed while he was in there. At times, God speaks to me prophetically in dreams - that night, the vision came to me clearly. In my dream I kept hearing the kid say, "if I'd took a second to think." *That was it, think!* When I woke, I knew God was showing me the next business venture - a film company. I had the idea to shoot a film called think!! The title was in lower case letters to represent simplicity to the thinking process and ended with two exclamation marks to show complexity of thinking.

I called Tyra immediately - I knew the only way I would pull this off was with her help. She would let me know the process and who I needed to talk to.

"You wanna shoot it where? Boy we have never let anyone, especially an ex-inmate, bring a camera crew into the prison and shoot a film. I like the idea and you know I got your back but I don't know about that idea. I'll set a meeting up with the warden and you can talk to her about it."

"Cool, that's all I ask is put me in front of the right people." I responded.

The next week I went to go meet with Warden Jackson.

"Ms. Jackson, I know I'm not MSNBC but I feel like God really wants me to shoot this film. The film will star younger inmates or inmates who have been here since there were young. It will be an interview style film, with actors reenacting their crimes. The purpose of the film is to help kids and young adults build critical decision making skills, that's why I called it think!!.

"Ronald I'm sold. I think it's a great idea. I can't promise you that the powers that be will approve it but, put a proposal together and send it to Columbus and see what they say." She replied.

After Tyra helped me construct a proposal, I sent it to the Ohio Department of Corrections office in Columbus. I knew if God had given me this vision, He would provide provision. Within one week I got a letter from the O.D.C. I was too nervous to open it. *What if they said no?* My heart raced as I opened the letter.

> **Dear Mr. Hummons,**
>
> **Your think!! Project proposal has been accepted and approved by the Ohio Department of Rehabilitation and Corrections. We are reviewing a list of potential interviewees and we will forward you a list soon.**
>
> **We look forward to working with you and wish you much success on your project.**

I sat and just stared at the letter. I knew God was with me. I couldn't have done any of this without Him. Once I got the approval letter I created the film company, Grapevine Media Group. I always kept the name Grapevine - it was the umbrella LLC to all of my business ventures. Next I needed a film crew who wouldn't be that expensive. I teamed up with some students from a local college who studied videography and film production. It was then time to write a storyboard and decide on film locations inside the prison. I didn't have a clue of what I was doing. I knew nothing at all about film production but God provided the right people who had experience to help me throughout the production of the film. I used black and white men and women inmates from different backgrounds and social statuses. I wanted to do a film that was relatable to anyone who would see it. During filming one inmate asked if I had a script to read from. I didn't want it to be scripted. I wanted their stories to make an impact and the only way to achieve that was for them to speak from their hearts.

"Nai'rashi I need you to look into the camera and act as if you're talking to your little brother or sister. Talk to them as if you were trying to convince them they don't wanna come here.

You think you can muster up some of those feelings?" I asked.

"Roll them cameras bruh, I got you." He responded.

Nai's segment was so heartfelt, he almost had me in tears. He spoke as if he was talking directly to the kids and the young adults who might benefit from his message. I took several trips to Murfreesboro Tennessee to have the film edited by a friend named Rick B. Once it was finished, I signed a distribution deal with a national bookstore chain and started accepting speaking engagements for the film. During the question and answer portion, someone asked me if there was a curriculum to go with the film. Of course I lied and said yes, but there really wasn't. When I got back to the Cincinnati I teamed up Bridgett, an educator friend who's been in the field for years. She helped me put a curriculum together and we developed think!!Campaign.org. Every major organization and school in the city used my film and curriculum. It was amazing to see how God was using this school dropout to make a tremendous impact on people's lives.

Chapter 17

My Son's "Death by Suicide"
June 2015

After taking a break from the clothing line business I decided to get back into the game. I had a new portfolio filled with a new hot look for a previous brand I'd created called C-town. C-town was a brand I created to represent everything Cincinnati related. The designs' signature look was a giant C on top of a map of the entire city of Cincinnati, with all the neighborhoods on it. When I first launched the brand, it's success made up for the major financial loss I took from Grapevine Collection defective shoes. C-town Apparel was the official brand of the city. After signing a distribution deal in 2009 with Finish Line Inc., C-town exploded in sales. After two of Cincinnati's hottest rap artists, Real Talk and Fame made a song about C-town. The song was uploaded on YouTube. At that point, I knew I had to take things to the next level. I decided to create a C-town Apparel flagship store. A friend had just closed down his store and gave me a good deal on the building. Getting the store ready for opening took months. After a lot of hard work and help from my cousin Kim, my friends Ken and JR, I had finally finished. I launched a grand opening right before Christmas and within two weeks we were nearly sold out. I was okay with running out of inventory though, we had suppliers in Cleveland. I was able to restock in a week.

After much success, I felt I needed a vacation to take a minute to look back over my life. I've definitely had my struggles but God had really blessed me. I had no complaints at that time. My marriage to Erica didn't work out but we grew to be good friends and the best co-parents to our son.

I was preparing the relaunch of my beverage company,

Jetti Juice. My sales director, Dan had just landed us a huge distribution deal with one of GNC's independent stores and there was a lot of preparation needed to be done to have us ready for our launch date. One morning while I was on a conference call with Dan, I got the worst phone call a parent could ever get.

"Daddy I think Tre dead!" My daughter screamed over the phone.

"What! Slow down Jelisa. Who did you hear this from? I asked.

"It's all on Facebook! Everyone is saying 'R.I.P Tre'."

"Oh God please not my child! Where are they saying it happened?"

"In Madisonville."

"I'm headed out there now. I'll call you soon as I find out what's up."

I jumped in my car right away and sped to Madisonville. I called Tre's aunt.

"Dora what's going on?" I asked.

"Ronald hurry! Tre been shot! We're on the corner of Whetsle and Erie!" she screamed.

"I'm pulling down now." My face streamed with tears as I pulled up to where the cops had the street blocked off.

"Please officer, I need to get through here. I was told my son had been shot."

"Son you're going to have to go down to Whetsle, park your car and walk up." He replied.

"Sir can you please tell me if my son is alive?"

"I'm sorry son, I don't have any information on the perp."

I left my car and ran down the street. I saw my son's aunt Dora.

"Oh God Ronald, the police shot Tre!"

All the oxygen left my body as I stood in the location my son had just been shot.

"Is he still alive?" I asked.

"Yes. The ambulance just took him to the University Hospital."

I ran to my car and rushed to the hospital. My eyes were so blurred from my tears that I could hardly see. I was speeding so fast and swerving all over the expressway trying to hurry and get to the hospital. When I pulled up, the police had the street blocked off to the emergency room.

"Officer can I please get through and park. That was my son involved in that shooting with the police."

"Let me call it in first and see if it's okay for you to come through."

The officer radioed the commanding officer on the scene to see what he could do.

Sarge we got the father of the kid that was shot here. Can we let him through so he can   park?"

"Please hurry up, my son is dying!" I yelled.

"Go ahead and pull right over there." The cop said.

I parked and ran into the emergency room. I saw Tre's grandmother first.

"Please tell me my baby is alive."

"Ronald it doesn't look good. They're working on him now." She replied.

"Oh my God, what the hell happened?" I asked.

"I don't have all the details yet but they said Tre shot a cop and then got into a shootout with two other cops and one of them shot him."

"What! Tre? Not my child. That doesn't even sound like Tre. Where is his mom?"

"They arrested her on the scene and took her downtown for questioning."

The nurse took us in this waiting room until the doctor could come out and give us the results of my son's surgery. This was the worst day of my life. None of this made any sense. My son Tre was a really sweet child. He had one of the most loving personalities you'd ever see in a kid. This had to be a nightmare. I had just talked to Tre on his birthday (June 1st) and here it is, almost three weeks later, my son is lying in the hospital dying.

"Please God, I'm begging you, please don't take my child...take my life in exchange!!" I pleaded with God.

I held on to my faith. I knew God wouldn't take one of mine. I had prayed for and over my kids everyday, so how could this be happening? When I saw the doctor's eyes I knew he didn't have god news.

"I need only the immediately family to remain and everyone else to step out please." He said.

"I'm sorry to say Trepierre didn't make it. We did everything we could but he had lost too much blood. I'm sorry." He walked out.

"OH MY GOD NOOOO!!! I yelled. I turned and punched a hole in the wall.

"NO, NO, NO!! Son I'm sorry. I should have been there to protect you."

I fell to my knees. I couldn't believe my child was gone. My baby was dead. I would never hear his voice again. I would never hear him say "I love you" every time we got off the phone.

I called my mom.

"Ma, Tre's dead."

"Wait, say it again baby. I can't understand you."

"Tre is dead! He was shot by the police!" I screamed.

"No, No, Nooo oh God Nooo. Ronald where are you?"

"At University Hospital."

"I'm on my way."

After finding out the news, I wouldn't let anyone touch or hug me, no one except Erica, after all she was Tre's step mom. She and I had been through rough times together. She knew the struggles I faced to be an active father in Tre's life. She was with me when I had to sneak to his school just to see him. My heart filled with so much hatred for the police. I didn't know the full details - I still really don't - but at that moment, all I could think was, the police had killed my son. A piece of me died when my son died. Life left my body when the doctor told me my son didn't make it. I felt everyone in a police uniform was a target. My mom and Erica walked me to my car. They were worried I was going to punch one of the officers, so they stayed on each side of me. The drive home from the hospital was the longest ride ever. I felt so much pain. I felt so much guilt, like it was my fault. I needed some answers and nobody had any answers for me.

All I had were my memories of my child and with those memories came so much more pain. I had always been a part of my son's life from the time he was born. I wasn't the best father but I was the best I knew how to be and I was always there for him, until I went to the penitentiary. When I came home one of the first things I did was visit my kids. Tre and I had a special bond. He was such a spiritual kid and filled with so much life. He told my mom when he 6 that he wanted to be a preacher when he got older. His mom and I got along -well, off and on during his childhood. When we were off, her way of getting back at me was to take my son from me. When she got mad at me she wouldn't let anyone on my side of the family see Tre. She was so busy trying to hurt me that she didn't realize she was hurting Tre in the process. I didn't let her stop from seeing him though. I would sneak to his school sometimes. His teacher appreciated me sitting in his classroom. She said he was a much better student when I was involved in his schooling. I didn't just involve myself with Tre at his school. I also included the rest of the kids - if they were good in class or if they all passed their weekly tests, I would sponsor a pizza party. There wasn't a week I wasn't there at his school. I was there at least 2 days out of the week, if not more.

One day while I was sitting in the back of the

class Tre raised his hand and asked the teacher if he could talk to me. When she said yes he came back with a long face.

"What's wrong son?"

"Dad it hurts when I sit down." Tre replied.

"Why, what's wrong?"

"My mom's boyfriend whooped me really hard and my legs and my back hurts."

"What!" I yelled. The teacher came back and asked if we were okay. I told her what happened. She called the office and asked for a substitute teacher to come to the class. She wanted to personally take us to the principal's office. When we got to there, she had him pull his pants down and pull his shirt up so we could check him out. When I saw the bruises and whelps I instantly teared up. All I could think about was what Walter used to do to me. She called 241-KIDS, as a result, Trepierre and his little sister was removed from the home. I wasn't satisfied though. I wanted blood. I went to Tre's mom's house and yelled for her boyfriend to come outside.

"Fred!" I yelled as loud as I could. He finally came to the door.

"What?!"

"Bring yo ass down off that porch, I need to talk to you." I shouted.

"Talk to me about what?" he asked.

"About you putting yo hands on my son. Bring yo ass off that porch and let's go behind this building and talk."

I tried not to threaten him, I had just gotten out of prison so I didn't want to bring too much attention to myself.

"Bro, bring yo bitch ass down off that porch. You man enough to put your hands on his mom and now you think you gon put yo hands on my son, man bring yo ass off that porch so I can fuck you up."

He closed the door for a minute before returning.

"Oh you still wanna see me?" He asked. He went and grabbed a knife.

"Bitch I don't care about you having no weapon. Bring yo ass down off that porch!"

He saw that I wasn't leaving and there was nothing he could do that would scare me. I was so filled with adrenaline, not even a gun could make me leave. He finally figured out the one thing that would scare me away, a telephone call.

"911 we need an officer out here. My girlfriend's baby daddy is out here threatening me." He said to the operator.

"Damn, serious bro? I knew you were a bitch when I first met you. I'ma see you and when I do I swear I'm gon beat yo ass."

I left before the police got there but they came to my house and issued me a court date. On the day we went to court the judge was confused. All she sees is two men standing there, on a domestic violence charge. I cleared things up really quick.

"Your honor if I could explain. This is not a relationship. I know it looks odd for two men to be here, but the honest truth is I went over my son's mom house to beat his ass." I explained.

"Is that what happened Mr. Johnson?" She asked.

"Yes your honor."

"Mr. Hummons you wanna tell me why you went to go fight Mr. Johnson?" The judge asked.

Fred didn't know I had the photos and the report from the Child and Family Service investigation for the abuse on my son. I gave them to the bailiff and then I started to explain.

"Your honor I went to my son's school, as I always do every week to spend time with him. When I got there, my son told me that Fred had whipped him really hard. When the principal and I checked him, we saw the bruises. The school had no choice but to call 241-KIDS. I was so angry when I saw the wounds that I just lost it. I admit it, I went to go whoop his ass."

"Thank you Mr. Hummons for being honest." The judge replied. Then she turned to Fred.

"Mr. Johnson, how long have you been with his

son's mom?" She asked.

"For about three months."

"Why are you putting your hands on this man's child and you've only been around for three months. I don't know how I would have reacted either. I'm dismissing this case but Mr. Hummons you have to stay away from Mr. Johnson." The judge ordered.

"Thank you judge." I responded.

The next morning I went down to the clerk of courts at the Juvenile Court and filed for emergency custody. Tre and his sister Chan were living with his grandmother but I felt they needed to be with me. At our first court hearing, Tre's mom showed up with her boyfriend. I couldn't say anything to him due to the court order so I tried not to even look at him. Just the sight of him made me angry. The judge ordered a paternity test even though paternity had already been established. I applied for custody of both of the kids because I thought they were both mine. I was present on the day of the test but Nina was a no show. I got a call from her later that night.

"Ronald can we talk?" Nina asked.

"About what? Why didn't you show up today?" I asked.

"That's what I wanted to talk to you about. I need to be honest with you. Chan is not yours....hello, hello?"

"You think I didn't know? I took on that roll because I wanted to, not because of your lies. That doesn't even matter at this point though. As far as I'm concerned she's mine and I'm her father and that's all she'll ever have to know."

"Ronald thank you."

"There is nothing to thank me for. I didn't do it for you." I replied.

Nina never showed up to court and my case for custody ended up getting dismissed. I had a letter from Tre and his teacher. Tre wrote that he wanted to be with his dad but the court didn't show me any love. I even tried to set a child support order on myself just so I can get visitation rights, she was a no show for that too.

When Nina found out I was going to the school to see Tre, she called the school and put a stop to that. I later found out that after I went to beat up her boyfriend, he was the one that told her to stop letting me see the kids and that he would play the role as dad. Fred smoked so much crack that the abuse on Tre's mom got worse. Tre's home life was so bad and there was nothing I could do. Drugs and alcohol played a major role in his mom's and her boyfriend's life that he felt obligated to his mom and sisters. Tre and his friend would sneak to my house before he graduated from high school and tell me how he had to fight Fred in order to get him off of his mom. I was willing to file custody for him even in his later teens, but Tre would always say his momma needed him. He played the role of the man in the house more than he played the role of her son. His mom made a remark after his death that he owed her money. I carry a lot of guilt. I don't know what more I could've done. I wish I could've been there to take the bullet that took his life.

Chapter 18

The Aftermath
July, 2015

The aftermath of my son's death was the worst day of my life. I didn't know everything that lead up to my son's death. No one would give me the entire story. I knew my son was not a stone cold killer. He was a sweet kid, like Ronald - he was nothing like Diamond. My mind was reeling. I was trying to wrap my mind about my baby being gone. I had a great reputation in the city years before with my work with C-Town and my program at the prison, but after my son's death - I was persona non grata in the city. The messages from relatives on Faccbook were crazy. Some of my family members were police and firefighters and they didn't know who the "perp" was… they just felt like he must be the scum of the earth and they voiced their opinions. I was fighting battles on every front because I refused to believe that my son was a cop killer. I knew there was more to the story that I was not being told. I knew something was being kept from me.

Why was Tre's mother, Nina arrested? She was released hours later, but couldn't or wouldn't explain what was going on and why she was held. I was trying to be there for my daughter's and my other son who had to deal with all that was being said on social media and the news about their brother. I had women try to come and be close to me but I didn't want them near me at all. One of the old church members had organized a vigil to remember the officer that was killed and my son. She knew me as a child. She knew my son was not the man that he was portrayed to be. She tried - but it went horribly wrong.

The officers that were there and supporters of the officers that were there screamed at me and my mother saying that I didn't belong. The anger that filled me was blinding. I was invited there and at that moment I felt like once again I was failed... I was set up. My son was being demonized on Social Media and in the press and I hadn't even been able to see him. I never saw him in the hospital. His body was sent to the medical examiner and I wasn't able to see him there. The image of my son, that I saw was of him at school telling me that it hurt when he sat down. That was by baby and that is who I wanted the city to see and the city to know. I prayed when I could. I cried out to God begging him to make this one bad dream and to bring my son back to me.

I got a message on Facebook from someone that I hadn't heard from in 20 years. She knew me when I lived in the basement at the church and went to the church school. She lived in Atlanta and asked me simply what did I need? Her name was Nikki. I couldn't tell her what I needed. Hell, I didn't know. I just knew that I felt like I was drowning in my grief and I was trying to stop people from seeing my son as a young thug. I knew better. I knew my son!

Nikki messaged, "Skip, (my childhood nickname) it is Nikki. I am so sorry. What do you need? How can I help?"

I gave her the general message of thanks for the well wishes. I didn't really want to be bothered. It wasn't until she started answering the family members that didn't realize that it was their little cousin that was killed - and gently but firmly telling them to fall back and delete posts that I actually believed that she was trying to help.

I started asking her to help with little things, but things that were just too painful for me to do. She and my partner Edward became my legs and arms. They helped me plan a vigil for my son, and prepare and release statements about who my son was. Edward was able to get a video of the shooting - something I still have been unable to watch to this day. He watched it for me - and that is when I knew, something was very wrong with my son the day he died. My son was asking the officers to shoot him, before he fired the gun that he had. My question was why?! I knew that my son thought he was being charged with rape, but that couldn't have been why he wanted to die.

We found out that my son was the person that called the police to report a man with a gun. He called the police on himself. We also found out that my son was drunk and high and had been drinking and doing drugs with his mother for hours the night before and even that morning. Tre was walking around with a gun and his mother was fighting with him because he wanted to call his girlfriend and ask her to drop the non-existent charges. Tre was bouncing from being depressed to running in the streets like someone or something was chasing him. His mother could not control him. A probation officer that knew both my son and myself tried to tell his mother to take him home before he got into trouble. His mother couldn't control him. Her hatred towards me wouldn't allow her to call me for help. I wish that she had, I would have been there.

My son had reached the lowest point of depression and had decided that he couldn't live with anymore pain. He lived through the pain of his mother's addiction, her abusive relationship, the abuse from his mother's boyfriend, my absence during my time in prison, and being isolated from me and my family - this last pain of being lied on my the woman that he loved was just one blow too many. I needed to hear from a sober voice. I needed to know what really happened to lead him to this point.

But first I had to bury my son. I had to plan a funeral with a woman that I knew was lying to me about how my son died. I knew Nina was there when he was killed, but she couldn't stay sober long enough to say anything helpful at all. I planned my son's funeral. I dealt with the social media attacks and even the attacks on my business - all of that didn't really matter to me. I had to get to the bottom of this. I need to understand. I needed closure so I could be begin the mission of making my son's life matter.

Nina and her family tried to get me to stop searching for the truth. They tried to get me to believe the version of events that was being played out in the media - but I knew better. I knew my son! My son was not the type of kid to want to hurt anyone. He was nothing like Diamond and everything like Ronald. I didn't know if I was coming or going, but I knew that I had a new mission. I would make my son's life count and use his death to prevent the deaths of others.

Chapter 19
Lost and Found

      After meeting with officer Troy, officer Kim's partner, I learned of the details that led up to the altercation that resulted in my son and officer Kim's death. Officer Troy was one of the officers that responded to a call from Tre's girlfriend the night before the incident. He and I met for breakfast recently. He gave me a full report of what really happened when he arrived at her house.

      "Hi Ronald. It's good to see you again," he said. "I know you have a lot of questions, so tell me where you'd like to start."

      "I guess it would be best to start from the beginning." I replied

      "First, I wanted to tell you that I don't want you to carry the guilt of your son's actions. I know it's easier said than done, but I know you did everything you could to raise your son, despite his mom's interference. I hope I can help give you some closure with what I'm about to tell you."

      "Thanks sir.....I appreciate that." I said.

      "Okay, so at about 1:30 am, I received a call from his girlfriend, Sheila. Once I arrived at her house, her mom instantly started trying to explain what happened. She said Tre had forced her daughter to give him oral sex. There were no visible marks on Sheila and she didn't seem to be at all shaken up by the situation. I observed her very well. Her posture was very relaxed, and she was acting very nonchalant for a woman who had supposedly been assaulted. I asked her if she wanted to go to the emergency room, she declined. Since there was no penetration we couldn't do a rape kit, and there were no signs of assault so we had nothing to go on. As her mom continuously tried to explain, Sheila seemed as if she didn't want to agree when we would ask if the information given was accurate. Ronald,   honestly, I could tell she was lying but for whatever reason, she was trying to get to get   back at Trepierre. After I left, the case was closed and that was it. There were never   any charges pressed against your son."

"So, you're telling me that there were no rape or any other charges filed on my son at all? I asked.

"Rape? Not at all. When we left her house that was it. No charges, no pursuit, no   nothing. Where did Tre get that we were charging him for rape?" officer Troy asked.

"When he was heading back to the house, he saw the cop cars in the driveway. He texted Sheila to ask her why the police were there, and she responded back and said he was being charged with rape. After reading the text, he tried calling her and kept texting, but she never responded back. He then went back to his mom's house and took some of her valium and began to drink alcohol. It was then that he began to fall into a deep depressive state. He couldn't believe he was being charged with rape. He told his mom that he wasn't going to jail for something he didn't do and he especially was not going to be labeled a sexual predator. I can imagine he probably thought life as he knew it, was over. He had planned to join the Navy in three weeks."

"Ronald I'm so sorry. It all makes sense now. I knew Tre, and one thing's for sure, he was not a killer. I had no idea Sheila lied to him. I wish I could have talked to him the night before. I would have assured him that we were not filing any charges. That text from Sheila is the cause of the death of your son and my friend. If she had never sent that text, I believe they both would still be alive. Now I understand Tre's state of mind at that time. I can see how and why he reacted out of fear." He said.

After the meeting with officer Troy, I felt empty. I never knew about the conversation between Sheila and the officers. She previously told me that their sexual activity was consensual, but she let her mom tell the cops that it wasn't. My son died because of a lie. I was glad to have some clarity though.

I finally had a much clearer understanding of the what and why. I didn't feel any better though. I visited Tre's grave site and had a long tearful conversation with him.

"Hey son. I had a meeting today that really deepened my sadness of losing you. I miss you so much. I'm so sorry that all of this was over a lie. I carry so much guilt over what happened to you. If I had been there, I would have taken those bullets for you. Losing you is the worst pain I've ever experienced. Son, I'm moving to North Carolina for awhile - I need to recuperate and rebuild. You'll always be with me. I won't be gone long. I promise I'm going to fight for you until the day I die. I love you and I miss you."

I closed my store, sold my house and moved to North Carolina. I didn't want to be in Cincinnati a second longer. Every street had a painful memory and I needed to be able to heal. No one could understand. I had taken a financial hit after my son's death. I had to pay for his funeral out of my pocket. I had to do everything. While in North Carolina - I started getting counseling. It was in North Carolina that I went through the real seven stages of grief. I will say that I felt every single stage.

After learning of Sheila's lies and her mother's hand in all of this - I was in shock. I couldn't leave Cincinnati fast enough. I had tried everything I could to keep busy so I wouldn't have to think about how my son had been pushed to this point of depression from betrayal from another woman that said that she loved him. I was in denial until I could no longer deny that lies are what killed my son. Lies are what kept my son from me as a child and lies were keeping people from knowing the truth about my son. Lies destroyed my son's life - just as lies destroyed Ronald and created Diamond.

Somewhere during the shock came the waves of guilt that felt like I was being crushed. Former Cincinnati Police Chief Jeffrey Blackwell termed the incident a "suicide by cop."

However, shortly there after the media and prosecutors began saying that my son was trying to kill as many police officers as possible. When the truth was that he was begging them to kill him. He had sent text messages saying he wanted to die and left a strange message on his Facebook page - but none of that was being told. The man that I worked side by side and got a recommendation for my program Think! was fueling the fire about my son's death and the unfortunate death of Officer Kim. With each word out of the prosecutor's mouth, the city that I loved dearly was turning against me. The city that I worked so hard to support and built an entire brand around was blaming me for not being in my son's life to prevent this. What is worse - I was blaming myself. Yes, I fought for years. Yes, I had proof - but I felt that I should have been able to fight harder. I felt that if I had just done something different, I would have been able to influence my son and I would have caught the signs of depression. I could have gotten him help. I could have done something and I could have saved two lives. I blamed myself for both my son's death and Officer Kim's death. No one believed me about fighting for my son through the courts and being denied every single time. I blamed myself for a long time. I blamed myself for not seeing the signs of my son's mental illness - when I knew so well the signs of his mother's. I stayed away and in counseling for 90 days.

When the depression came in and it wouldn't let me go! I refused to let depression win. The crazy part about everything, was even going through the NAMI training, I couldn't find any other way to deal with my depression other than to fight. I fought it with anger. I was angry! I was angry at everyone and everything that I thought let me down, let my son down, kept my son from me as a child, allowed Officer Kim to be killed… The angrier I got, the bigger my anger grew. It grew to the point that instead of depression trapping me, my anger trapped me. My anger at first was like the whale from the Bible story - Jonah and the Whale - it saved me from debilitating depression. I couldn't sleep. I couldn't eat. I couldn't maintain a relationship with a woman. I couldn't do anything, until I got angry.

Unfortunately, my anger was so great that it couldn't be handled by anyone other than God. I hated God with every fiber of my being. I began to blame God and even said that God could not exist, because nothing in my life was like I heard people of faith say it should be. I cursed God! I cursed God with everything in me. I hated everything that had anything to do with God. I blamed God for allowing me to be abused at the hands of a "educated church man" in Walter. I was having excruciating headaches and unable to sleep. It was getting worse. Doctors after several MRI's said that I have high levels of a protein called CLL11 which has been a proven link to CTE (Chronic Traumatic Encephalopathy). A CTE is a degenerative brain disease found in athletes, military veterans, and others with a history of repetitive brain trauma. I suffered 3 major head injuries that lead to my concussions before the age of 13 and 5 more by the age of 30- this was more than enough to cause this condition. This condition could lead to me becoming unable to take care of myself and ultimately my death. How could God allow this If he was real?! If God was real, why would he allow me to be born, as a product of rape?

I lost my faith! The one thing that had been keeping me sane, I lost! And what replaced it was anger and bitterness! I had valid reasons be be angry. I had valid reasons to be furious with God or whomever created this world we lived on. My anger forced me to stay away until I could get my life in order. My anger fueled me to fight for my son and his memory. My angry stage lasted longer than any of the other stages. I began to function in my anger. I began to be see my anger at God and the dismissal of His existence as normal.

One day I was driving to the airport and there was a strange cloud pattern that caught my attention. Then out of nowhere the sun broke through. It was the way that it broke through what seemed to be an impossible cloud pattern - that made me say - something greater than me created that. I don't know that I will ever believe in God the way that I was taught as a child. I just can't believe that the god that Walter said told him to abuse me could be the God that created the clouds and the sun that were shining so brilliantly. No, that man was using drugs himself - he couldn't have been praying to the same God that created this miracle. The God that created the sun and moon, was the God that created the process of a diamond being formed. That process is long and hard and to be honest is hell. The God that created the sky that had me so captivated was able to use all the hell that I had been through to be able to explain and educate others about the pain and despair that my son was feeling. It was in that moment that my faith returned. I had lost the baggage of the faith of a child, but I embraced in the moment when God made himself real to me. And for me, that is all that matters.

Chapter 20
Birth of the Mission

People say that the moments before a woman gives birth is when she experiencing the most pain. The pain of losing my son was the greatest pain in my life, but it also has birthed a passion in me and launched me into a position to create a platform to give young people like my son the voice that they never had. My platform is not for me. It isn't for Tre - my platform is for those that we can still save. One morning, I woke up and I knew my mission was to share my son's story and to show where the system is failing kids like my son. My mission was ignited out of the pain of my son's life.

My first step was understanding suicide and explaining it to others that were affected by a family member that attempted or committed suicide. I had made a vow that Tre's death will not be in vain. Soon after I returned to Cincinnati, I pursued the proper classes and I received a N.A.M.I (National Alliance on Mental Illness) certification. I created an organization called The Trepierre Foundation. My goal is to bring awareness, training and workshops to help break the stigma of mental illness. My prayer is that I can actively help save others that may be struggling with the disease. I wrote a blog called Suicidal Grace that speaks from the voice of the suicide victim. I want to help people affected by suicide gain a better understanding of their loved ones' mind set. I read a post on Facebook, written by a woman whose husband committed suicide. What she said about him broke my heart. She accused him of being selfish. What she fails to realize is that he probably thought the world would be a better place without him. I can understand because I used to be one of those victims who really believed the world would be a better place without Ronald - but God decided to spare my life. The blog was meant to provide a different perspective on suicide.

My son's death triggered all kinds of emotions and memories for me. I remember reading comments that implied that those who commit suicide are selfish. I'll be the first to say that I understand the pain of those who have attempted or has committed suicide. I do not come from a place of empathy, but from a place of first hand experience. I too attempted suicide years ago.

After coming home from prison, I made the decision to live a legitimate lifestyle and do everything "by the book." I didn't know how hard it would be to honor that decision. I found myself homeless with no job, no money, unable to provide for my children, literally sleeping on park benches and eventually living in a shelter. This was the lowest point in my life, the bottom of the barrel. I felt like I was a burden to my family and friends because I couldn't even provide my own basic needs.

The thought that those who commit suicide are selfish, couldn't be further from the truth. Suicide has nothing to do with being selfish. It has everything to do with being in such a dark and hopeless place, that you no longer fear what is on the other side. You are just looking for relief from the pain and the hurt. Once you get to the point of where you are so low and can't see any sign of light is when those suicidal thoughts rush in like a flood.

I didn't talk to anyone about what I was feeling. I was so far gone, no one could help or reach me. I remember telling God, "If you won't tell me why my life has been so painful, then I'll come and ask you face to face." I took a bunch of pills and woke up a day and half later in the hospital, blind and paralyzed. I couldn't speak, but I could hear what was going on around me. I was in that state for almost a week - a week of not being able to communicate with anyone but God. I remember being so angry at God for not letting me cross over to the other side. I just wanted to die and have solace. I wanted to cross over to a place where the pain couldn't follow me. I thought to myself, anywhere but here on this earth, facing my pain had to be better. It was then that I began to really think about my life and how I had gotten to that point. How did I get to a point where I had no more fight left in me? I realized that the prison I was living in, was filled with shame and guilt.

God spared me. I didn't understand it at the time. During my dark season, I couldn't see any future with a bright outcome. I didn't know God had purpose for me - purpose that led to success and greatness - not failure. It's hard to see anything in the dark except lies, lies that you're worthless and have no purpose. Looking into a mirror in the dark will reflect no value, only distrust of what the future could be once you let some light in. If you have family, friends, or close loved ones that have made the choice to commit suicide, please give them GRACE and forgiveness. If you are considering committing suicide, I LOVE YOU. Please try to find some light.

I received a lot of positive comments of the blog. A mother commented and said that it brought about her healing. I found healing in my writing as well. I continue to write on mental illness and suicide for different publications. I also wrote a couple of op-eds in the local paper, which also have gotten a lot of positive reactions and attention. I was even asked to be the opening speaker for actor and activist Dick Gregory. I was asked to speak about my son's death and his mental illness. It was by far the biggest and perhaps most important speaking opportunities I've had. I've spoken in many places about various topics, but this was the first time I would speak on mental illness. My life journey has been a long and difficult road. I sometimes still don't understand the reason for all of the madness I've gone through. However, I still believe God has a purpose for it all. Until the day God calls me home, I will continue to fight for those battling mental illness.

My determination took many forms. To some, it may have even looked like I was suffering from manic depressive disorder. I was all over the place - but I know my time may be limited because of the CTE and I came back to Cincinnati with a passion to fight like never before.

I filled out the paperwork to register as a candidate for Mayor of Cincinnati. I was under the impression that the Mayor of our great city could make changes to the departments that failed my son. I was not going to be a traditional politician. However, I put that on the back burner once I realized that the problem was bigger than Cincinnati.

I reached out to Ohio Senators Cecil Thomas to discuss what could be done to protect children who were facing the same kind of hell my son was forced to live in, when the courts work against the best long term interest of the child. We came up with a proposal for Tre P Law. The proposed Ohio State law reads:

An Act prohibiting parents or guardians being investigated under Child Protective Services for abuse access to the child/ victim.

WHEREAS, access the children whose parents/ guardians are under investigation for child abuse has proven to be a danger to the child and the integrity of the investigation.

WHEREAS, according to data from the National Child Abuse and Neglect Data System (NCANDS), 50 States reported a total of 1,546 fatalities. Based on these data, a nationally estimated 1,580 children died from abuse and neglect in due to negligence by CPS.

WHEREAS, Research indicates that very young children (ages 4 and younger) are the most frequent victims of child fatalities. NCANDS data for 2014 demonstrated that children younger than 1 year accounted for 44.2 percent of fatalities; children younger than 3 years accounted for 70.7 percent of fatalities. These children are the most vulnerable for many reasons, including their dependency, small size, and inability to defend themselves.

WHEREAS, dozens of children have been killed in Ohio alone due to easy access to the abused child. Parents/ guardians under investigation for abuse with access to children have been proven to manipulate children into recanting their claims of abuse and as a result have been placed back into living conditions that result in the child's death, growing up in environments conducive to the development of mental illness, and or prison.

BE IT ENACTED BY THE STATE OF OHIO LEGISLATION:

Section 1. The parent or guardian shall have no/ limited access with caseworker on site. Discussions of the investigation shall be prohibited.

Section 1. Guardian where child is placed during investigation will face consequences if parent/ guardian are allowed access to the child without caseworker present.

Section 1. This act shall take place at June 1, 2017
Senate:
Sherrod Brown, State of Ohio
Rob Portman, State of Ohio

The proposed law is there, but due to my son being responsible for the death of Office Kim - lawmakers and the police union as well as the city are not in support of this bill becoming a law. There are other reasons that CPS does not support becoming law. I have been told that it would cost too much money to enforce the law. However, I will not be stopped. Children that are dealing the abuse that Tre and myself dealt with as children should be able to be avoided. There has to be a way to protect them. Two generations of my family had to deal with life altering abuse. No other family should have to deal with this.

While I was working to get this bill to become law, the records that I had been working on for months finally came through. I had every court record and transcript of every case concerning my son. I could now prove to anyone that would listen that my son needed serious help! In high school after his brush with Juvenile Court it was discovered that my son was suffering from Post Traumatic Stress Syndrome. Counseling was recommended but his mother refused to follow the treatment plan. Instead she began to allow and encourage my son to drink alcohol and smoke drugs and to take her prescription drugs. I letters from the school psychologist and the court records proving why my son and daughter should be removed from their mother's care.

During one meeting I presented this information to a journalist that wanted to interview me about my proposal Cop Block. Cop Block was a proposal to get the community involved with policing their own streets along with the police. Originally the former Police Chief was supportive - however as soon as it was discovered that I was the father of the young man that was responsible for the death of Officer Kim - all support ceased instantly. I wanted to help to provide the solution to the problem that Cincinnati has with police and the community. There is an US vs THEM atmosphere in Cincinnati that has been ingrained in the culture of the city for years. Yes, my son was responsible for the death of a police officer. Yes, police officers have been responsible for the deaths of black men and women - but we can't continue to draw a line in the sand and refuse to understand the other side's point of view. I tried and I will continue to try, but I can't say when the Police Department will be willing to work with me on finding a solution. Most are good men and women. I want them all to go home to their families at the end of their shifts. I also want all those that they have to encounter live to face trial and tell their side of the story.

While I was trying to get Cop Block put into place, the prosecutors office decided to release the dash cam video of the officer that shot my son. I asked that it not be released. Officer Kim's family asked that it not be released, but our voices fell on deaf ears. After it was released, I asked to see the dash cam footage of Officer Kim's car - so I can see exactly what my son was saying when Officer Kim arrived. My request was denied. My only guess is that Officer Kim's dash cam will show that my son was asking to be killed before he shot and fired at Officer Kim. I am still requesting that I see that footage - but I know that no one wants to say that they were wrong.

I was starting to feel discouraged, but the fight was not over. I launched another initiative to develop a mobile app which was called Strike Back. Strike Back is an app to assist those battling depression and manic depressive disorders and PTSD. The goal of #strikeback to give kids and young adults necessary tools to battle this debilitating disease. The app #strikeback gives the user a direct connection into their own community support group and reminds them of their core values in life. The app will send a text message to three categories that the user will set up in your profile with their counselor and family. The three support categories are spiritual, family and friends. The user can place two phone numbers in each category that will contact the support team at any point that the user feels that they are in crisis and they trigger the app. After your community group receives the text explaining the user's current struggle with suicide or depressive thoughts they will also get a GPS location directing them to the user. Once the text have gone out an automatic slide show will appear on the user's phone showing pictures that the user uploaded of their loved ones, family, or friends to remind them that there is a reason for living. Loved ones could also then contact authorities and advise them of the mental health issues before they arrive. The reason why this was important to me, was because I found through taking the NAMI course that police are usually the first responders in mental health crisis - but they have the least amount of training. People with undiagnosed mental illness are 16 times more likely to die in an encounter with the police. I read an article during my research into developing the app that made my heart sink.

It said, "By dismantling the mental illness treatment system, we have turned mental health crisis from a medical issue into a police matter," said John Snook, executive director and a co-author of the study. "This is patently unfair, illogical and is proving harmful both to the individual in desperate need of care and the officer who is forced to respond."

In my son's case it proved that Mr. Snook's opinion was indeed correct. I knew I had to do everything in my power to get this app up and going. As I began to share my idea with people, they loved it. They said it was a great idea. I started attempting to raise the $86,000 it would cost to develop the app and have it available for download and I ran into the same issues that I had with Cop Block. Many people were not willing to help the father of the man that killed a cop with anything. People were committed to being angry instead of looking for a solution to the issues. I was frustrated and hurt. I was trying to be proactive and fix the issues that lead to my son's death - but no one could hear me. I started to feel like the powers that be would rather continue to allow those with undiagnosed mental health issues to be criminalized instead of treated. I could be wrong, but that is how it felt.

I was driving down the road and I got a call from the one person that could not only understand my pain - but he could also help me understand why I had to fight as hard as I did. That call was from Tracy Martin - the father of Trayvon Martin.

Chapter 21
This is bigger than me - bigger than Cincinnati

Tracey Martin's call was not out of the blue. I expected his call. My friend Nadia reached out to me about speaking with Trayvon Martin's parents. I was hesitant at first because of all the push back I had been getting in the city. It was like I would take 2 steps forward and then 10 steps back.

Finally I agreed and I spoke first to Trayvon's mother, Sybrina Fulton. We didn't speak long, but she said I needed to speak with Tracey. I wasn't sure if anything would come of it because our son's lost their lives in very different circumstances. I was driving when Tracey Martin called. He was the one person that I needed to speak with, but never knew that I needed him.

As a man, he was able to speak to the pain that I felt that no one could understand. My pain as a father and a black man fighting against impossible odds - he understood. Don't get me wrong, women had been trying to help me since this happened. My childhood friend, Nikki, was handling a lot of my Public Relations from Atlanta - and as close as we had become - she could not understand what I was feeling. My mother, tried. My brother tried. Even my business partners that were men tried - but Tracey understood the place of conflict that had become my everyday reality. Do I continue to fight for children like my son - or do I just go about my life and stay out of the spotlight. I lost my business after my son's death. I was getting death threats daily the more I tried to fight for my son's memory and to pull the curtain back on the pipeline from DCS to prison. Tracey knew exactly what to say and in that hour that we spoke, I pulled over and cried like a baby. There was no judgement. Only understanding and a bond that was forged in the pain of two father's losing their son's to violence and the trauma of us surviving.

That conversation between Tracey and I lead to him inviting me to come speak at the Trayvon Martin Remembrance Dinner and Gala in February, 2017. This would be my first speaking engagement on my son's story outside of Cincinnati. Now that I could prove everything I was saying about the fight that I had for my son - people outside of Cincinnati were open and receptive to hear what I had to say. I was received with open arms and everyone there was supportive of my mission to end the criminalization of mental health crisis when minorities are involved.

Speaking here was the encouragement I needed to know that I was on the right path. Little did I know that it would also open the door for me to begin speaking all over the country. I have been flying all over the country speaking about mental health and our young people dying from violence that could have been avoided. I am out of town more often than I am in town. This is good for me and my family. The city of Cincinnati isn't ready to embrace me and my mission , but I speak whenever and wherever I am invited to speak. I often travel with Tracey Martin and we speak at the same events - but the more I spoke, the more I started to see that I was not alone in this fight. I now work within a network of men who have lost sons to violence. We talk about solutions and different approaches - which is what men do. Men find the solution instead of just complaining about the problem. This has been therapeutic for me and it also pushes me to continue to find solutions to end the DCS to prison pipeline that I have found after receiving all the DCS reports about my son over the years.

Working with Tracey Martin and the other has put me in different arenas to share my son's story. I was able to meet and be mentored by the late great Dick Gregory. The biggest platform, however has been once again with my brother in the journey Tracey Martin, when we appeared on VH1's Black Ink

Chicago at 9Mag Tattoo Shop to get tattoos that represent our sons and to discuss their lives and deaths. Kat worked on my tattoo and did a wonderful job.

The network of fathers speak all over the country in an effort to find solutions to prevent other families from enduring the pain that we have had to endure. It has been painful. I has been a roller coaster. I cannot lie, I would rather have my son back than to be sharing this story with you.

BUT

My story is far from over. I have a long road ahead of me. My mission is to be the change that I want to see in our country. I will continue to fight to bring awareness to the long-term effects childhood trauma on the child, their family and the community at large.

Violence and trauma will not win in my city, my state, or my country!

WE MUST RAISE THE LEVEL OF AWARENESS TO A LEVEL OF IMPACT

Ronald A. Hummons

AFTERWORD

Ronald Hummons spoke often times about the pipeline to prison that he felt was coming from the Department of Children and Family Services often as he processed the death of his son. As his friend, I wanted to show him that what he was feeling could not possibly be true. I spent months researching and trying to find hard facts that would disprove his theory. How naive I was.

I read scholarly article after scholarly article that stated that between 60% and 75% of all male felons had experienced some form of physical abuse or neglect. This information broke my heart. I knew that Ronald's son had been involved with Hamilton County's Department of Children and Family Services over 35 times. There could have been therapy that was required of the family - however that did not happen. I began to ask myself why?

I thought about a lesson that I learned in high school economics - supply and demand. If you have a high demand for a product, you will find a way to supply that demand.

Ok, but who would want people who are suffering from mental illness to go untreated? Everyone in the world knows that hurt people are more likely to hurt people. So no one would want children who were victims of childhood trauma to go untreated. And that may be correct - no ONE person may want that, but industry wants are not personal. Industry wants are all about profits and losses.

The prison industry is a multi-million dollar industry. For prisons to make money, they must be filled with prisoners - which would lead one to think that crime is good for business. If we know that hurt people, hurt people, then we can see why it isn't in the state's best interest to invest in providing all the necessary treatment opportunities to victims of childhood trauma. A human being is worth more to the state and federal government as a prison inmates than they are as college educated tax paying citizens.

Once I understood this, I understood that Ronald's gut feeling was indeed correct. In addition to the work that Ronald is doing to bring attention to childhood trauma and the long term impact to the city - I think it is important to follow the money. Our country can no longer continue to criminalize mental health. We have to see the value in raising whole children, instead of trying to repair broken adults. We as a country cannot be more interested in profiting on prisons than we are on keeping young people out of prisons.

Nicole Riggins

References

Abernethy, A. D., Houston, T. R., Mimms, T., & Boyd-Franklin, N. (2006). Using prayer in psychotherapy: Applying sue's differential to enhance culturally competent care. Cultural Diversity and Ethnic Minority Psychology, 12(1), 101-114. doi:http://dx.doi.org.pearl.stkate.edu.ezproxy.stthomas.edu/10.10 37/1099-9809.12.1.101

American Psychiatric Association. (2000). Diagnostic and statistical manual of mental disorders (4th ed., text rev.). Washington, DC: Author.

Anderson, L. B. (2012). African American males diagnosed with schizophrenia: A phenomenological study. 72(12), 7276. Retrieved from https://digarchive.library.vcu.edu/bitstream/handle/10156/3537/L orraineBAnderso nDissertation_08%2011%2011%20%5b2%5d.pdf?sequence=1

Angelou, M. (1993). The Inaugural Poem: On The Pulse Of Morning. Retrieved from https://poetry.eserver.org/angelou

Alexander, M. (2010). The New Jim Crow: Mass Incarceration In The Age Of Colorblindness. New York, NY: The New Press

Baker, F. M. & Bell, C. C. (1999). Issues in psychiatric treatment of African Americans. Psychiatric Services, 50(3), 362-368. Retrieved from http://fc9en6ys2q.search.serialssolutions.com/?ctx_ver=Z39.88-2004&ctx_enc=info%3Aofi%2Fenc%3AUTF8&rfr_id=info:sid/ summon.serialssol utions.com

Bankole, K. (2009). Sankofa, film. In M. Asante, & A. Mazama (Eds.), Encyclopedia of African religion. (pp. 588-590).

Thousand Oaks, CA: SAGE Publications, Inc. doi:
http://dx.doi.org/10.4135/9781412964623.n365

Barnes, A. (2008). Race and hospital diagnoses of
schizophrenia and mood disorders. Social Work, 53(1), 77.
Retrieved from
http://go.galegroup.com/ps/i.do?id=GALE%7CA209801162&v=
2.1&u=clic_sttho
mas&it=r&p=HRCA&sw=w&asid=9bb7692bcc3b441a3295eaed
a78346f5

Berg, B. L., & Lune, H. (2009). Qualitative research
methods for the social sciences(8th ed). Edinborough Gate,
Harlow: Pearson.

Bhugra, D., Mallett, R., & Leff, J. (1999). Schizophrenia
and African-Caribbeans: A conceptual model of aetiology.
International Review of Psychiatry, 11(2), 145-152.
doi:10.1080/0954026997431 1

Borowsky, S. J., Rubenstein L.V., Meredith L. S., Camp,
P., Jackson-Triche, M., & Wells, K.B. Who is at risk of
nondetection of mental health problems in primary care? J Intern
Med, 15(6), 381-388. Retrieved from
http://www.ncbi.nlm.nih.gov/pmc/articles/PMC1495467/

Boyd-Franklin, N. (2003). Black families in therapy:
understanding the African American experience. New York, NY.
The Guilford Press.

Boyd-Franklin, N. (1987). The contribution of family
therapy models to the treatment of black families.
Psychotherapy: Theory, Research, Practice, Training, 24(3S),
621- 629.
doi:http://dx.doi.org.pearl.stkate.edu.ezproxy.stthomas.edu/10.10

37/h0085760

Bronfenbrenner, U. (2000). Ecological systems theory. (pp. 129-133). New York, NY, US: Oxford University Press. doi:10.1037/10518-046

Broussard, B., Goulding, S. M., Talley, C. L., & Compton, M. T. (2010). Beliefs about causes of schizophrenia among urban African American community members. Psychiatric Quarterly, 81(4), 349-362. doi:10.1007/s11126-010-9143-1

Brown, J. A. (2004). African American church goers' attitudes toward treatment seeking from mental health and religious sources: The role of spirituality, cultural mistrust, and stigma toward mental illness. (Order No. 3129678, The University of North Carolina at Chapel Hill). ProQuest Dissertations and Theses, 77-77 p. Retrieved from http://search.proquest.com/docview/305169067?accountid=26879. (305169067).

Center of Excellence for Cultural Competence. (2009, July 23). Schizophrenia: the impact of race on diagnosis: Cultural Competence Matters. Retrieved from http: http://nyspi.org/culturalcompetence/what/pdf/Cultural_Competence_Matters_Issue_4.pdf

Constance-Huggins, M. (2012). Critical race theory in social work education: a framework for addressing racial disparities. Critical Social Work, 13(2), 1-16. Retrieved from http://www1.uwindsor.ca/criticalsocialwork/system/files/Constance-Huggins.pdf

Danzer, G. (2012). African-Americans' historical trauma: Manifestations in and outside of therapy. Journal of Theory

Construction & Testing, 16(1), 16-21. Retrieved from http://ezproxy.stthomas.edu/login?url=http://search.ebscohost.co m.ezproxy.sttho mas.edu/login.aspx?direct=true&db=aph&AN=75165742&site= ehost-live

DeCoux Hampton, M. (2007). The role of treatment setting and high acuity in the over diagnosis of schizophrenia in African Americans. Archives of Psychiatric Nursing, 21(6), 327-335. doi:http://dx.doi.org.ezproxy.stthomas.edu/10.1016/j.apnu.2007. 04.006

Degrury-Leary, J. (2005). Post traumatic slave syndrome: America's legacy of enduring injury and healing. Milwaukie, OR: Uptone Press.

Ellis, M. C. & Carlson, J. (2009). Cross cultural awareness and social justice in counseling. New York: Taylor & Francis.

Estrada, A. L. (2009). Mexican Americans and historical trauma theory: A theoretical perspective. Journal of Ethnicity in Substance Abuse, 8(3), 330-340. Retrieved from http://ezproxy.stthomas.edu/login?url=http://search.ebscohost.co m.ezproxy.stthom as.edu/login.aspx?direct=true&db=swh&AN=78447&site=ehost-live

Fook, J. (2002). Social work: Critical theory and practice. London: Sage Publications.

Fralich-Lesarre, N.M. (2012). Beyond cultural competency: understanding contemporary problems with historical roots using an African-centered/Black psychology lens. (Doctoral dissertation). ProQuest LLC. Retrieved from http://pqdtopen.proquest.com/pqdtopen/doc/1103346420.html?F

MT=AI (3539696).

Glover, T. M. (2012). Exploration of culturally proficient mental health assessment and treatment practices of Black/African American clients. (Order No. 3528626, Oregon State University). ProQuest Dissertations and Theses, 285. Retrieved from http://search.proquest.com/docview/1048218940?accountid=14756. (1048218940).

Hall, C. A. (2008). The African American experience of overcoming barriers and participating in therapy. (Order No. 3333569, Syracuse University). ProQuest Dissertations and Theses, 228. Retrieved from http://search.proquest.com/docview/304389145?accountid=26879. (304389145).

Hackett, J. S. (2014). Mental Health in the African American Community and the Impact of Historical Trauma: Systemic Barriers. (Master of Social Work Clinical Research Papers). Paper 320. Retrieved from http://sophia.stkate.edu/msw_papers/320

Hines-Martin, V., Malone, M., Kim, S., & Brown-Piper, A. (2003). Barriers to mental health care access in an African American population. Issues in Mental Health Nursing, 24(3), 237. Retrieved from http://ezproxy.stthomas.edu/login?url=http://search.ebscohost.com.ezproxy.sttho mas.edu/login.aspx?direct=true&db=keh&AN=9303876&site=ehost-live

Holden, K. B. & Xanthos, C. (2009). Holden, K. B. & Xanthos, C. (2009). Disadvantages in mental health care among African Americans. Journal of Health Care for the Poor and Underserved 20(2A), 17-23. The Johns Hopkins University

Press. Retrieved September 29, 2013, from Project MUSE Database., 20(2A), 17.

Keyes, C. L. M., & Ryff, C. D. (2003). Somatization and mental health: A comparative study of the idiom of distress hypothesis. Social Science & Medicine, 57(10), 1833- 1845. doi:http://dx.doi.org.ezproxy.stthomas.edu/10.1016/S0277-9536(03)00017-0

Knapp, M., Funk, M., Curran, C., Prince, M., Grigg, M., & McDaid, D. (2006). Economic barriers to better mental health practice and policy. Health Policy and Planning, 21(3), 157.

Lonnie R. Snowden, P. D., Ray Catalano, P. D., & Martha Shumway, P. D. (2009). Disproportionate use of psychiatric emergency services by African Americans. Psychiatric Services, 60(12), 1664. doi:10.1176/appi.ps.60.12.1664
Mason, P. L. (2013). Encyclopedia of race and racism. Detroit: Macmillan Reference USA.

Metzl, J. M. (2009). The protest psychosis: How schizophrenia became a black disease.
Boston, MA, US: Beacon Press.

Miller, M. J. (2010). Ancestral indigenous culture and historical-transgenerational trauma: Rethinking schizophrenia in African Americans. (Order No. 3419756, Institute of Transpersonal Psychology). ProQuest Dissertations and Theses, 201. Retrieved from http://search.proquest.com/docview/756862781?accountid=2687 9. (756862781).

Mohamed, R. A. (1980). Race, sex, and therapist's perceived competence. ProQuest Information & Learning). 41(6), 2337.

Monette, D.R., Sullivan, T.J., & Dejong, C.R. (2011).
Applied Social Research. Belmont, CA: Brooks/Cole.
National Association of Social Workers. (2008). Code of
ethics of the National Association of Social Workers.
Washington, DC. NASW Press.

National Institute on Mental Health. (2009). African
American community mental health. Retrieved from
    http://www.nami.org/Content/ContentGroups/Multicultur
al_Support1/Fact_Sheets
1/AfricanAmerican_MentalHealth_FactSheet_2009.pdf

Okeke, A. (2013). "A Culture of Stigma: Black Women
and Mental Health" Undergraduate Research Awards. Paper 13.
http://scholarworks.gsu.edu/univ_lib_ura/13

Ojanuga, D. (1993). The medical ethics of the father of
gynecology, dr. j. Marion Sims. Journal of Medical Ethics, 19
(1), 28-31. Retrieved from
    http://www.jstor.org.ezproxy.stthomas.edu/stable/277172
50?seq=

Perdue, B., Singley, D., & Jackson, C. (2006). Assessing
spirituality in mentally ill African
    Americans. ABNF Journal, 17(2), 78-81. Retrieved from
http://ezproxy.stthomas.edu/login?url=http://search.ebscohost.co
m.ezproxy.stthom
as.edu/login.aspx?direct=true&db=keh&AN=21836448&site=eh
ost-live

Possaint, A. F. & Alexander, A. (2000). Lay my burden
down: suicide and mental health crises among African
Americans. Boston, Massachusetts: Beacon Press Books.

Ridley, C. R. (1984). Clinical treatment of the

nondisclosing black client: A therapeutic paradox. American Psychologist, 39(11), 1234-1244. doi:10.1037/0003-066X.39.11.1234

Roberts, J. D. (1974). A Black Political Theology. (p.58) Philadelphia, PA: The Westminster Press

Rosa, M. E. (1996). Cognitive-behavioral processes that affect substance-dependent schizophrenic african-american males' completion of inpatient treatment. ProQuest Information & Learning). 57(6), 3659.

Schnittker, J. (2003). Misgivings of medicine?: African Americans' skepticism of psychiatric medication. American Sociological Association, 44(4), 506-524.

Sheafor, B. W., & Horejsi, C. R. (2006, 2012). Techniques and guidelines for social work practice. Upper Saddle River, NJ: Pearson Allyn & Bacon.

Snowden, L. R. (2001). Barriers to effective mental health services for African Americans. Mental Health Services Research, 3 (4), 2-7. Retrieved from http://link.springer.com/article/10.1023/A:1013172913880

Snowden, L. R. (2003). Bias in mental health assessment and intervention: theory and evidence. American Journal of Public Health, 93(2), 239-243. Retrieved from http://fc9en6ys2q.search.serialssolutions.com/?ctx_ver=Z39.88-2004&ctx_enc=info%3Aofi%2Fenc%3AUTF

Sotero, M. M. (2006). A conceptual model of historical trauma: implications for public health practice and research. Journal of Health Disparities Research and Practice. Vol. 1(1), pp. 93-108. Retrieved from http://ssrn.com/abstract=1350062.

Stewart, P. E. (2004). Afrocentric approaches to working with African American families. Families in Society, 85 (2), 221-228. Retrieved from http://yt2js5ru4z.scholar.serialssolutions.com/?sid=google&auinit=PE&aulast=Stewart&atitle=Afrocentric+approaches+to+working+with+African+American+famili es&id=doi:10.1606/1044-3894.326&title=Families+in+society&volume=85&issue=2&date=2004&spage=2 21&issn=1044-3894

Substance Abuse and Mental Health Services Administration (SAMHSA). (n.d.). How being trauma informed improves criminal justice system: responses. Retrieved from http://gainscenter.samhsa.gov/cms-assets/documents/93078-842830.historical-trauma.pdf

Trierweiler, S. J., Muroff, J. R., Jackson, J. S., Neighbors, H. W., & Munday, C. (2005). Clinical race, situational attributes, and diagnoses of mood versus schizophrenia disorders. Cultural Diversity and Ethnic Minority Psychology, 11(4), 351-364.

Trierweiler, S., Neighbors, H. W., Munday, C., Thompson, E., Jackson, J., & Binion, V. (2006). Differences in patterns of symptom attribution in diagnosing schizophrenia between African American and non-African American clinicians. American Journal of Orthopsychiatry, 76, 154-160.

Thompson, A. O. (2008). The African maafa: The impact of the transatlantic slave trade on western Africa. The Journal of Caribbean History, 42(1), 67-VIII. Retrieved from http://search.proquest.com.ezproxy.stthomas.edu/docview/211116014?accountid=1 4756

U.S. Census Bureau. (2007, January 12). State & county Quick facts: Allegany County, N.Y. Retrieved January 25, 2007, from http://quickfacts.census.gov.

Van Wormer, K., Sudduth, C., & Jackson, D.W, III. (2011). What we can learn of resilience from older african-american women: Interviews with women who worked as maids in the deep south. Journal of Human Behavior in the Social Environment, 21(4), 410-422. Retrieved from http://ezproxy.stthomas.edu/login?url=http://search.ebscohost.com.ezproxy.stthom as.edu/login.aspx?direct=true&db=swh&AN=81751&site=ehost-live

Wallace, V. E. (2012). Differences in mental health resiliency in young African Americans. American Journal of Health Studies, 27 (1), 8-12. Retrieved from http://web.ebscohost.com.pearl.stkate.edu/ehost/pdfviewer/pdfviewer?vid=5&sid= 9c9cc420-4d87-440e-a234-35bc3c66eb54%40sessionmgr4004&hid=4206

Ward, E. C. (2005). Keeping it real: A grounded theory study of African American clients engaging in counseling at a community mental health agency. Journal of Counseling Psychology, 52(4), 471-481. doi:10.1037/0022-0167.52.4.471

Ward, E. C., Clark, L., & Heidrich, S. (2009). African American women's beliefs, coping behaviors, and barriers to seeking mental health services. National Institutes of Health, 19 (11), 1598-1601. doi: 10.1177/1049732309350686

Whaley, A. L. (1998). Cross-cultural perspective on paranoia: A focus on the black American experience. Psychiatric Quarterly, 69(4), 325. Retrieved from http://ezproxy.stthomas.edu/login?url=http://search.ebscohost.com.ezproxy.stthom as.edu/login.aspx?direct=true&db=keh&AN=11303801&site=ehost-live

Whaley, A. L. (2001). Cultural mistrust: An important psychological construct for diagnosis and treatment of African Americans. Professional Psychology: Research and Practice, 32(6), 555-562. doi:10.1037/0735-7028.32.6.555

Whaley, A. L. (2002). Confluent paranoia in African American psychiatric patients: An empirical study of ridley's typology. Journal of Abnormal Psychology, 111(4), 568- 577. doi:10.1037/0021-843X.111.4.568

Whaley, A. L., & Hall, B. N. (2009). Effects of cultural themes in psychotic symptoms on the diagnosis of schizophrenia in African Americans. Mental Health, Religion & Culture, 12(5), 457-471. doi:10.1080/13674670902758273

Wiener, H. W., Klei, L., Irvin, M. D., Perry, R. T., Aliyu, M. H., Allen, T. B., Go, R. C. P. (2009). Linkage analysis of schizophrenia in african-american families. Schizophrenia Research, 109(1–3), 70-79.
doi:http://dx.doi.org.ezproxy.stthomas.edu/10.1016/j.schr es.2009.02.007

Wilkins, E., Whiting, J., Watson, M., Russon, J., & Moncrief, A. (2013). Residual effects of slavery: What clinicians need to know. Contemporary Family Therapy: An International Journal, 35(1), 14-28. doi:10.1007/s10591-012-9219-1

Williams, D. R., & Williams-Morris, R. (2000). Racism and mental health: The African American experience. Ethnicity and Health, 5(3/4), 243. Retrieved from http://search.proquest.com.ezproxy.stthomas.edu/docview/21705 4191?accountid=1 4756

Williams-Washington, K. N. (2009, Feb 2009). Do African Americans suffer from historical trauma? Take Pride! Community Magazine. Retrieved from

Made in the USA
Middletown, DE
23 April 2023

28942623R00156